Seven Principles of Brilliant Sales and Marketing

Whatever you sell and whatever the size of your business, these simple and universal practices can help you market more effectively:

- **Never miss an opportunity to present yourself well.** Everything from your clothing and business card to the envelope in which you send an invoice must work toward your marketing goals.
- **Spend at least ten minutes a day marketing your company.** So many people don't do marketing routinely – and then complain that they don't have enough customers or revenue.
- **Know what you want to get out of your marketing before you write the first cheque.** You can lose your focus all too easily and invest in useless activities. In a field as complex and multifaceted as marketing, have a simple, clear objective in sight at all times.
- **Know what makes you special to customers and prospects, so that you can remind them of your strengths in every marketing communication.** They buy from you for this reason alone.
- **Experiment.** Great businesses are built on great marketing formulas, and you have to arrive at those formulas through trial and error.
- **Sort out the people who don't want what you sell and eliminate them from your marketing straight away.** Wasting time and effort on the wrong prospects is the single biggest cause of inefficiency in sales and marketing.
- **If your plan looks complicated, you haven't finished it yet.** The best marketing is blindingly simple. You want to aim for a one-page marketing plan, because you may actually be able to implement it!

Ten Ways to Spend Less on Marketing

Because marketing is a creative activity, you can always find new and better ways to make an impact and attract sales, even on a small budget. Here are some ideas that help you maximise your impact while minimising your budget:

- **Make your communications more visually striking** by including images of people and using creative, dynamic layouts. This visual style gets more reader attention than any letter, brochure, or ad you put out there, making it more effective and efficient for you.
- **Improve the appearance of your logo.** Most logos are boring, but great companies always have great logos. Wonder which came first?
- **Buy visibility on the Google and Yahoo! search engines.** This is inexpensive enough to work for local as well as global markets.
- **Release a survey or host an interesting event** to generate publicity.
- **Send out a press release** to your local media once every quarter or whenever you have valuable news to release, updating them on events in your business. Getting local news coverage isn't that hard, and it often attracts new business.
- **Find something simple and inexpensive to offer** along with your most popular product or service in order to pick up add-on sales.
- **Give out coupons to encourage prospects to try your product or service,** so that its qualities become obvious to them. Don't, however, give away price-cutting coupons or discounts for no good reason – think of other ways to increase sales appeal.
- **Offer (or improve) a guarantee,** one with no small print. If you have a good product or service, stand behind it!
- **Vow never to lose a customer.** Whenever you have a customer who's upset or at risk, find out why and win them back.
- **Discover where you lose the most prospects or potential customers** and then concentrate your marketing at this point to convert more of them into customers.

For Dummies: Bestselling Book Series for Beginners

Marketing For Dummies®

Seven Rules for Avoiding Business Trouble

A dangerous area of marketing arises when people try to bypass regulations that ensure fair pricing, safety, and honest advertising. In the UK, as in Europe and North America, there are regulations as well as self-regulatory industry guidelines.

- Always make sure your pricing is fair to customers and competitors (because unfair competitive practices are usually illegal).
- Always clarify the limits of warranties for services or goods.
- Always provide full warnings and details about your product's content and source on labels.
- Always follow an open and honest policy with the media.
- Never say anything deceptive or misleading in ads or other communications – remember the watchwords 'legal, decent, honest, and truthful'.
- Never distribute products that can do significant harm to anyone.
- Never discuss prices with competitors (that's called *price fixing*).

The Seven Ps of Marketing

Knowing and evaluating how your customer interacts with your business are important in creating a successful marketing plan, so keep the seven Ps of marketing – the key contact points between your customer and your business – in mind. Note: You can read more about these in Chapter 1.

- Product: What aspects (both rational and emotional) of the product have an influence on customer perception and purchase intentions?
- Price: What does it cost the customer to use your product, including but not limited to list price?
- Place: When and where, in terms of time and space, is your product available to customers?
- Promotion: How do you communicate with your customers?
- People: What are the important points of human contact between your customer and your business?
- Process: What are the processes involved in delivering your products and services to the customer?
- Physical presence: What are all the physical spaces viewed by your customers, from your reception area through to your delivery vehicles and drivers?

For Dummies: Bestselling Book Series for Beginners

Marketing

FOR

DUMMIES®

Marketing FOR DUMMIES®

by Craig Smith and Alexander Hiam

JOHN WILEY & SONS, LTD

Marketing For Dummies®

Published by
John Wiley & Sons, Ltd
The Atrium
Southern Gate
Chichester
West Sussex
PO19 8SQ
England

E-mail (for orders and customer service enquires): cs-books@wiley.co.uk

Visit our Home Page on www.wileyeurope.com

Wiley also publishes its books in a variety of electronic formats. Some content that appears in print may not be available in electronic books.

British Library Cataloguing in Publication Data: A catalogue record for this book is available from the British Library.

ISBN-13: 978-0-7645-7056-8 (PB)

Printed and bound in Great Britain by Bell and Bain Ltd, Glasgow

10 9 8 7 6 5 4

WILEY

About the Authors

Craig Smith is the editor of *Marketing*, the UK's highest circulation weekly magazine, and PPA Weekly Business Magazine of the Year, serving the marketing and advertising industries. He has worked as a business journalist for 18 years and is a regular commentator on marketing issues to the national press and broadcast media.

Craig works closely with industry trade bodies the Association of Publishing Agencies and Business in the Community to promote best practice in the areas of customer magazines and cause related marketing.

Alex Hiam is a consultant, corporate trainer, and public speaker with 20 years of experience in marketing, sales, and corporate communications. He is the director of Insights, which includes a division called Insights for Marketing that offers a wide range of services for supporting and training in sales, customer service, planning, and management. His firm is also active in developing the next generation of leaders in the workplace through its Insights for Training & Development. Alex has an MBA in marketing and strategic planning from the Haas School at U.C. Berkeley and an undergraduate degree from Harvard. He has worked as marketing manager for both smaller high-tech firms and a *Fortune* 100 company, and did a stint as a professor of marketing at the business school at U. Mass. Amherst.

Alex is the co-author of the best-seller, *The Portable MBA in Marketing* (Wiley) as well as *The Vest-Pocket CEO* and numerous other books and training programs. He has consulted to a wide range of companies and not-for-profit and government agencies, from General Motors and Volvo to HeathEast and the U.S. Army (a fuller list of clients is posted at www.insightsformarketing.com).

Alex is also the author of a companion volume to this book, the *Marketing Kit For Dummies* (Wiley), which includes more detailed coverage of many of the hands-on topics involved in creating great advertising, direct mail letters, Web sites, publicity campaigns, and marketing plans. On the CD that comes with the *Marketing Kit For Dummies*, you'll find forms, checklists, and templates that may be of use to you. Also, Alex maintains an extensive Web site of resources that he organized to support each of the chapters in the book.

Publisher's Acknowledgements

We're proud of this book; please send us your comments through our Dummies online registration form located at www.dummies.com/register/.

Some of the people who helped bring this book to market include the following:

Acquisitions, Editorial, and Media Development

Executive Project Editor: Martin Tribe

Content Editor: Simon Bell

Development Editor: Tracy Barr

Copy Editor: Kate O'Leary

Proofreader: Helen Heyes

Technical Editor: John Bills

Executive Editor: Jason Dunne

Cover Photo: Corbis/Royalty Free

Cartoons: Ed McLachlan

Composition

Project Coordinators: Maridee Ennis, Jennifer Theriot

Layout and Graphics: Beth Brooks, Andrea Dahl, Lauren Goddard, Brooke Graczyk, Denny Hager, Stephanie D. Jumper, Alicia South, Erin Zeltner

Proofreader: Susan Moritz

Indexer: Techbooks

Publishing and Editorial for Consumer Dummies

    Diane Graves Steele, Vice President and Publisher, Consumer Dummies

    Joyce Pepple, Acquisitions Director, Consumer Dummies

    Kristin A. Cocks, Product Development Director, Consumer Dummies

    Michael Spring, Vice President and Publisher, Travel

    Kelly Regan, Editorial Director, Travel

Publishing for Technology Dummies

    Andy Cummings, Vice President and Publisher, Dummies Technology/General User

Composition Services

    Gerry Fahey, Vice President of Production Services

    Debbie Stailey, Director of Composition Services

Contents at a Glance

Table of Contents

· ·

Introduction

● ●

Marketing is the most important thing that you can do in business today, even if your job title doesn't have the word *marketing* in it. Marketing, in all its varied forms, focuses on attracting customers, getting them to buy, and making sure that they're happy enough with their purchase that they come back for more. What could be more important? Ever try to run a business without customers?

About This Book

We wrote this book to help you do that critical job of marketing as well as you possibly can. We wrote with a variety of marketers in mind, including small business owners and entrepreneurs who wear the marketing and sales hat along with several other hats. We also wrote for managers and staffers of larger organisations who work on marketing plans, product launches, ad campaigns, printed materials, Web sites, and other elements of their organisation's outreach to customers and prospects.

We kept in mind that some of our readers market consumer products, others sell to businesses, and some market physical products, while others offer services. The different types of business have many important distinctions, but good marketing techniques can work wonders anywhere.

Marketing can be a great deal of fun – it is, after all, the most creative area of most businesses. In the long run, however, marketing is all about the bottom line. So, although we had fun writing this book, and we think you can enjoy using it, we take the subject matter very seriously. Any task that brings you to this book is vitally important, and we want to make sure that the advice you get here helps you perform especially well.

Conventions Used in This Book

We refer to any organised, coordinated use of product development, price, promotion, distribution and sales as your *marketing plan*. There is an important distinction between a marketing plan and your *marketing campaign* – some people start off down the campaign route thinking that marketing is all about advertising and promotion. It isn't. We want you to have a marketing plan. Creating a plan means avoiding random or disconnected activities. It also means thinking about how everything the customer sees, whether that be your prices, premises or staff, interlinks and contributes to achieving your marketing goals. Whether you work in a large organisation or own a small business, you need a coherent, well-thought-out marketing plan!

We refer to whoever buys what you sell as the *customer*. This customer can be a person, a household, a business, a government department, a school, or even a voter. We still call them your customers, and the rules of sound marketing still apply to them.

What you sell or offer to customers we refer to as your *product*, whether it's a good, service, idea, or even a person (such as a political candidate or a celebrity). Your product can be animate or inanimate, tangible or intangible. But if you offer it, it's a product in marketing jargon, and using just one term for whatever the reader wants to sell saves us all a lot of time and wasted printer's ink.

We also treat person-to-person sales as one of the many possible activities under the marketing umbrella. You need to integrate selling, which is its own highly sophisticated and involved field, into the broader range of activities designed to help bring about sales and satisfy customers. We address ways of managing sales better as part of our overall efforts to make all your marketing activities more effective.

Foolish Assumptions

In writing this book, we made a few assumptions about you:

- ✔ You're clever, caring, and persistent, butyou don't have all the technical knowledge that you may need to do great marketing.

- ✔ You're willing to try new ideas in order to improve sales results and grow your organisation. Marketing is challenging, after all, and requires an open mind and a willingness to experiment and try new ideas and techniques.

- ✔ You're willing and able to switch from being imaginative and creative one moment to being analytical and rigorous the next. Marketing has to take both approaches. Sometimes, we ask you to run the numbers and do sales projections. Other times, we ask you to dream up a clever way to catch a reader's eye and communicate a benefit to them. These demands pull you in opposite directions. If you can assemble a team of varied people, some of them numbers orientated and some of them artistic, you can cover all the marketing bases more easily. But if you have a small business, you may be all you have, and you need to wear each hat in turn. At least you never get bored as you tackle the varied challenges of marketing!

✔ You have an active interest in generating new sales and maximising the satisfaction of existing customers. This sales orientation needs to underlie everything you do in marketing. Keep in mind that the broader purpose on every page of this book is to try to help you make more and better sales happen!

How This Book Is Organised

This book is organised into parts that we describe in the following sections. Check out the Table of Contents for more information on the topics of the chapters within each part.

Part 1: Where You Are, Where You're Going

Military strategists know that great battles must be won first in the general's tent, with carefully considered plans and accurate maps, before the general commits any troops to action on the field of battle. In marketing, you don't have any lives at stake, but you may hold the future success of your organisation in your hands! We advocate just as careful an approach to analysis and planning as if you were a general preparing on the eve of battle.

In this part, we show you how to make the most of your marketing by focusing on your customers and what your organisation delivers to them and give you strong, aggressive marketing strategies that can maximise your chances of sales and success. You'll also get the help you need to put a plan of action together that you can be reasonably confident will actually work.

Part 11: Creative Thinking, Powerful Marketing

Great marketing requires a wide range of special skills. If you don't already have all of them, this part shores up any gaps and helps you take advantage of specialised tools and techniques.

We cover an essential marketing skill: How to find out what you need to know in order to develop better strategies and design better ads and other elements of your marketing activity. Where can you find the best customers? What do they respond to? What is the competition up to? Imagining, communicating, and researching make up the power skills of great marketers, and we want to make their benefits available to you!

We share with you that most precious and hard-to-capture of marketing skills: The marketing imagination. When marketers can bottle up a little of this magic and work it into their marketing plans, good things begin to happen. We also address another fundamental marketing skill: Communicating with customers. Good ideas plus clear, interesting communications add up to better marketing.

Part III: Advertising Everyone Can Do

Advertising is the traditional cornerstone of marketing. Firms combined advertisements with sales calls back in the early days of marketing, and great things happened to their revenues. In this part, we show you how to create compelling, effective ads, brochures, and fliers on paper – the traditional medium of marketing. You can run full-page, colour ads in national magazines if you have a big budget, or you can place small, cheap black-and-whites in a local newspaper – and either one may prove effective with the right creativity and design. Everyone can access radio and TV these days, too, regardless of budget, if you know how to use these media economically and well. However, you may also want to use perhaps the simplest – and most powerful – form of advertising: The simple sign; from signs on buildings, vehicles, and doors to posters at airports and advertising hoardings next to main roads. You can put advertising to good use in your business in so many different ways.

Part IV: Powerful Alternatives to Advertising

Many marketers are discovering the power of publicity and discovering how to help the media cover their stories and to get more exposure at far less cost than if they had advertised. Special events also provide you with a powerful alternative or supplement to ad campaigns and can bring you high-quality sales leads. Also take a good look at how you use direct mail, the Web, and other options for bringing in prospects and closing high-quality sales.

Part V: Connecting with Your Customers

The classic marketing plan has seven components (the 7 Ps), but much of what marketers do (and what is covered throughout Parts II to IV) falls into the fourth P: Promotion. In this part, we go deeper into the other Ps: Product design and branding, pricing and discounting to create incentives for purchase, the aggressive use of distribution strategies to place your product in front of consumers when and where they are most likely to buy, and selling and servicing customers. We draw your attention to the all-important product and make sure yours is naturally brilliant enough to shine out and beckon customers to you. We also encourage you to examine your distribution, sales, and service, because these can make or break a marketing plan (and a business), too.

Part VI: The Part of Tens

The Part of Tens is a traditional element of *For Dummies* books, and it communicates brief but essential tips that didn't fit easily into the other parts. We recommend that you look at this part whenever you need insights or ideas because it encapsulates much of the essential philosophy and strategies of good marketing practice. And reading this part also helps you avoid some of the dead ends and traps that await the unwary marketer.

Icons Used in This Book

Look for these symbols to help you find valuable stuff throughout the text:

This icon flags specific advice that you can try out in your marketing plan straight away. The icon uses a pound sign for the filament of the light bulb because the acid test of any great idea in business rests in whether it can make you some money.

Sometimes, you need the right perspective on a problem to reach success, so this icon also flags brief discussions of how to think about the task at hand. Often, a basic principle of marketing pops up at this icon to help you handle important decisions.

All marketing is real-world marketing, but this icon means that you can find an actual example of something that worked (or didn't work) in the real world for another marketer.

In marketing, lone rangers don't last long. Successful marketers use a great many supporting services and often bring in graphic artists, ad agencies, research firms, package designers, retail display designers, publicists, and many other specialists. You can't do it all. Sometimes, the best advice we can give you is to pick up your phone and make a call. And this icon marks a spot where we give you leads and contacts.

 You can easily run into trouble in marketing because so many mines are just waiting for you to step on them. That's why we've marked them all with this symbol.

 When we want to remind you of essential or critical information you need to know in order to succeed, we mark it with this icon. Don't forget!

Where to Go from Here

If you read only one chapter in one business book this year, please make it Chapter 1 of this book. We've made this chapter stand alone as a powerful way to make the most of your marketing and upgrade or enhance the things that you do to make profitable sales. We've packed the rest of the book with good tips and techniques, and it all deserves attention. But whatever else you do or don't get around to, read the first chapter with a pen and action-list at hand!

Or maybe you have a pressing need in one of the more specific areas covered by the book. If fixing your Web site is the top item on your to-do list, go to Chapter 10 first. If you need to increase the effectiveness of your sales force, try Chapter 17, instead. Or are you working on a letter to customers? Then Chapters 6 and 11 on marketing communications and direct mail can really help out your project. Whatever you're doing, we have a feeling that this book has a chapter or two to help you out. So don't let us slow you down. Get going! It's never too early (or too late) to do a little marketing.

Part I
Where You Are, Where You're Going

In this part . . .

Management's job is to see the company not as it is, but as it can be. Helping you recognize that vision is the purpose of this part. Whatever your current business or service is and does, this part helps you to imagine and plan what it may be best become in the next quarter and year. How do you do that?

You need, first, to understand your marketing program – the integrated ways in which you reach out to motivate customers and win their loyal support. Next, we highly recommend that you come to grips with the big strategy questions in a marketer's life – who are we and what makes us so special that our sales and profits deserve to grow? Finally, we also recommend that you write down your big picture insights to help organise and simplify later decisions about the details of marketing. A plan, even a simple one-page plan, can help you a lot as you make marketing decisions throughout the coming year.

Chapter 1

Making the Most of Your Marketing

In This Chapter

▶ Focusing your marketing by understanding your customers

▶ Clarifying what your marketing is trying to achieve

▶ Leveraging your marketing with focus and control

▶ Identifying your customer touchpoints

▶ Maximising the appeal of your product, service, or business

*E*ven though you are reading Chapter 1 of a book called *Marketing For Dummies*, you're probably already 'doing' quite a bit of marketing, maybe without even knowing it. If you have a product or service that is selling, know who your best customers are and what they want, and have plans to develop new products for them or to find more customers, then you're already addressing some of the fundamentals of marketing. A lot of companies, and even some of the biggest ones, mistake marketing for advertising. But promotion is just one aspect of marketing; many of the other elements that go into doing good marketing are things that you may think of as essential and everyday parts of doing business, such as setting price and getting your product into the hands of your customers.

You may be good at doing some or all of these things, but unless you're co-ordinating all of these activities under a formal marketing framework, then your efforts are not nearly as efficient or effective as they could be. Your marketing activity (by which we mean everything about your business that makes a difference to your customers) is crucial because it's what gets your business from where it is now to where you want it to be. In this chapter, we go over lots of simple, quick steps you can take to make progress with your marketing activities.

Your Marketing Strategy: A Map to Success

Any marketing you do ought to be based on a *marketing strategy,* which is the big-picture idea driving your success. In order to make your marketing strategy happen you need to work out how you're going to achieve it, which involves writing up a *marketing plan.*

We like to use a simple analogy to stress the importance of doing all this in a co-ordinated way, which involves a destination, a starting point, and a map. Your marketing strategy is your destination – where you want to be by a certain time. Your marketing plan is your map, which tells you where you are now, and sets the best course to get to your destination. This analogy is effective because it demonstrates the importance of getting everything working together. You can have a destination and try to feel your way to it, but you'll get there quicker and more efficiently if you know where you're starting from, what the most direct route is, and what obstacles lie in your way. There's a final part to the map analogy: You can plan the most perfect route to your destination, but unless you start putting one foot in front of the other you'll never get there!

We swear, it works . . .

Time was when French Connection was an everyday high street clothing chain with not much to distinguish it from the competition. That was before an executive from its advertising agency reportedly glanced at a fax that had come in from one of the company's overseas offices addressed to French Connection UK, or fcuk for short. That led to the idea to start printing the acronym fcuk – something you want to be very careful you get in the correct order in memos to your boss – on the company's advertising, t-shirts, bikinis, and even his and hers fragrances. Over the years innuendos using the acronym have appeared over all kinds of products and all over the world, and lots of people have been offended, complained, and even tried to boycott the stores. You'd think that a company would shy away from that kind of bad publicity, but not French Connection, which knows the acronym appeals to their core customers of teens and young adults – and works internationally, too. And the more parents (and even some people in the advertising industry!) complain, the more French Connection sells.

Knowing Your Customer

There are lots of definitions of marketing created by experts with too much time on their hands. The Chartered Institute of Marketing (CIM) defines marketing as 'the management process responsible for identifying, anticipating, and satisfying customer requirements profitably'. Wow. We prefer our own, simpler version – 'selling more stuff to more people'. We're being a little unfair to the wordier version, because it does reflect one of the more important changes in modern marketing. You don't get very far in business these days by just making stuff and then finding people to buy it. Instead, you've got to find out what customers want from you and then create a product to meet those needs. This view is the difference between being what the experts call product-orientated and customer-orientated.

Whether you're product- or customer-orientated, however, the first and most important principle of marketing is this: Know your customer. When you understand how customers think and what they like, you can develop products or services that meet those needs and come up with appropriate and appealing ways to communicate them.

You need to understand your customer on two levels: The rational, functional dimension of making a purchase decision, and the irrational, emotional dimension. Every purchase, whether of a fizzy drink, a software program, a consulting service, a book, or a manufacturing part, has both rational and emotional elements. So to truly know your customer, you must explore two primary questions:

- **How do they feel about your product?** Does it make them feel good? Do they like its personality? Do they like how it makes them feel about themselves?

- **What do they think about your product?** Do they understand it? Do they think its features and benefits are superior to the competition and can meet their needs? Do they feel that your product is good value given its benefits and costs?

Sometimes, one of these dimensions dominates for the customer you want to sell to. In other instances, all dimensions are equally important. Which is true of your customers? You need to take one of the three following approaches:

- **Informational approach.** The approach you use if your customers buy in a rational manner. This is the case for many business-to-business marketers. This approach involves showing the product and talking about its benefits. Comparisons to worse alternatives are a great idea when using an informational approach. Use this approach when you think buyers are going to make a careful, thoughtful, informed purchase decision or when you have strong evidence in favour of their buying *your* product or service instead of others.

- ✔ **Emotional approach.** This approach pushes emotional instead of rational buttons. For example, a marketer of virus-scanning software may try to scare computer users by asking them in a headline, 'What would it cost you if a virus destroyed everything on your computer right now?' That emotional appeal can be much more powerful than a pile of statistics about the frequency and type of viruses on the Web. Use an emotional approach when your customers have strong feelings you can tap into and relate to your product or service, or when you think people are going to make an impulse decision.

- ✔ **Balanced mix.** This approach uses a combination of informational and emotional appeals. We would choose this approach to sell anti-virus software, and many other products, because it engages both the rational and emotional sides of the buyer's mind. For example, after a scare-tactic (emotional) headline asking what would happen if a virus destroyed everything on your computer, we would follow up with a few statistics such as, 'One out of every ten computer users suffers a catastrophic virus attack each year.' The facts reinforce the nervous feelings the headline evoked, helping move the prospect toward purchase.

Decide which of these three approaches to use, and use it consistently in all your communications. And when in doubt, use the balanced mix to hedge your bets.

Getting focused

You begin to organise and focus your marketing activities when you define as clearly as possible who you're targeting with your marketing. Your marketing may include sales, service, product design and packaging, all marketing and media communications, and anything else that helps win loyal customers. Marketing can encompass tens to hundreds of contributing elements, so you need a clear focus to keep them all on target. Remember that your target is a clearly defined customer.

To help you focus, write a detailed description of this customer, as if you were developing their character for use in a novel or screenplay you plan to write. (The plot of this story is, of course, that the character falls in love – with your product.)

When you try to identify distinct groups of customers that your product or service may appeal to, it's called segmentation – and there are any number of ways to cut the cake. If your customers are other businesses, then you can group them by the type of product or service they offer or by the industry sector they are in. If your customers are people, the common ways to define them are by demographics (age and location), socio-economic status or by attitude and behaviour. Whichever way you try to identify the group or groups of customers most likely to buy from you, the objective is the same: to create a specific product and tailored marketing message that will have the best effect on them.

You further increase your focus when you decide whether your target customers prefer marketing that takes a rational, information-based approach, an emotional, personality-based approach, or a balanced mix of the two. By simply being clear about whom to target and whether to market to them in an informational or emotional manner, you've taken a great leap in providing a clear focus. You know whom to target, and you have an important clue as to how to target them and communicate with them in every element of your marketing.

Another aspect of your customer focus is whether you want to emphasise attracting new customers, or retaining and growing existing customers. One or the other may need to dominate your marketing, or perhaps you need to balance the two. Marketing to new prospects is usually a different sort of challenge from communicating with and satisfying existing customers, so knowing what is most important helps you to improve the effectiveness of your marketing.

As a marketer, you face a great many decisions and details. Marketing tends to be fragmented, so that marketing efforts spring up with every good idea or customer demand, rather like rabbits. In most organisations, hundreds of marketing rabbits are running around, each one in a slightly different direction from any other. Focus gets every element of your marketing moving in the right direction.

Finding out why customers like you

In marketing, always think about what you do well, and make sure you build on your strengths in everything you do.

You can't be all things to all customers. You can't be the best on every rational and emotional dimension. If you try to meet the competition on their ground, you remain in second place. So now we want you to clearly and succinctly define (notes, please!) what your special strength or advantage is. Start your sentence like this: 'My product (or service) is special because . . .'

The way you complete that sentence reflects whatever it is that is outstanding about your product or business. Use this strength-based method to add an additional degree of focus to your marketing. Take a minute to think about what makes your firm or product special and different, and why customers have been attracted to that excellence in the past. Then make sure your marketing leverages that strength wherever possible.

For example, if you're known for good customer service, make sure to train, recognise, and reward good service in your employees, and to emphasise good service in all communications with your customers and prospects. A photo of a friendly, helpful employee ought to be featured in your advertising, brochures, or Web page, because friendliness personifies your excellence in customer service. You can also quote customer testimonials that praise your service. And you may want to offer a satisfaction guarantee of some sort, too. Focus on your strength in all that you do, and your marketing becomes more profitable.

Working out the best way to find customers

We periodically survey managers of successful businesses to ask them about their marketing practices. And the first and most revealing question we ask is, 'What is the best way to attract customers?' Now, the interesting thing about this question is that the answer differs for every successful business. So, you need to answer this question yourself; you can't look the answer up in a book.

Take a look at the following list to see some of the most common answers – things that businesses often say are most effective at bringing them customers:

- ✔ **Referrals.** Customers sell the product (see coverage of word of mouth in Chapter 12 for how to stimulate them).
- ✔ **Trade shows and professional association meetings.** Contacts sell the product (see Chapter 13).
- ✔ **Sales calls.** Salespeople sell the product (see Chapter 17).
- ✔ **TV, radio, or print ads.** Advertising sells the product (see the chapters in Part III).
- ✔ **Product demonstrations, trial coupons, or distribution of free samples.** Product sells itself (see Chapters 14 and 15).
- ✔ **Web sites and newsletters.** Internet information sells the product (see Chapter 10).
- ✔ **Placement and appearance of buildings/shops.** Location sells the product (see Chapter 16).

As the preceding list indicates, each business has a different optimal formula for attracting customers. However, in every case, successful businesses report that one or two methods work best – their marketing is therefore dominated by one or two effective ways of attracting customers. These businesses put one-third to two-thirds of their marketing resources into the top ways of attracting customers, and then use other marketing methods to support and leverage their most effective method. And successful businesses don't spend any time or money on marketing activities inconsistent with their best method or that rob resources from it.

 You need to find the one best way to attract customers to your business. If you already know that way, you may not be focusing your marketing around it fully. So you need to make another action note and answer another question: What is your best way to attract customers, and how can you focus your marketing to take fuller advantage of it?

When you answer this question, you're taking yet another important step toward highly focused marketing that leverages your resources as much as possible. Your marketing can probably be divided into three lists of activities:

✔ Works best

✔ Helpful

✔ Doesn't work

If you reorganise last year's budget into these categories, you may well find that your spending isn't concentrated near the top of your list. If not, then you can try to move your focus and spending up. Think of this as a *marketing pyramid* and try to move your spending up the pyramid so that your marketing resources are concentrated near the top. What does your marketing pyramid look like? Can you move up this pyramid by shifting resources and investments to higher-pulling marketing activities?

Defining Your Marketing Methods

Peter Drucker, one of few justly famous management gurus, has defined marketing as the whole firm, taken from the customer's point of view. This definition is powerful, because it reminds you that your view from the inside is likely to be very different from the customer's view. And your own view is totally irrelevant to customers. The success of any business comes down to what customers do, and they can only act based on what they see. That's why marketing and advertising gurus often say, 'Perception is everything.' You must find ways to listen to your customers and to understand their perceptions of your firm and offerings, because your customers (not you) need to define your marketing methods.

This section requires you to think about and write down some ideas, so get out a pencil and some paper to jot down notes while you're reading.

Finding your customer touchpoints

From the customer's point of view, identify the components of your marketing. (The components include everything and anything that the customer sees, hears, talks to, uses, or otherwise interacts with.) Each customer interaction, exposure, or contact is what we call a touchpoint, where good marketing can help build customer interest and loyalty.

We want to warn you that, if you have a marketing plan or budget already, it probably doesn't reflect this customer perspective accurately. For example, in many firms, the marketing department is separate from product development, yet customers interact with your products so, to them, this is a key component of your marketing.

Similarly, some of the people who sell your product may not be in your plan or even on your company's payroll. A salesperson in the field, a distributor, a wholesaler, or anyone else who sells, delivers, represents, repairs, or services your product is on the marketing frontline from the customer's perspective. All these people may be seen to represent or even be the product, from the customer's point of view. Are they all representing your firm and product properly – with the focus and professionalism you want? Are they available when and where needed? Are they likeable? Is their presentation and personality consistent with your strategy for your marketing? If not, you must find ways to improve these people's impact on the customer, even though you may not have formal authority over them.

Analysing your seven Ps

In marketing, the only things that really matter are points of contact between the customer and your communications, products, and people. These interactions with you constitute your marketing, from the customer's point of view. These are touchpoints, and we find that most of them aren't itemised in a firm's marketing budget or plan.

When does your customer interact with your people, your product, or information about your people and product? Take a few minutes to make up your master list of touchpoints, which will form the basis of a more extensive and accurate marketing plan. To help you do this, we suggest you use the seven Ps of marketing: Product, price, place, promotion, people, process, and physical presence. Now think about your touchpoints using these seven Ps.

There used to be just four Ps of marketing (product, price, place, and promotion), which are sometimes referred to as the *marketing mix*. Every marketing expert seems to have his or her own set of Ps, and wants to interfere with what is a very useful framework for trying to target a specific group of customers with a specific product. All these different ideas are okay – marketing is about challenging orthodoxy, after all. But don't get too hung up on which set of Ps is the right one. The list we give here is the most up to date, and covers all the key touchpoints.

Product

What aspects of the product itself are important – have an influence on customer perception and purchase intentions? Include tangible features that relate to how well the product is meeting current and future customer needs, and intangibles like personality, look and feel, and also packaging. Remember that first impressions are important for initial purchase, but that performance of the product over time is more important for repurchase and referrals.

List the aspects (both rational features and emotional impressions) of your product that influence customer perception.

Price

What does it cost the customer to obtain and use your product? The list price is often an important element of the customer's perception of price, but it isn't the only one. Discounts and special offers are part of the list of price-based touchpoints, too. And don't forget any extra costs the customer may have to incur, like the cost of switching from another product to yours. This can really affect the customer's perception of how attractive your product is. (If you can find ways to make it easier/cheaper to switch from the competitor's product to yours, you may be able to charge more for your product and still make more sales.)

List the aspects of price that influence customer perception.

Place

When and where is your product available to customers? Place is a big influence, because most of the time, customers aren't actively shopping for your product. Nobody runs around all day every day looking for what you want to sell. When someone wants something, they are most strongly influenced by what is available. Getting the place and timing right is a big part of success in marketing and often very difficult. When and where do you currently make your product available to customers?

List the aspects of place (in both time and space) that influence accessibility of your product.

Promotion

This fourth P incorporates any and all ways you choose to communicate to customers. Do you advertise? Send mailings? Hand out brochures? Promotion includes all aspects of communicating with customers: Advertising, personal selling, direct marketing, sales promotion, and public relations. Do distributors or other marketing partners also communicate with your customer? If so, include their promotional materials and methods because they help shape the customer's perception, too. And what about other routine elements of customer communication, like bills? Routine admin forms part of the impression your marketing communications make, too.

List all the ways you have to promote your offering by communicating with customers and prospects.

People

Almost all businesses offer a variety of human contacts to customers and prospective customers, including salespeople, receptionists, service and support personnel, collections, and sometimes shipping, billing, repair, or other personnel, too. All these points of human contact are important parts of marketing, even though they may not all be working well to help keep your marketing focused and effective right now. People need to be trained and motivated to put across the right image for your marketing – and that's down to you, not them.

List all the points of human contact that may be important to the success of your marketing.

Process

You need to think not only about the point when customers buy your product, but everything that happens before and after that. These are the processes through which you connect the product with the customer. Are you identifying prospective customers properly and professionally? Do you keep them informed about deliveries and can you avoid delays? Do you have a proper complaints procedure to alert you to dissatisfaction early on? All these issues aren't as back-office as many companies believe, and they all affect the way your customers perceive your business.

List all the processes involved in delivering your products and services to the customer.

Physical presence

Not all businesses make a tangible product and this latest addition to the list of marketing Ps covers those organisations, and the image they portray to customers. Physical presence means your company's premises, vehicles, and even the appearance of your staff. If you offer services rather than tangible products, you need to provide prospective customers with an image to communicate what your organisation represents (you do anyway, you probably just haven't thought about it or formally planned it).

List all the physical spaces viewed by your customers, from your reception area through to your delivery vehicles and drivers.

Adding to your list

You need to find efficient, effective ways to positively influence customer perception. You want to use elements of your marketing to motivate customers to buy and use your product (service, firm, whatever). The list of your current touchpoints for each of your seven Ps is just a starting point on your journey to an optimal marketing mix.

Now ask yourself what else can be added. Think about each of the Ps and try to add more possible touchpoints. Look to competitors or successful marketers from outside your product category and industry for some fresh ideas. The longer your list of possibilities, the more likely you are to find really good things to include in your marketing.

For example, the energy drink Red Bull uses student ambassadors to talk about the product to other students and to run marketing activities like sampling campaigns on university campuses. The company makes heavy use of advertising as well, but finds that using students to target other students is an effective way of communicating credibly with a core target audience.

Can you think of one or more new ways to reach and influence your customers and prospects in each of the seven Ps? If so, add them to your list as possibilities for your future marketing activity.

Determining what works best for each P

Within each of the seven Ps of marketing, one or two things have the biggest impact and give you the most improvement for your effort. Make your best guess or do some research to find out what works best.

Observe the results from different activities in an experimental way and then focus on those activities that produce the best results. Or you can ask customers or industry experts their opinion to find out what elements of each of the Ps have the biggest impact on your customers and their purchase decisions. Should you concentrate your resources on a bigger presence at industry trade shows, or build up your Web site? Should you use print advertising or hire a public relations consultant to get editorial coverage? The answers to these questions depend on what works best for your marketing strategy, customers, and industry.

Deciding which P is most important

Ask yourself which of the seven Ps needs to be most important in your marketing. If you've already identified what customers like about you (for example, your special quality or a distinct point of difference from competitors), this may point you toward one of the Ps.

The company that sells the quality of its service, for example, obviously needs to emphasise people and process in its marketing and business plan. In contrast, the company whose products are technically superior needs to make sure its marketing investments focus on maintaining the product edge.

Don't be tempted to make price the main focus of your marketing. Many marketers emphasise discounts and low prices to attract customers. But price is a dangerous emphasis for any marketing activity; you're buying customers instead of winning them, and that is a very, very hard way to make a profit in business. So unless you actually have a sustainable cost advantage (a rare thing in business), don't allow low prices or coupons and discounts to dominate your marketing. Price reasonably, use discounts and vouchers sparingly, and look for other things to focus on in your marketing.

Catching the uncontrolled Ps

You can easily lose control of one or more of the seven Ps. In fact, you may never have had control of them in the first place! Small companies often have to use intermediaries or part-time sales staff, while big companies employ so many staff that it can be hard to align them all behind the image you want to portray to customers. Does your marketing display this kind of inconsistency and does it also miss opportunities to get the message across fully and well? If so, you can increase your marketing effectiveness by eliminating these pockets of inconsistency to prevent out-of-control marketing. Given the reality that some of your touchpoints may be partially or fully uncontrolled right now, draw up a list of inconsistent and/or uncontrolled elements of your marketing. You'll probably find some in each of the seven Ps – these inconsistencies are common. And if you can make even one of the elements work better and more consistently with your overall marketing plan and its focus, you're improving the effectiveness of your marketing. Use Table 1-1.

Table 1-1	Getting Your Marketing in Focus
Customer Focus	
Define your customers clearly: Who are they? Where and when do they want to buy?	
Are they new customers, existing customers, or a balanced mix of both?	
Understand what emotional elements make them buy: What personality should your brand have? How should customers feel about your product?	
Understand what functional elements make them buy: What features do they want and need? What information do they need to see in order to make their decision?	
Product Attraction	
What attracts customers to your product?	
What is your special brilliance that sets you apart in the marketplace?	
Do you reflect your brilliance through all your marketing efforts?	
Most Effective Methods	
What is the most effective thing you can do to attract customers?	

(continued)

Table 1-1 *(continued)*	
Most Effective Methods	
What is the most effective thing you can do to retain customers?	
Which of the seven Ps (product, price, place, promotion, people, process, physical presence) is most important in attracting and retaining customers?	
Controlling Points of Contact	
What are all the ways you can reach and influence customers?	
Are you using the best of these right now?	
Do you need to increase the focus and consistency of some of these points of contact with customers?	
What can you do to improve your control over all the elements that influence customer opinion of your product?	
Action Items	
Draw up a list of things you can do based on this analysis to maximise the effectiveness of your marketing.	

Clarifying Your Marketing Expectations

When you make improvements to your marketing, what kind of results can you expect? As a general rule, the percentage change in your marketing activity will at best correspond with the percentage change you see in sales. For example, if you only change 5 per cent of your marketing from one year to the next, you can't expect to see more than a 5 per cent increase in sales over whatever their natural base would be.

Projecting improvements above base sales

Base sales are what you can reasonably count on if you maintain the status quo in your marketing. If, for example, you have seen steady growth in sales of 3 to 6 per cent per year (varying a bit with the economic cycle), then you may reasonably project sales growth of 4 per cent next year, presuming everything else stays the same. But things rarely do stay the same, so you may want to look for any threats from new competitors, changing technology, shifting customer needs, and so on, and be careful to adjust your natural base downward if you anticipate any such threats materialising next year. Your base, if you don't change your marketing, may even be a negative growth rate, because competitors and customers tend to change even if you don't.

After you have a good handle on what your base may be for a status quo sales projection, you can begin to adjust it upward to reflect any improvements you introduce. Be careful in using this tactic, however, because some of the improvements are fairly clearly linked to future sales, while others aren't. If you have tested or tried something already, then you have some real experience upon which to project the improvement's impact. If you're trying something that is quite new to you, be very cautious and conservative about your projections at first, until you have your own hard numbers and real-world experience to go on.

Planning to fail, understanding why, and trying again

Start small with new ideas and methods in marketing so that you can afford to fail and gain knowledge from the experience, and then adjust and try again. Effective marketing formulas are usually developed through a combination of planning and experimentation, not just from planning alone. In marketing, you don't have to feel bad about making mistakes, as long as you recognise the mistakes and take away useful lessons.

When it comes to marketing, we're positive pessimists. Our philosophy is, 'What can go wrong, will go wrong . . . and we'll be fine!' We advise you to avoid being too heavily committed to any single plan or investment. Keep as much flexibility in your marketing as you can. For example, don't buy ads too far in advance even though it would be cheaper, because if sales drop you don't want to be stuck with the financial commitment to a big ad campaign. And favour monthly commissions for salespeople and distributors, because then their pay is variable with your sales and goes down if sales fall – so you don't have to be right about your sales projections.

Flexibility, cautious optimism, and contingency planning give you the knowledge that you can survive the worst. That way, you have the confidence to be a creative, innovative marketer and the courage to grow your business and optimise your marketing. And you can afford to profit from your mistakes.

Don't expect to solve all your company's problems through your marketing. If the product is flawed from the customer's perspective, the best thing you can do as a marketer is to present the evidence and encourage your company to improve the product. Marketing can't make a dog win a horse race, so don't let others in your company try to tell you otherwise.

Finding More Ways to Maximise Your Marketing Impact

We want to end this chapter by sharing our conviction that you can improve your marketing and increase the sales and profits of your business in an infinite number of ways. The preceding sections look at some of the most important ways to focus your marketing, but we want to encourage you to keep searching for more ideas and to implement as many good ideas as you can.

Here, for example, are some additional ways to make the most of your marketing:

- ✔ **Talk to some of your best customers.** Do they have any good ideas for you? (Ignore the ideas that are overly expensive, however. You can't count on even a good customer to worry about your bottom line.)

- ✔ **Thank customers for their business.** A friendly 'Thank you' and a smile, a card or note, or a polite covering letter stuffed into the invoice envelope are all ways to tell your customers you appreciate their business, and people tend to go where they're appreciated and may spread the news – WOM is a powerful tool.

- ✔ **Change your marketing territory.** Are you spread too thinly to be visible and effective? If so, narrow your focus to your core region or customer type. But if you have expansion potential, try broadening your reach bit by bit to grow your territory.

✔ **Get more referrals.** Spend time talking to and helping out people who can send customers your way. And make sure you thank anyone who sends you a lead. Positive reinforcement increases the behaviour.

✔ **Make your marketing more attractive (professional, creative, polished, clear, well written, well produced).** Often, marketing activities can pull better simply by upgrading the look and feel of all the communications and other components. (Did you know that the best-dressed consultants get paid two to five times as much as the average in their fields?)

✔ **Be pleasant, to attract and retain business.** Make sure your people have a positive, caring attitude about customers. If they don't, their negativity is certainly losing you business. Don't let people work against your marketing – spend time making sure they understand that they can control the success of it, and help them through training and good management so that they can take a positive, helpful, and productive approach to all customer interactions.

✔ **Offer a memorable experience for your customer or client.** Make sure that doing business with you is a pleasant, memorable experience. Plan to do something that makes it memorable (in a good way, please!).

✔ **Know what you want to be best at and invest in being the best.** Who needs you if you're ordinary or average? Success comes from being clearly, enticingly better at something than any other company or product. Even if it is only a small thing that makes you special, know what it is and make sure you retain that excellence. It is why you deserve the sale.

✔ **Try to cross-sell additional products (or related services) to your customer base.** Increasing the average size of a purchase or order is a great way to improve the effectiveness of your marketing. But keep the cross-sell soft and natural. Don't sell junk that isn't clearly within your focus or to your customer's benefit.

✔ **Debrief customers who complain or who desert you.** Why were they unhappy? Could you have done something simple to retain them? (But ignore the customers who don't match your target customer profile, because you can't be all things to all people.) A well-handled complaint can teach you a lot and may even turn an angry customer into one of your most loyal – research reveals that customers who have been 'turned around' will even become ambassadors for your business, and spread the word about how good your service is.

Every time you put your marketing hat on, seek to make at least a small improvement in how marketing is done in your organisation and for your customers.

Marketing activity needs to constantly evolve and improve. Most companies fall far short of their full potential, which is why for every hundred businesses, only a few really succeed and grow. The others don't have the right marketing needed to maximise their success. Think big when it comes to marketing. You can always do something more to improve your effectiveness and your results.

Chapter 2

Clarifying Your Marketing Strategy

. . . .

In This Chapter

▶ Thinking about a market expansion strategy

▶ Targeting your customers

▶ Deciding what your market share should be

▶ Rethinking your strategy as you go forward

▶ Keeping your strategy in mind by writing it down

. . . .

Strategies are the big-picture insights that guide your marketing activity and make sure all those activities add up to success. A good strategy gives a special kind of high-level direction and purpose to all you do. This chapter shows you how to take your focus to an even higher level, by centring your marketing on a single, core strategy that gives you an overarching goal. With a core marketing strategy, your marketing begins to fall into place naturally.

The Beauty of Having a Core Strategy

The key to using a core strategy is to make sure that your strategy is the hub around which all your marketing activities rotate.

In Figure 2-1, you can see how a strategy provides an organising central point to a range of marketing activities. This example is for the gift shop at an art gallery and their strategic goal was to get gallery visitors to come into the shop and make a substantial purchase. Gift shop staff developed a variety of tactics for their marketing, each of which is clearly helpful in achieving the strategy or the goal.

As you create your own core strategy, make sure you can draw a solid arrow from your chosen strategy to each of the activities on the rim. Also try to explain in simple words how the activity helps implement your strategy and achieve your strategic goal. If the link to the big-picture strategy isn't clear, modify or eliminate the activity.

Figure 2-1:
A strategy
wheel for
a gallery's
gift shop.

The figure shows a strategy wheel with "Strategy: Increase the average sale size" at the hub, with spokes to:
- Offer more and better products.
- Place low-priced impulse-purchase items by tills.
- Teach salespeople to cross-sell.
- Spend resources on finding and buying unique selection of gift items.
- Offer pre-wrapped gifts during holiday seasons.
- Use brochures to let gallery visitors know what we offer.
- Advertise in magazines with wealthy readers.
- Clearly reflect that all purchases help the gallery.

If you have more than one strategy, draw more than one wheel. But avoid too many or your resources get spread so thinly that you can't achieve *any* of your goals. Also, try to select strategies that have some synergy. The strategy wheels need to belong on the same wagon or they can't move you forward.

Expanding with a Market Expansion Strategy

Market expansion is the most common strategy in marketing. The idea is dis-armingly simple. Just pick some new territory and head out into it. Oh, and don't come back until you've struck gold.

The market expansion strategy has two variants: You can expand your market by finding new customers for your current products (often this means going into new geographic territory to do so), or your can try to sell new products to your existing customers and market.

If you choose to adopt a market expansion strategy as your main focus – the hub of your marketing wheel – then make sure a majority of your marketing activity is working toward this goal. For example, if you seek publicity, make sure most of it is about your new product or in your new market, not about the old. It may take all your resources to effectively expand your market. And the faster you get through the transition and achieve your growth goal, the better, because extra costs are associated with the transition.

Risk increases if you experiment with new products – defined as anything you're not accustomed to making and marketing. And so you should discount your first year's sales projections for a new market by some factor to reflect the degree of risk. A good general rule is to cut back the sales projection by 20 to 50 per cent, depending upon your judgement of how new and risky the product is to you and your team.

Risk also increases if you enter any new market – defined as new kinds of customers at any stage of your distribution channel. You should discount those sales projections by 20 to 50 per cent if you're entering a new market to reflect your lack of familiarity with the customers.

What if you're introducing a new product into a new market? *Start-up firms* often run both these risks at once, and need to discount sales projections even further to reflect this risk. Sometimes a market expansion strategy is so risky that you really should not count on any revenues in the first year. Better to be conservative and last long enough to work out how to correctly handle the marketing than to over-promise and have your marketing die before it succeeds.

Expanding sales within your territory

Innocent Drinks is expanding its market without expanding its geographic territory. In fact, as the company makes fresh fruit smoothies, it's hard to expand geographically, as the nature of its products mean they don't store or ship particularly well. Innocent Drinks' expansion plans are based on increasing the range of drinks it offers. So now, as well as offering single-serve smoothies, it sells family-size cartons, fruit-flavoured waters, and even a product just for kids. With a longer product line, Innocent Drinks can occupy more shelf space in the cafes and sandwich bars where it sells – and get a larger 'share of throat' as a result. The bigger pack size also means the smoothies can make it into people's fridges at home, pushing out traditional rivals like standard fruit juices. Innocent Drinks' sales goals can be increased to reflect its market expansion strategy. But by how much? The answer to that question depends not only on the increase in Innocent Drinks' potential market due to its product expansion, but also on the strategic risks of growing its market. The main risks are that new sales won't really be new, but may be replacement sales for its original smoothies, and that customers won't like the new products as much as the old. Innocent Drinks needs to make sure it keeps product quality high and that the new range is different enough not to cannibalise sales from the original product line.

Specialising with a Market Segmentation Strategy

A *market segmentation strategy* is a specialisation strategy in which you target and cater to (specialise in) just one narrow type or group of customer. If you're in the consulting business, you can specialise in for-profit businesses, or you can specialise in not-for-profit businesses. You can even design and market your services to individuals – as, for example, a career development consultant does. Each of these types of customer represents a subgroup, or segment, of the larger consulting industry. And you can drill down even further to define smaller segments if you want. You can specialise in consulting to the healthcare industry, or to manufacturers of boxes and packaging, or to start-up firms in the high-tech sector. Certain consultants use each of these strategies to narrow down their markets.

The advantage of a segmentation strategy is that it allows you to tailor your product and your entire marketing effort to a clearly defined group with uniform, specific characteristics. For example, the consulting firm that targets only the healthcare industry knows that prospective clients can be found at a handful of healthcare industry conferences and that they have certain common concerns around which consulting services can be focused. Many smaller consulting firms target a narrowly defined market segment in order to compete against larger, but less specialised, consulting firms.

Specialising to outdo the competition

Use the segmentation strategy if you think your business can be more profitable by specialising in a more narrowly defined segment than you currently service. This strategy works well when you face too many competitors in your broader market and you can't seem to carve out a stable, profitable customer base of your own. Also use the specialisation strategy if it takes better advantage of things you're good at. It goes along well with the idea of focusing better, based on your unique qualities (see Chapter 1).

Adding a segment to expand your market

If you're running out of customers and market and need to expand (see the 'Expanding with a Market Expansion Strategy' section earlier in this chapter), one way to do it is to decide to target a new segment. For example, the consultant specialising in coaching executives in the healthcare industry could decide to start offering a similar service to not-for-profit organisations. A different approach and different marketing may be needed, because the two industries are different in many ways and have only partial overlap (much of the healthcare industry is not-for-profit, but many not-for-profit organisations are not hospitals). By specialising in two segments instead of just one, the consulting firm may be able to grow its total sales significantly.

Developing a Market Share Strategy

Another common and powerful strategy is to increase your market share through your marketing activities. In essence, this means taking some business from your competitors. *Market share* is, very simply, your sales as a percentage of total sales for your product category in your market (or in your market segment if you use a segmentation strategy, too).

Calculating your share of the market

If you sell £2 million worth of inflatable paddling pools and the world market totals £20 million per year, then your share of the global inflatable paddling pool market is 10 per cent. The calculation is almost that simple. Or is it? Not quite. To accurately identify your market share, you need to consider what units to use to measure sales, the total sales in your market, your product category, and more. The following sections explain.

Choosing a unit

What unit should you measure sales in? Sterling, euros, units, containers, or grams are fine, as long as you use the same unit throughout. You can calculate your share of the European market for fibre optic cable in metres sold, so long as both your sales and industry sales are measured in metres sold, and euro sales or metric tonnes aren't mixed into the equation by mistake. Just pick whatever seems to make sense for your product and the information you have access to.

For example, if you are a distributor of speciality teas to UK grocery stores and specialist shops, you can buy a market intelligence report on the tea sector (the figures we use here are from a Mintel report) to discover that the total tea market was worth £623 million in 2004. If your sales are £21.8 million, then your market share is 21.8 ÷ 623 or 3.5 per cent.

Alternatively, the report tells you that nearly two-thirds of the market is made up of standard teabag sales that don't compete directly with you, in which case you can calculate your market share of the 16.6 per cent of total sales that are similar speciality teas: $21.8 \div (0.166 \times 623)$ or 21 per cent – a much larger share, based on a narrower definition of the market. Which calculation is right?

Defining your product category

What is your product category? This may be the most important strategic question you ever ask or answer. If you sell speciality teas, are you competing with the mass-market brands like Tetley and PG Tips, or not? Should you count these products' sales in your market share calculations and try to win sales from them?

Ask your customers. Are they choosing among all the tea options, or just some of them? What matters is *customer perception*: How the customers see the category. So watch your customers or ask them to find out what their purchase options are (see Chapter 4 if you want to conduct a formal study). Get a feel for how customers view their choices – then include all the likely or close choices in your definition of the market. With speciality teas, you may find that a majority of consumers do sometimes drink the cheaper mass-market brands, too. And you may also find that you must as a distributor fight for grocery shelf space and room on restaurant menus against the mass-market brands. So you probably do need to use total market sales as your base, not just speciality sales.

Researching the total sales in your market

To calculate market share, you need to estimate the total sales in your market. Doing so requires some research on your part. (Sorry, you can't avoid the research.) While you're at it, why not try to get some historical data – the sales in your market for the past five or ten years, for example? This information allows you to look at the growth rate of your market – which is an indicator of its future potential for you and your competitors.

Such data is most easily obtained from industry trade associations or from marketing research firms, many of which track sales by year in different product categories. There are many companies that offer these market reports, but some of the best known are Mintel (www.mintel.co.uk) or Datamonitor (www.datamonitor.co.uk). Market reports will cost you between £600 and £2,500, depending on the source and size of the report. A cheaper option for more rudimentary data is the trade magazines for the industry of your choice (that generally cover industry size and trends at least once a year). *Marketing*, for example, publishes an analysis on a different consumer goods sector every week. Trade magazines are often the best source for the business-to-business marketer.

Such data is now increasingly available on the Web, too. For keyword searches, enter the name of your product combined with **sales figures** or **market size** and see what you can find. Sites with marketing information abound.

Using the napkin method for estimating market share

Take a look at this simple method for estimating market size and share that you can sketch on the back of a napkin if you haven't the time or money for fancier approaches:

1. **Estimate the number of customers in your market (how many people in your country are likely to buy toothpaste, how many businesses in your city buy consulting services?).**

2. **Estimate how much each buys a year, on average (six tubes, fifteen hours of consulting service).**

   You can check your sales records, or ask some people what they do, to improve this estimate.

3. **Now, just multiply the two figures together to get the total size of the annual market, and then divide your unit sales into it to get your share.**

Setting market share goals

Market share gives you a simple way of comparing your progress with your competitors from period to period. If your share drops, you're losing; if your share grows, you're winning – it's that simple. And so most marketing plans are based at least partly on a *strategic market share goal,* such as: 'Increase share from 5 per cent to 7 per cent by introducing a product upgrade and increasing our use of trial-stimulating special offers.' A tea wholesaler, for example, whose product competes primarily with speciality teas and secondarily with mass-market teas, may develop strategic goals that look something like this:

- ✔ Increase value sales of our products to end consumers of tea from 3.5 per cent to 5 per cent.

- ✔ Protect our share of the speciality tea market by keeping it at 21 per cent or higher.

- ✔ Differentiate ourselves even more from Lipton, Tetley, and other mass-market tea brands by emphasising what makes our tea special to avoid having to compete directly against much larger marketers.

Post mortems on last year's marketing plan should always be based on an examination of what market share change accompanied it. If you don't already do routine post mortems, or careful analyses of what happened and why it differed from your plans, you should. If the past period's marketing doubled your market share, seriously consider replicating it. But if share stayed the same or fell, you're ready for something new. So whether you make share gain the focus of your marketing or not, at least keep it in mind and try not to lose any share.

Should you invest in growing your share?

In addition to its use as a benchmark, market share may also give you insights into the realities of your potential success – well, at least into the future profitability of your product and business. Many experts believe that market share is a good long-term predictor of profitability, arguing that market share leaders are more profitable and successful than other competitors. This belief is taken so seriously in some companies that low-share brands are dropped so as to focus spending on those brands with a chance at category leadership.

If this theory is correct, then you need to build market share aggressively. We favour share-growth strategies because some good studies are showing that high-share businesses have higher returns on investment on average. The Strategic Planning Institute (a consulting firm in Cambridge, USA) has extensive data on market share and financial returns in its PIMS (Profit Impact of Marketing Strategy) database. We like their database because it looks at *business units* (divisions or subsidiaries in a single market) rather than whole companies, so it's more marketing orientated. And those business units with higher market shares have higher pre-tax ROIs (or *returns on investment;* the percentage yield or the amount earned as a percent of the amount invested). The relationship is roughly as shown in Table 2-1.

Table 2-1	Profiting from Market Share
Market Share (%)	*ROI (%)*
Less than 7	10
7 to 15	16
15 to 23	21
23 to 38	23
38 or more	33

Also impressive is some PIMS data suggesting that a gain in market share seems to lead to a corresponding gain in ROI (although the ROI gain is a half to a quarter as large on a percentage basis). You can visit www.pimsonline.com for more details of their research on effective marketing strategies.

Oh, by the way, we must warn you that loss of share leads to loss of ROI. So a good strategy for many plans is to defend existing market share. You can accomplish this by keeping your brand's image well polished, by innovating to keep your product fresh, and by designing good marketing campaigns in general. So we generally advise marketers to defend leading shares, and to try to grow their low shares into leading positions. For example, if you're a strong third-place finisher in the share race, you should probably consider investing in a growth effort in order to leapfrog the number two player and get within striking distance of the number one slot.

But not all studies say the same thing about market share. If you're a small firm with a narrow market niche, trying to grow your share by expanding aggressively can get you in trouble. Balance share growth with the need to avoid excessive risks.

Achieving your market share goals

How can these market share goals be achieved? Consider the tea wholesaler example (refer to the section 'Setting market share goals' earlier in this chapter). For starters, a distributor needs retail shelf space, so you may need to push to win a larger share of shelf space from retailers. And to earn the right to this shelf space, you may need to do some consumer advertising or publicity, provide the stores with good point-of-purchase displays or signs, improve your product packaging, or do other things to help ensure that consumers take a stronger interest in buying your products.

This plan needs to revolve around the goal of increasing share by 1½ percentage points. Each point of share is worth £6.23 million in annual sales (1 per cent of the total sales in the market), so a plan that involved spending, say, an extra £1 million to win a 1.5 per cent share gain can provide an extra £9.35 million if it works. But will it work? To be cautious, the marketer may want to discount this projection of £9.35 million in additional sales by a risk factor of, say, 25 per cent, which cuts it back to a projected gain of £7 million.

Then consider timing. Remember that the plan can't achieve the full gain in the first month of the year. A sales projection starting at the current level of sales in month one and ramping up to the projected increase by, say, the sixth month, may be reasonable. Dividing £7 million by 12 to find the monthly value of the risk-discounted 1.5 share point increase gives you £583,000 in extra monthly sales for the sixth month and beyond. Lower increases apply to earlier months when the marketing is just starting to kick in. But the marketing expenses tend to be concentrated in the early months, reflecting the need to invest in advance in order to grow your market share.

Perhaps the most important research you can do for the market share strategy is to simply study your closest and/or most successful competitors. What do they do well? How do they take business from you now? What new initiatives are they trying this year? The better you understand your competitors, the more easily you can take customers away from them. Talk to customers, suppliers, distributors, and anyone else with good knowledge of your competitors' practices, and gather any online information about them from their Web sites. Also collect your rivals' marketing materials and brochures, and keep track of any information you come across on how they market. For example, if your rivals are picking up good business by having a stand at a trade show you don't attend, then consider getting a booth next time to make sure you're able to compete against them there.

Revising Your Strategy over the Life of the Product Category

Every *product category* – the general grouping of competitive products to which your product belongs (be it merchandise or a service), has a limited life. At least in theory – and usually in all-too-real reality – some new type of product comes along to displace the old. The result is a never-ending cycle of birth, growth, and decline, fueled by the endless inventiveness of competing businesses. Categories of products arise, spread through the marketplace, then decline as replacements arise and begin their own life cycles. Marketing works differently depending on where in its life cycle your product is. In this section, we show you a practical version of the life-cycle model that helps you choose the most applicable of three powerful marketing strategies.

To use the life-cycle model, you must look at the long-term trend in the overall market, as indicated by the sales of your brand and its major competitors.

Interpreting and predicting market growth

Over a long period of time, sales (in sterling, units, or as a share of the potential market) will

- ✔ Follow a sigmoid growth curve (like a stretched-out, right-leaning S, or sigma, in shape).

  Having trouble visualizing that? See the bottom half of Figure 2-2 for a picture of this life-cycle curve. Because of this characteristic pattern, products generally go through a series of four life-cycle stages.

- ✔ Level off to grow at the rate that the customer base grows.

- ✔ Fall off when a replacement product enters the market.

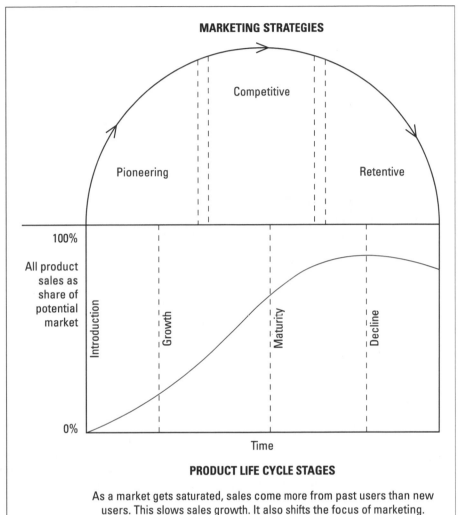

MARKETING STRATEGIES

Competitive

Pioneering

Retentive

100%

All product sales as share of potential market

Introduction

Growth

Maturity

Decline

0%

Time

PRODUCT LIFE CYCLE STAGES

Figure 2-2: Growth rates and market conditions over the product life cycles.

As a market gets saturated, sales come more from past users than new users. This slows sales growth. It also shifts the focus of marketing.

The introduction phase

Sales start slowly because a new product concept takes time to gain momentum and catch on. That situation makes the introductory phase of the life cycle a tough one for marketers. You have to educate consumers about the advantages of the new product. And the more unfamiliar the product is, the more change the product demands from users, and the longer this introductory phase takes. In the introduction phase, marketers emphasise coaching prospective customers about their exciting new product. Here, marketers worry less about competition than about converting the dubious to their cause.

The growth phase

After a while – often after 10 to 20 per cent of the potential market is reached – the idea gains momentum. The life cycle enters its growth stage. Consumers accept the product, and begin to adopt it in greater numbers. Growth rates shoot upward. Unfortunately, the obvious success of the new product attracts more competitors – the number of competing products always grows during the growth phase, so the market leaders generally lose market share. But still, the rapid growth usually enriches all viable competitors and everybody is happy. In this phase of the life cycle, marketers jockey for position by trying to maximise their share of distribution and of consumption, hoping to emerge in maturity as one of the leaders.

The maturity phase

A sad thing happens to end the growth-stage party: Marketers begin to run out of market. After most able-bodied people who like to skate have bought their first pair of in-line roller skates, for example, the nature of the roller skate market has to change. Now you can't get rich just by spreading the good news about this new product. You have to wait until people are ready to replace their old skates, and then you have to fight tooth-and-nail with competitors to make the sale. At best, you keep most of your old customers and pick up a share of the new people who have thoughtfully managed to be born and grow up with a proclivity for roller-skating. The days of heady growth are over because your market is becoming *saturated*, meaning that most potential customers have already found out about and started using the product. In-line roller skates reached this point a few years ago and the mobile phone market will reach it within the next few years.

When a market is saturated, you can no longer grow just by finding new customers. Your ambitions are limited by the rate at which customers replace the product and your ability to steal customers from your competitors. Competitive, share-orientated marketing is the way to go, and you should focus on refining your points of difference from competitors and communicating them clearly to customers.

Stimulating a second childhood

Sometimes markets seem to have matured and then are revived with a new growth phase by creative marketers. The market for television sets was originally assumed to be limited to one TV per household, as it was presumed that watching TV was a family activity. While some homes have had two or more TVs for years, it's only since the rapid growth of multi-channel TV that marketers have really started to push the idea that you can have more individual choice over what you watch when you have multiple TVs and subscriptions to services like Sky.

Reincarnation: Life after the death phase

Some marketers refuse to give up. They think a dose of imagination and some clever marketing can revive a dying product. And sometimes these marketers are right. When Heinz recognised that the market for its Salad Cream was diminishing and wasn't coming back, they decided to kill off the brand. When the news leaked (or was leaked), there was a public outcry and Heinz got enough valuable media coverage to reinvigorate the brand. But it was more than just a PR stunt. The company ran some heavyweight advertising, giving people new ideas on how to use the product on dishes and in recipes. It also changed the pack sizes and packaging. Heinz managed to uncover all the loyal users of Salad Cream, and some new ones to boot. Sales climbed, and so did the price people were prepared to pay for it. Voilà. Life after death. (Old LPs are also having a reincarnation now because of a new generation of DJs and music enthusiasts who prefer the format.)

The death phase

Finally, so the product life-cycle model says, people stop replacing their old products with similar new ones because something even better has come along. Who buys new LP records now that the same music is available on CDs? What will music downloads eventually do to the CD market? Most products eventually enter a decline stage in which sales fall, profits evaporate, and most of the competitors exit. Sometimes you can make good money by hanging on to serve the die-hard loyals, but often this stage is a waste of time. Best to make hay while the sun shines and then switch your product line into some hot new growth markets.

Choosing your life-cycle strategy

In the upper half of Figure 2-2 is the advertiser's version of the life cycle with its helpful emphasis on what to do to win sales. We have redrawn it slightly (usually the model looks like half of a wagon wheel) to make it tie into the product life-cycle drawing. Put the two together, and you have that finest of combinations: Situation diagnosis plus practical prescription.

The advertising life-cycle model says that products go through three stages, each requiring a different marketing strategy: *Pioneering* (use it when the majority of prospects are unfamiliar with the product), *competitive* (use it when the majority of prospects have tried at least one competitor's product), and *retentive* (use it when attracting new customers costs more than keeping old customers). By tying these to the life-cycle model, you can choose the right strategy based on the current growth rate trend in your market. Table 2-2 shows the strategic objectives of each of these stages.

Table 2-2	What to Do in Each Product Stage	
Pioneering	*Competitive*	*Retentive*
Educate consumers	Build brand equity	Retain customers
Encourage trial usage	Position against competitors	Build relationships with customers
Build the distribution channel	Capture a leading market share	Improve quality
Segment market to better serve specific needs	Improve service	Upgrade product

Everything about your marketing follows from these simple strategies. And you can tell when you need them by looking at where you are in your product's life cycle. That makes your strategic thinking fairly simple.

For example, if you're marketing a radical new product that has just begun to experience accelerating sales, then you know you're moving from the introduction to the growth stage of the product life cycle. Table 2-2 indicates that a pioneering strategy should apply. And the table tells you that you need to educate consumers about the new product, encourage them to try it, and make sure that the product is widely distributed. Now you have a clear strategic mandate as you move on to define your marketing activity.

How should you price this pioneering product – high or low? Well, price should be low enough to keep from discouraging new customers, so the high end of the price range may be a mistake. On the other hand, no mandate exists to compete head-to-head on price (that would be more appropriate to the competitive strategy later on). So the best time to use low prices is probably in special offers to stimulate trial. In fact, perhaps free samples are appropriate now, especially if coupled with a moderately high list price.

And your advertising? It certainly needs to be informative, showing potential consumers how to benefit from the product. Similarly, you know you need to encourage distributors to stock and push the product, so special offers to the trade and a strong sales effort (through your own salespeople or through reps or distributors) should get a fair share of your marketing budget.

All these conclusions are fairly obvious – if you stay focused on the strategic guidelines in the model. And that is the beauty of strategy – it makes the details of your tactics so much clearer and simpler.

Designing a Positioning Strategy

A positioning strategy takes a psychological approach to marketing. This strategy focuses on getting customers or prospects to see your product in a favourable light. The positioning goal you articulate for this kind of strategy is the position your product holds in the customer's mind.

When you go to the trouble of thinking through your positioning statement, you have – a positioning statement. So what? You can't use the statement to sell products. But you can use a positioning statement to design all your marketing communications. Everything you do in your marketing, from the product or service's packaging to its advertising and publicity, should work to convince customers of the points your positioning statement contains. So put the statement up over your desk and refer to it to make sure that you communicate the right information and feelings to get the point across and help customers think about your product in the right way.

For example, you may decide to emphasise speed and reliability if you're advertising a courier service. You may even make a grid or positioning map with one axis representing a range from low to high speed and the other from low to high reliability, and then stake out the quadrant where both are as high as your goal, as Figure 2-3 shows.

Figure 2-3: A positioning map for a courier service.

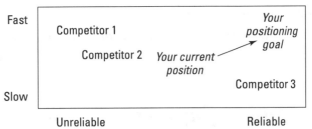

Here are some of the more common options for a positioning strategy:

- ✔ **You may position against a competitor.** 'Our interest rates are lower than Citibank's.' (This tactic is a natural in a mature product category, where the competitive strategy applies.)

- ✔ **You may emphasise a distinctive benefit.** 'The only peanut butter with no harmful transfats.' (This positioning strategy can be combined with a pioneering strategy or a competitive one.)

✔ **You can affiliate yourself with something the customer values.** 'The toothpaste most often recommended by dentists.' (Doing so allows some of the virtues of this other thing to rub off on your brand.) A celebrity endorser, an image of a happy family playing on the beach, a richly appointed manor house set in beautiful gardens, a friendly giant: All have been used to position products favourably in consumers' minds.

You can write down your positioning strategy in big print and pin it above your desk to make sure that you actually stay focused on its execution. Handing out copies of your positioning statement to your ad agency, distributor, PR firm, salespeople, and anyone else who works on or in your product marketing also pays off.

Writing a positioning statement is pretty easy. First you must decide:

✔ What type of customer you target

✔ What you do for that customer

✔ How you do it

✔ Why you do it better than competitors

Next, you should fill in the following with your own words:

✔ Our product offers the following benefit:

✔ To the following customers (describe target segment): _____

✔ Our product is better than competitors in the following manner:

✔ We can prove we're the best because of (evidence/differences): _____

Considering Other Core Strategies

Are there other winning marketing strategies? Certainly. In fact, strategy, like everything in marketing, is only limited by your imagination and initiative. If you can think of a better approach to strategy, go for it. This section goes over a few examples of other strategies that marketers have proven to be effective in recent years. Perhaps one of them may work for you.

Simplicity marketing

After years promoting the latest services and functions you can get through your mobile phone (and thereby the handsets themselves), Vodafone announced the launch of Vodafone Simply. Simply is a basic handset that doesn't do much else than make calls and send text messages. You can still get the fancy 3G phones from Vodafone, but the Simply handsets are designed to appeal to a whole new group of customers – 35-year-olds and older who are put off by complex technology they don't need. Vodafone's new handset is an example of a simplicity strategy.

Use this strategy in your business to position yourself as simpler, easier to understand, and easier to use or work with than the competition. So-called simplicity positioning is a new opportunity according to research firm Datamonitor. This firm predicts that people are going to be increasingly attracted to simple brands that are easy to buy and use. In fact, Datamonitor's studies indicate that many customers are willing to pay a premium in order to avoid complexity and make purchase decisions simply and quickly. Can this approach be useful to customers in your market? Look for technologies or processes that can make your customers' lives simpler and easier.

Quality strategies

Most marketers grossly underrate quality. All else being anywhere near equal, a majority of customers choose the higher-quality option. But be careful to find out what your customers think quality means – they may have a different view from you. Quality as an end itself can be a wasteful and unsuccessful strategy, if your customers plan to replace the product every couple of years. A mobile phone company that made a durable mobile that would last 20 years is adding cost all round – quality should mean better than the competition, not better than is required. And also be careful to integrate your quality-based marketing messages with a genuine commitment to quality in all aspects of your business.

You can't just say you're better than the competition; you really have to deliver. But if customers see you as superior on even one dimension of quality – then by all means emphasise this in your marketing. Quote customer testimonials praising your quality, describe your commitment to quality in your marketing materials, and make trial usage easy for prospective customers so that they can experience your quality, too. And also make sure your pricing is consistent with a high-quality image. Don't focus on advertising big discounts, as these signal cheapness, not quality.

Reminder strategies

A reminder strategy is good when you think people would buy your product if they thought of it – but may not without a reminder. A lot of routine purchases benefit from this strategy. The theme of a recent TV ad made by the British Egg

Industry Council is quite simply to remind people that when they've got eggs in the fridge, they've got enough to cook a meal – 'Eggs make a meal out of anything'.

Point-of-purchase marketing (POP) is often an effective way to implement the reminder strategy. Point-of-purchase marketing simply means doing whatever advertising is necessary to sway the consumer your way at the time and place of their purchase. For retail products, this strategy often means a clever in-store display or sign to remind the consumer.

Writing Down Your Strategy

What is your marketing strategy? Is your strategy a pure version of one of the strategies reviewed in this chapter, or is it a variant or even a combination of more than one of them? Whatever it is, take some time to write your marketing strategy down clearly and thoughtfully. Put your strategy in summary form in a single sentence. (If you must, add some bullet points to explain it in more detail.)

Looking at an example

Here is what one company's marketing strategy looks like:

> Our strategy is to maximise the quality of our security alarm products and services through good engineering and to grow our share of a competitive market by communicating our superior quality to high-end customers.

What you have here is a nice, clear statement of strategy. Now you know what the big-picture game plan is and can set to work designing good products and packaging, friendly services, and impressive ads that communicate your quality to consumers.

Dusting it off and reading it, for goodness sake

Is your strategy obvious in all you do? When you adopt a specific marketing strategy, you must actually read it from time to time and check that you're following it. We're often amazed at the lack of relationship between companies' strategies and their actions.

For example, take the case of a car parts manufacturer emphasising efficiencies as a way to win contracts from the big carmakers. Efficiencies include quicker order turnaround, computer systems to manage orders and inventories better, and substitutable component parts to simplify repairs. Companies like Ford or Toyota want to buy from suppliers who make good component parts quickly, reliably, and cheaply. But this particular firm isn't consistent in communicating its efficiency strategy to its customer base. The firm purchased very handsome full-colour brochures illustrating its marvellous efficiency; however, it hired an inexpensive direct-mail service to send these brochures to its entire customer list. The result was that many of the labels had errors in them, and the envelopes used were so light and cheap that many of them tore during mailing. The impression made was a poor one, and quite inconsistent with the intended strategy.

After you develop a marketing strategy, make sure you follow it. You may need to write your strategy down and display it so that you (and others) can't forget it. In fact, we highly recommend that you do some formal planning to figure out exactly how you will implement your strategy in all aspects of your marketing. And we show you how to develop a plan as painlessly as is possible in Chapter 3.

Chapter 3

Writing a Marketing Plan

· ·

In This Chapter

▶ Avoiding common marketing errors

▶ Writing a powerful executive summary

▶ Clarifying and quantifying your strategic objectives

▶ Gaining an advantage through your situation analysis

▶ Defining your marketing mix

▶ Projecting and controlling revenues and expenses

· ·

*Y*ou don't have to write a marketing plan to use this book or even to benefit from this chapter. But you may want to, because doing so is not as hard as you may think, and, most important, a good plan increases the odds of success. In fact, most of the really successful businesses we know – small or large, new or old – write a careful marketing plan at least once a year.

Marketing combines lots of activities and expenditures in the hope of generating or increasing sales and maintaining or increasing market share. You won't see those sales numbers rise without a coherent plan linking a strategy based on the strengths of your position to your sales and marketing activities that can convince targeted customers to purchase. Marketing can get out of control or confused in a hurry unless you have a plan. Every successful business needs a marketing plan. (Yes, even if you're in a small or start-up business. In fact, especially if you are. You don't have the resources to waste on unplanned or ineffective marketing.)

Identifying Some Planning Rules and Tips

Marketing plans vary significantly in format and outline from company to company, but all have core components covering

- **Your current position** in terms of your product, customers, competition, and broader trends in your market.

- **For established businesses, what results you achieved in the previous period** in terms of sales, market share, and possibly also in terms of profits, customer satisfaction, or other measures of customer attitude and perception. You may want to include measures of customer retention, size, and frequency of purchase, or other indicators of customer behaviour, if you think them important to your new plan.

- **Your strategy,** that is the big picture that will help you get improved results.

- **The details of your marketing activities,** including all your company's specific activities, grouped by area or type, with explanations of how these activities fit the company's strategy and reflect the current situation.

- **The numbers,** including sales projections and costs. Consider whether knowing these additional numbers would help your business: Market share projections, sales to your biggest customers or distributors, costs and returns from any special offers you plan to use, sales projections and commissions by territory, or whatever helps you quantify your specific marketing activities.

- **Your *learning plans,*** if you have a new business or new product, or if you're experimenting with a new or risky marketing activity, **and** want to set up a plan for how to test the waters or experiment on a small scale first. You need to determine what positive results you want to see before committing to a higher level. Wisdom is knowing what you don't know – and planning how to work it out.

The more unfamiliar the waters, the more flexibility and caution your plan needs. If you're a start-up, for example, consider a step-wise plan with a timeline and alternatives or options in case of problems. And if you're writing a marketing plan for the first time, make flexibility your first objective. Avoid large advance purchases of media space or time, use short runs of marketing materials at the copy shop over cheaper off-set printing of large inventories, and so on. (We cover details such as these in Parts III and IV.) Optimising your plan for flexibility means preserving your choice and avoiding commitments of resources. Spending in small increments allows you to change the plan as you go.

If your business has done this all before, however, and your plan builds on years of experience, you can more safely favour _economies of scale_ over flexibility. (It is cheaper and more efficient to advertise, for example, if you do it on a large scale, because you get bigger discounts on design of ads and purchase of media space or airtime.) If you know a media investment is likely to produce leads or sales, go ahead and buy media in larger chunks to get good rates. And don't be as cautious about testing mailing lists with small-scale mailings of a few hundred pieces. A good in-house list supplemented by 20 per cent or fewer newly purchased names probably warrants a major mailing without as much emphasis on advance testing. Adjust your plan to favour economies of scale if you feel confident that you can make sound judgements in advance.

But always leave yourself at least a _little_ wiggle room. Reality never reflects your plans and projections 100 per cent of the time. Aim for an 80 per cent match in marketing, and plan accordingly.

The following sections share a few other suggestions to follow if you want to increase your marketing plan's chances of success.

Avoiding common mistakes

Marketing campaigns end up like leaky boats very easily, so be sure to total up your costs fully and carefully. Each activity seems worthy at the time, but too many of them fail to produce a positive return – ending up like holes in the bottom of your boat: Too many of those holes, and the water starts rising. To avoid the costly but all-too-common mistakes that many marketers make, follow these suggestions:

- **Don't ignore the details.** You build good plans from details like customer-by-customer, item-by-item, or territory-by-territory sales projections. Generalising about an entire market is hard. Your sales and cost projections are easier to get right if you break them down to their smallest natural units (like individual territory sales or customer orders), do estimates for each of these small units, and then add those estimates up to get your totals.

- **Don't imitate the competitors.** Even though everyone seems to market their products in a certain way, you don't have to imitate them. High-performing plans clearly point out what aspects of the marketing are conventional and why – and these plans also include some original, innovative, or unique elements to help differentiate your company from and outperform the competition. Your business is unique, so make your plan reflect your special talents or advantages.

✔ **Don't feel confined by last period's budget and plan.** Repeat or improve the best-performing elements of the past plans, but cut back on any elements that didn't produce high returns. Every plan includes some activities and spending that aren't necessary and can be cut out (or reworked) when you do it all over again next year. Be ruthless with any underperforming elements of last year's plan! (If you're starting a new business, at least this is one problem you don't have to worry about. Yet.)

✔ **Don't engage in unnecessary spending.** Always think your plan through and run the numbers before signing a contract or writing a cheque. Many of the people and businesses you deal with to execute your marketing activities are salespeople themselves. These people's goal is to get *you* to buy their ad space or time, to use their design or printing services, or spend money on fancy Web sites. They want your marketing money and they don't care as much as you do whether you get a good return or not. You have to keep these salespeople on a tight financial rein.

Breaking down your plan into simple sub-plans

If all your marketing activities are consistent and clearly of one kind, a single plan is fine. But what if you sell services (like consulting or repair) and also products? You may find that you need to work up one plan for selling products (perhaps this plan aims at finding new customers) and another plan for convincing product buyers to also use your services. The general rule is that if the plan seems too complicated – divide and conquer! Then total everything up to get the big picture – overall projections and budgets.

If you have 50 products in five different product categories, writing your plan becomes much easier if you come up with 50 sales projections for each product and five separate promotional plans for each category of product. (Believe it or not, this method sounds harder but really is much simpler.) We've included some methods to break down your planning, making it easier and simpler to do:

✔ Analyse, plan, and budget sales activities by sales territory and region (or by major customer if you're a business-to-business marketer with a handful of dominant companies as your clients).

✔ Project revenues and promotions by individual product and by industry (if you sell into more than one).

✔ Plan your advertising and other promotions by product line or other broad product category, as promotions often have a generalised effect on the products within the category.

✔ Plan and budget publicity for your company as a whole. Only budget and plan publicity for an individual product if you introduce it or modify it in some way that may attract media attention.

✔ Plan and budget for brochures, Web sites, and other informational materials. Be sure to remain focused in your subject choices: One brochure per topic. Multipurpose brochures or sites never work well. If a Web site sells cleaning products to building maintenance professionals, don't also plan for it to broker gardening and lawn-mowing services to suburban homeowners. Different products and customers need separate plans.

Remember that every type of marketing activity in your plan has a natural and appropriate level of breakdown. Find the right level, and your planning will be simpler and easier to do.

Writing a Powerful Executive Summary

An executive summary is a one-page plan. This wonderful document conveys essential information about your company's planned year of activities in a couple of hundred well-chosen words or less. If you ever get confused or disorientated in the rough-and-tumble play of sales and marketing, this clear, one-page summary can guide you back to the correct strategic path. A good executive summary is a powerful advertisement for your marketing, communicating the purpose and essential activities of your plan in such a compelling manner that everyone who reads it eagerly leaps into action and does the right things to make your vision come true.

Draft the executive summary early in the year as a guide to your thinking and planning. But revise this summary often, and finish it after finishing all the other sections, because it needs to summarise them.

Help yourself (and your readers, if others in your company are going to be involved in approving or implementing the plan) by giving an overview of what's the same and what's different in this plan, compared with the previous period's plan. Draft a short paragraph covering these two topics.

Summarise the main points of your plan and make clear whether the plan is

✔ **Efficiency orientated:** Say that your plan introduces a large number of specific improvements in how you market your product.

✔ **Effectiveness orientated:** Say that your plan identifies a major opportunity or problem and adopts a new strategy to respond to it.

Make sure that you summarise the bottom-line results – what your projected revenues will be (by product or product line, unless you have too many to list on one page) and what the costs are. Also show how these figures differ from last year's figures. Keep the whole summary under one page in length if you possibly can.

If you have too many products to keep the summary under one page in length, you can list them by product line. But a better option is to do more than one plan. You probably haven't clearly thought out any plan that can't be summarised in a page. We've worked with many businesses in which marketing prepares a separate plan for each product. Divide and conquer.

Clarifying and Quantifying Your Objectives

Objectives are the quantified, measurable versions of your strategies. For example, if your strategy involves raising the quality of service and opening a new territory in order to grow your sales and market share, you need to think through how you'll do all that and set a percentage increase goal for sales and a new, higher goal for market share. These numbers become your objectives. The objectives flow from your thinking about strategies and tactics, but put them up near the front of your plan to help others quickly understand what you're saying.

What objectives do you want your plan to help you accomplish? Will the plan increase sales by 25 per cent, reposition a product to make it more appealing to upmarket buyers, introduce a direct marketing function via the Internet, or launch a new product? Maybe the plan will combine several products into a single family brand and build awareness of this brand through print and radio advertising, which will gain market share from several competitors and cut the costs of marketing by eliminating inefficiencies in coupon processing, media buying, and sales force management. Address these sorts of topics in the objectives section of the plan. These points give the plan its focus.

If you write clear, compelling objectives, you'll never get too confused about what to write in other sections – when in doubt, you can always look back at these objectives and remind yourself what you're trying to accomplish and why.

Try to write this part of the plan early, but keep in mind that you'll rewrite it often as you gather more information and do more thinking. Objectives are such a key foundation for the rest of the plan that you can't ever stop thinking about them. However, for all their importance, objectives don't need a lot of words – half a page to two pages, at most. (Paradoxically, we have to tell you more about these short upfront sections than about the longer, detail-orientated sections in the back because planners find the short sections more conceptually challenging.)

Preparing a Situation Analysis

The context is different for every marketing plan. A *situation analysis* examines the context, looking at trends, customer preferences, competitor strengths and weaknesses, and anything else that may impact sales. The question your situation analysis must answer is, 'What's happening?' The answer to this question can take many forms, so we can't give you an easy formula for preparing the situation analysis. You should analyse the most important market changes to your company – these changes can be the sources of problems or opportunities. (See Chapter 4 for formal research techniques and sources.)

But what most important changes have occurred since you last examined the situation? The answer depends on the situation. See the difficulty? Yet somehow you have to gain enough insight into what's happening to see the problems and opportunities clearly.

Seeing trends more clearly than others do

Your goal is to see the changes more clearly than the competition. Why? Because if your situation analysis isn't as accurate as the competition's, you'll lose market share to them. If your analysis is about the same as your competition's, then you may hold even. Only if your situation analysis is better than your rivals' can you gain market share on the competition.

What you want from your situation analysis is

- ✔ **Information parity:** When you know as much as your leading competitors know. If you don't do enough research and analysis, your competitors will have an information advantage. Therefore, you need to gain enough insight to put you on a level playing field with your competitors. (That includes knowing about any major plans they may have. Collect rumours about new products, new people, and so on. At a minimum, do a weekly search on a Web-based search engine for any news about them.)

- ✔ **Information advantage in specific areas:** Insight into the market that your competitors don't have. Information advantage puts you on the uphill side of an uneven playing field and that's an awfully good place from which to design and launch a marketing campaign. Look for new fashions, new technologies, new ways to segment the market – anything that you can use to change the rules of the game even slightly in your favour.

Most marketing plans and planners don't think about their situation analysis in this way. We're telling you one of our best-kept secrets because we don't want you to waste time on the typical *pro forma* situation analysis, in which the marketer rounds up the usual suspects and parades dull information in front of them without gaining an advantage from it. That approach, although common, does nothing to make the plan a winner.

Using a structured approach to competitor analysis

What kinds of information can you collect about your competitors? You can gather and analyse examples of competitors' marketing communications. You may have (or be able to gather) some customer opinions from surveys or informal chats. You can group the information you get from customers into useful lists, like discovering the three most appealing and least appealing things about each competitor. You can also probably get some information about how your competitors distribute and sell, where they are (and aren't) located or distributed, who their key decision-makers are, who their biggest and/or most loyal customers are, and even (perhaps) how much they sell. Gather any available data on all-important competitors and organise the information into a table for easy analysis.

Building a competitor analysis table

Here's an example of a format for a generic Competitor Analysis Table. Make entries on the following rows in columns labelled for Competitor #1, Competitor #2, Competitor #3, and so on:

- ✔ **Company.** Describe how the market perceives it and its key product.

- ✔ **Key personnel.** Who are the managers, and how many employees do they have in total?

- ✔ **Financial.** Who owns it, how strong is its *cash position* (does it have spending power or is it struggling to pay its bills), what were its sales in the last two years?

- ✔ **Sales, distribution, and pricing.** Describe its primary sales channel, discount/pricing structure, and market share estimate.

- ✔ **Product/service analysis.** What are the strengths and weaknesses of its product or service?

- ✔ **Scaled assessment of product/service.** Explore relevant subjects like market acceptance, quality of packaging, ads, and so on. Assign a score of between 1 and 5 (with 5 being the strongest) for each characteristic you evaluate. Then add the scores for each competitor's row to see which seems strongest, overall.

- ✔ **Comparing yourself to competitor ratings.** If you rate yourself on these attributes, too, how do you compare? Are you stronger? If not, you can include increasing your competitive strength as one of your plan's strategic objectives.

Explaining Your Marketing Strategy

Many plans use this section to get specific about the objectives by explaining how your company will accomplish them. Some writers find this task easy, but others keep getting confused about the distinction between an objective and a strategy. The objective simply states something your business hopes to accomplish in the next year. The strategy emphasises the big-picture approach to accomplishing that objective, giving some good pointers as to what road you'll take.

An objective sounds like this: Solidify our leadership of the home PC market by increasing market share by 2 points.

A strategy sounds like this: Introduce hot new products and promote our brand name with an emphasis on high quality components, in order to increase our market share by 2 points.

Is your strategy flaky?

What do you do if you're the leading producer of breakfast cereals, but the total market for breakfast cereals is declining? Find new and exciting ways for people to consume breakfast cereals, obviously. When Kellogg decided to launch its Cereal Mates product, it thought it was following changes in customer behaviour rather than asking people to radically change their ways. The pattern of breakfast consumption had changed, with fewer people having the time or inclination for a sit-down breakfast at home. The trend was for breakfast on the go, so Kellogg created cereal to go.

Cereal Mates was an all-in-one single serve version of Kellogg's most popular breakfast cereal. It came with its own spoon and was sealed in such a way that the milk didn't need refrigerating. Mistake number one – consumers didn't want warm milk on their cereal. So Kellogg changed tactic and situated Cereal Mates in supermarket chill cabinets. Mistake number two – who looks in the chill cabinets for breakfast cereal?

Consumers were even more confused by the advertising, which showed kids helping themselves at home while their parents slept. Finally, the price was prohibitive (certainly too high to encourage trial) at around 65p. You could buy a family-sized box for not much more than that.

Cereal Mates was killed off in the end, when Kellogg finally realised they had mistaken a change in consumer eating habits with a change in the way people wanted to consume breakfast cereal – not the same thing at all. The company got the strategy right when it eventually launched a product that could be eaten on the go but was only dimly related to cereal at all – its NutriGrain bars. You have to sense-check your strategy, especially when you're asking your customers to try something radically different.

Combining strategies and objectives

Some people view the difference between objectives and strategies as a pretty fine line. If you're comfortable with the distinction, write a separate *Strategy* section. If you're not sure about the difference, combine this section with the objectives section and title it *Objectives and Strategies*; what you call the points doesn't matter, as long as they're good. For more details about how to develop and define marketing strategies, see Chapter 2.

Your strategies accomplish your objectives through the tactics (the seven Ps) of your marketing plan. (See Chapter 1 for a discussion of the seven Ps, sometimes also known as the *marketing mix*.) The plan explains how your tactics use your strategies to accomplish your objectives.

Giving your strategy common sense

This advice is tough to realise. Unlike a mathematical formula or a spreadsheet column, you don't have a simple method to check a marketing strategy to make sure that it really adds up. But you can subject a marketing strategy to common sense and make sure that it has no obvious flaws – as outlined in the following sections.

Strategy fails to reflect limitations in your resources

Don't pull a Napoleon. If you're currently the tenth-largest competitor, don't write a plan to become the number one largest by the end of the year simply based on designing all your ads and mailings to claim you're the best. Make sure that your strategy is achievable. Would the average person agree that your strategy sounds attainable with a little hard work? (If you're not sure, find some average people and ask them.) And do you have enough resources to execute the strategy in the available time?

Strategy demands huge changes in customer behaviour

You can move people and businesses only so far with marketing. If you plan to get employers to give their employees every other Friday off so those employees can attend special workshops your firm sponsors, well, we hope you have a back-up plan. Employers don't give employees a lot of extra time off, no matter how compelling your sales pitch or brochure may be. The same is true of consumer marketing. You simply cannot change strongly held public attitudes without awfully good new evidence.

A competitor is already doing the strategy

This assumption is a surprisingly common error. To avoid this mistake, include a summary of each competitor's strategy in the *Strategy* section of your plan. Add a note explaining how your strategy differs from each of them. If you're marketing a computer installation and repair service in the Liverpool area, you really need to know how your strategy differs from the multiple competitors also trying to secure big corporate contracts in that area. Do you specialise in certain types of equipment that others don't? Do you emphasise speed of repair service? Are you the only vendor who distributes and supports CAD/CAM equipment from a leading maker? You need a distinctive strategy to power your plan. You don't want to be a me-too competitor.

Strategy requires you to know too much that you don't already know

You can't use some brilliant strategies for your business because they would require you to do too many things you don't know anything about. For example, there is a growing need for computer skills training, but if your business is in selling and servicing computer equipment, that doesn't automatically give you experience in developing, selling, or delivering computer courses. Strategies that involve doing a lot of things you have little or no expertise in are really start-up strategies, not marketing strategies. If you want to put a minority of your resources into trying to start a new business unit, go ahead. But don't put your entire marketing plan at risk by basing it on a strategy that takes you into unfamiliar waters.

Summarising Your Marketing Mix

Your *marketing mix* is the combination of marketing activities you use to influence a targeted group of customers to purchase a specific product or line of products. Creating an integrated and coherent marketing mix starts, in our view, with an analysis of your *touchpoints* (see Chapter 2) – in other words, how your organisation can influence customer purchases. And the creative process ends with some decisions about how to use these touchpoints. Usually you can come up with tactics in all seven of the marketing Ps: Product, price, place (or distribution), promotions, people, process, and physical presence.

Prioritising your touchpoints and determining cost

Prioritise by picking a few primary touchpoints – ones that will dominate your marketing for the coming planning period. This approach concentrates your resources, giving you more leverage with certain components of the mix. Make the choice carefully; try to pick no more than three main activities to take the lead. Use the (usually many) other touchpoints in secondary roles to support your primary points. Now you begin to develop specific plans for each, consulting later chapters in this book as needed to clarify how to use your various marketing components.

Say that you're considering using print ads in trade magazines to let retail store buyers know about your hot new line of products and the in-store display options you have for them. That's great, but now you need to get specific. You need to pick some magazines. (Call their ad departments for details on their demographics and their prices – see Chapter 7 for how.) You also need to decide how many of what sort of ads you'll run, and then price out this advertising campaign.

Do the same analysis for each of the items on your list of marketing components. Work your way through the details until you have an initial cost figure for what you want to do with each component. Total these costs and see if the end result seems realistic. Is the total cost too big a share of your projected sales? Or (if you're in a larger business), is your estimate higher than the boss says the budget can go? If so, adjust and try again. After a while, you get a budget that looks acceptable on the bottom line and also makes sense from a practical perspective.

A spreadsheet greatly helps this process. Just build formulas that add the costs to reach subtotals and a grand total, and then subtract the grand total from the projected sales figure to get a bottom line for your campaign. Figure 3-1 shows the format for a very simple spreadsheet that gives a quick and accurate marketing campaign overview for a small business. In this figure, you can see what a campaign looks like for a company that wholesales products to gift shops around the UK. This company uses personal selling, telemarketing, and print advertising as its primary marketing components. The company also budgets some money in this period to finish developing and begin introducing a new line of products.

This company's secondary influence points don't use much of the marketing budget when compared with the primary influence points. But the secondary influence points are important, too. A new Web page is expected to handle a majority of customer enquiries and act as a virtual catalogue, permitting the company to cut back on its catalogue printing and postage costs. Also, the company plans to introduce a new line of floor displays for use at point of purchase by selected retailers. Marketers expect this display unit, combined with improved see-through packaging, to increase turnover of the company's products in retail stores.

Marketing plans for multiple groups

If your marketing plan covers multiple groups of customers, you need to include multiple spreadsheets (such as the one in Figure 3-1) because each group of customers will need a different marketing mix.

Overview of Campaign to Target Retail Store Buyers	
Components	**Direct Marketing Costs (£)**
Primary influence points:	
– Sales calls	£265,100
– Telemarketing	162,300
– Ads in trade magazines	650,000
– New product line development	100,000
	Subtotal: £1,177,400
Secondary influence points:	
– Quantity discounts	£45,000
– Point-of-purchase displays	73,500
– New Web page with online catalogue	15,000
– Printed catalogue	30,500
– PR	22,000
– Packaging redesign	9,200
	Subtotal: £195,200
Projected Sales from This Programme	£13,676,470
Minus Campaign Costs	– 1,372,600
Net Sales from This Marketing Campaign	**£12,303,870**

Figure 3-1:
A campaign budget, prepared on a spreadsheet.

For example, the company whose wholesale marketing campaign you see in Figure 3-1 sells to gift shops. But the company also does some business with stationery shops. And even though the same salespeople call on both, each of these customers has different products and promotions. They buy from different catalogues. They don't use the same kinds of displays. They read different trade magazines. Consequently, the company has to develop a separate marketing campaign for each customer, allocating any overlapping expenses appropriately. (For example, if you make two-thirds of your sales calls to gift shops, then the sales calls expense for the gift shop campaign should be two-thirds of the total sales budget.)

Exploring Your Marketing Components

In this part of your plan, you need to explain the details of how you plan to use each component of your marketing mix. Devote a section to each component, which means that this part of your plan may be quite lengthy (give it as many pages as you need to lay out the necessary facts). The more of your thinking you get on paper, the easier implementing the plan will be later – as will rewriting the plan next year.

Although this portion is the lengthiest part of your plan, we're not going to cover it in depth here. You can find details about how to use specific components of a marketing mix, from product positioning to Web pages to pricing, in Chapters 7 to 17 of this book.

At a minimum, this part of the plan should have sections covering the *seven Ps* – the product, pricing, place (or distribution), promotion, people, process, and physical presence. But more likely, you'll want to break these categories down into more specific areas. You can even get as detailed as this book does, having a section corresponding to each of Chapters 7 to 17, for example.

Don't bother going into detail in your marketing plan on components that you cannot alter. Sometimes, the person writing the marketing plan can't change pricing policy, order up a new product line, or dictate a shift in distribution strategy. Explore your boundaries and even try to stretch them, but you need to admit they exist or your plan can't be practical. If you can only control promotion, then this section of the plan should concentrate on the ways that you'll promote the product – in which case, never mind the other Ps. Acknowledge in writing any issues or challenges you have to cope with, given that you can't change other factors. Now write a plan that does everything you can reasonably do given your constraints. (A section called *Constraints* ought to go into the *Situation analysis* if your company has such constraints.)

Managing Your Marketing

The main purpose of the management section of the plan is simply to make sure that enough warm bodies are in the right places at the right times to get the work done. The management section summarises the main activities that you, your employees, or your employer must perform in order to implement the components of your marketing mix. The section then assigns these activities to individuals, justifying the assignments by considering issues such as an individual's capabilities, capacities, and how the company will supervise and control that individual.

Sometimes this section gets more sophisticated by addressing management issues, like how to make the sales force more productive or whether to decentralise the marketing function. If you have salespeople or distributors, develop plans for organising, motivating, tracking, and controlling them. Also develop a plan for them to use in generating, allocating, and tracking sales leads. Start these subsections by describing the current approach, and do a strengths/weaknesses analysis of that approach, using input from the salespeople, reps, or distributors in question. End by describing any incremental changes/improvements you can think to make.

Make sure that you've run your ideas by the people in question *first* and received their input. Don't surprise your salespeople, sales reps, or distributors with new systems or methods. If you do, these people will probably resist the changes, and sales will slow down. So schmooze and share, persuade and propose, and enable them to feel involved in the planning process. People execute sales plans well only if they understand and believe in those plans.

Projecting Expenses and Revenues

Now you need to put on your accounting and project management hats. (Neither hat fits very well, perhaps, but try to bear them for a day or two.) You need these hats to

- ✔ Estimate future sales, in units and by value, for each product in your plan.

- ✔ Justify these estimates and, if they're hard to justify, create worst-case versions, too.

- ✔ Draw a timeline showing when your marketing incurs costs and when each component begins and ends. (Doing so helps with the preceding section and also prepares you for the unpleasant task of designing a monthly marketing budget.)

- ✔ Write a monthly marketing budget that lists all the estimated costs of your activity for each month of the coming year and breaks down sales by product or territory and by month.

If you're a start-up or small business, we highly recommend doing all your projections on a *cash basis*. In other words, put the payment for your year's supply of brochures in the month in which the printer wants the money, instead of allocating that cost across 12 months. Also factor in the wait time for collecting your sales revenues. If collections take 30 days, show money coming in during December from November's sales, and don't count any December sales for this year's plan. A cash basis may upset accountants, who like to do things on an accrual basis – see *Accounting For Dummies*, 2nd Edition, by John A. Tracy (Wiley) if you don't know what that means – but cash-based accounting keeps small businesses alive. You want a positive cash balance (or at least to break even) on the bottom line during every month of your plan.

If your cash-based projection shows a loss some months, fiddle with the plan to eliminate that loss (or arrange to borrow money to cover the gap). Sometimes a careful cash-flow analysis of a plan leads to changes in underlying strategy. One business-to-business company adopted as its primary marketing objective the goal of getting more customers to pay with credit cards instead of on invoices. The company's business customers co-operated, and average collection time shortened from 45 days to under 10, greatly improving the cash flow and thus the spending power and profitability of the business.

Several helpful techniques are available for projecting sales, such as build-up forecasts, indicator forecasts, and time-period forecasts. Choose the most appropriate technique for your business based on the reviews in this section. If you're feeling nervous, just use the technique that gives you the most conservative projection. Here's a common way to play it safe: Use several of the techniques and average their results.

Build-up forecasts

These predictions go from the specific to the general, or from the bottom up. If you have sales reps or salespeople, ask each one to project the next period's sales for their territories and justify their projections based on what changes in the situation they anticipate. Then aggregate all the sales force's forecasts to obtain an overall figure.

If you have few enough customers that you can project per-customer purchases, build up your forecast this way. You may want to work from reasonable estimates of the amount of sales you can expect from each shop carrying your products or from each thousand catalogues sent out. Whatever the basic building blocks of your marketing, start with an estimate for each element and then add these estimates up.

Indicator forecasts

This method links your forecast to economic indicators that ought to vary with sales. For example, if you're in the construction business, you find that past sales for your industry correlate with *GDP* (gross domestic product, or national output) growth. So you can adjust your sales forecast up or down depending upon whether experts expect the economy to grow rapidly or slowly in the next year.

Multiple scenario forecasts

You base these forecasts on what-if stories. They start with a straight-line forecast in which you assume that your sales will grow by the same percentage next year as they did last year. Then you make up what-if stories and project their impact on your plan to create a variety of alternative projections.

You may try the following scenarios if they're relevant to your situation:

- What if a competitor introduces a technological breakthrough?
- What if your company acquires a competitor?
- What if the government deregulates/regulates your industry?
- What if a leading competitor fails?
- What if your company has financial problems and has to lay off some of your sales and marketing people?
- What if your company doubles its ad spending?

For each scenario, think about how customer demand may change. Also consider how your marketing would need to change in order to best suit the situation. Then make an appropriate sales projection. For example, if a competitor introduced a technological breakthrough, you may guess that your sales would fall 25 per cent short of your straight-line projection.

The trouble with multiple scenario analysis is that . . . well, it gives you multiple scenarios. Your boss (if you have one) wants a single sales projection, a one-liner at the top of your marketing budget. One way to turn all those options into one number or series of numbers is to just pick the option that seems most likely to you. That's not a very satisfying method if you aren't at all sure which option, if any, will come true. So another method involves taking all the options that seem even remotely possible, assigning each a probability of occurring in the next year, multiplying each by its probability, and then averaging them all to get a single number.

For example, the Cautious Scenario projection estimates £5 million, and the Optimistic Scenario projection estimates £10 million. The probability of Cautious Scenario occurring is 15 per cent, and the probability of Optimistic Scenario occurring is 85 per cent. So you find the sales projection with this formula: [(£5,000,000 × 0.15) + (£10,000,000 × 0.85)] ÷ 2 = £4,630,000.

Time-period projections

To use this method, work by week or month, estimating the size of sales in each time period, and then add these estimates for the entire year. This approach helps you when your marketing activity or the market isn't constant across the entire year. Ski resorts use this method because they get certain types of revenues only at certain times of the year. And marketers who plan to introduce new products during the year or to use heavy advertising in one or two *pulses* (concentrated time periods) also use this method because their sales go up significantly during those periods. Entrepreneurs, small businesses, and any others on a tight cash-flow lead need to use this method because you get a good idea of what cash will be flowing in by week or month. An annual sales figure doesn't tell you enough about when the money comes in to know whether you'll be short of cash in specific periods during the year.

Creating Your Controls

This section is the last and shortest of your plan – but in many ways, it's the most important. This section allows you and others to track performance.

Identify some performance benchmarks and state them clearly in the plan. For example:

- ✔ All sales territories should be using the new catalogues and sales scripts by 1 June.
- ✔ Revenues should grow to £75,000 per month by the end of the first quarter if the promotional campaign works according to plan.

These statements give you (and, unfortunately, your employers or investors) easy ways to monitor performance as you implement the marketing plan. Without these targets, nobody has control over the plan; nobody can tell whether or how well the plan is working. With these statements, you can identify unexpected results or delays quickly – in time for appropriate responses if you have designed these controls properly.

A good marketing plan gives you focus, a sense of direction and increases your likelihood to succeed, but writing a good one takes time and many businesses don't have a lot of that to spare. A sensible rule is to spend time on your marketing plan, but not so much that you don't have a chance to look up and see whether the market has changed since you started writing it. If the plan you wrote at the start of the year is no longer relevant because business conditions have changed quickly then tear it up and start again – don't stick rigidly to it.

Using Planning Templates and Aids

Referring to model plans can help you in this process. Unfortunately, most companies don't release their plans – they rightly view them as trade secrets. Fortunately, a few authors have compiled plans or portions of them, and you can find some good published materials to work from.

You can look at sample marketing plans and templates in several different books. These texts show you alternative outlines for plans, and they also include budgets and revenue projections in many formats – one of which may suit your needs pretty closely:

- *The Marketing Kit For Dummies*, by Alex Hiam (Wiley) includes a five-minute marketing plan worksheet if you're the impatient sort

- *The Marketing Plan*, by William Cohen (Wiley), is a practical step-by-step guide that features sample plans from real businesses

- *The Marketing Planning Tool* is an online planning tool available free through the 'Marketing Shop' section of the Chartered Institute of Marketing's Web site (www.cim.co.uk)

Part II
Creative Thinking, Powerful Marketing

"Are you sure this stunt is going to sell our custard pies, Colin?"

In this part . . .

Albert Einstein once said that imagination is more important than knowledge. But still, knowledge can be useful too. In Part II we help you ground your marketing efforts in both. We share ways of increasing your knowledge of your customers, competitors, and market, and we also help you turn your imagination into profitable marketing ideas and actions.

Several basic skill sets underlie everything else you do in marketing. Great marketing demands skills in analysis, so we show you how to do some simple market research in this part. But great marketing also requires creativity and imagination, and we devote an entire chapter to helping you dip into this free and easy-to-leverage asset of your business. A little imagination can increase the return on a marketing or advertising effort by a factor of ten, so please make sure that you tap into the power of your marketing imagination!

The third essential skill is communications, the key to almost every aspect of marketing. In this section of the book, we help you translate the insights from your research and creativity into really powerful marketing communications, no matter which of the many media you choose to communicate though (which we talk about in later sections of this book).

Chapter 4

Researching Your Customers, Competitors, and Industry

● ●

In This Chapter

▶ Why research matters

▶ Planning and doing original research

▶ Finding quick research techniques

▶ Profiting from existing information sources

● ●

*W*hat makes your product or service better or worse than that of your competitors? That question, and more like it, can help you tighten up your strategy, make more accurate sales projections, and decide what to emphasise (visually or verbally) in your marketing communications. A little research can go a long way toward improving the effectiveness of your marketing.

One per cent of companies do 90 per cent of all market research. Big businesses hire research firms to do extensive customer surveys and to run discussion groups with customers. The marketers then sit down to 50-page reports filled with tables and charts before making any decisions. I don't recommend this expensive approach, which can lead to analysis paralysis – where those that can afford to spend more time pouring over the mountains of data they have generated than they do on actually acting on it.

Instead, in this chapter, I help you adopt an inquisitive approach by sharing relatively simple and efficient ways of learning about customers, competitors and the environment. As a marketer, you need to challenge assumptions by asking the questions that lead to useful answers – something you can do on any budget. In the end, not only will you know what you need to know about your customers and competitors, but you'll also better understand your own business.

Why Research Matters – and What to Focus On

Many large companies do so much research, in part, to cover the marketer's you-know-what if the marketing campaign subsequently fails, and more than half of all market research expenditure really just builds the case for pursuing strategies the marketers planned to do anyway. These marketers use research in the same way a drunk uses a lamppost – for support rather than illumination. Other business people refuse to research anything at all because they know the answers already, or think they do. Gut instinct will only get them so far before the ideas, customers, or both run out.

Doing research to cover your derriere or to bolster your already-decided-upon plans is a waste of time and money spent doing endless surveys and focus groups. A *focus group* is a group of potential or actual customers who sit behind a one-way mirror discussing your product while a trained moderator guides their conversation and hidden video cameras immortalise their every gesture and phrase. Of course, you don't have to be so formal with your research techniques. You can always just ask your customers what they think of your product or service – it's not as impartial, but it may tell you everything you need to know without having to pay professional researchers.

So, what are good reasons to do research? Basically, if you can get a better idea or make a better decision after conducting market research, then research is worth your while. You should embrace research because it is the first step to making your company customer-orientated rather than product-orientated. In other words, asking what your customers want from your business is a better starting point than merely trying to sell them what you've already got – and makes for a more profitable business. If you can find out where your customers are, what they want, and how best to reach them, then you are on the right path to doing better business.

Research for better ideas

Information can stimulate the imagination, suggest fresh strategies, or help you recognise great business opportunities. So always keep one ear open for interesting, surprising, or inspiring facts. Don't spend much money on this kind of research. You don't need to buy in an expensive trendwatching service to keep a businesslike eye on new consumer developments that may affect your market. Instead, take subscriptions to a diverse range of publications and make a point of talking to people of all sorts, both in your industry and beyond it, to keep you in the flow of new ideas and facts. Also, ask other people for their ideas and interests.

Every marketer should carry an ideas notebook with them wherever they go and make a point of collecting a few contributions from people every day. This habit gets you asking salespeople, employees, customers, and complete strangers for their ideas and observations. You never know when a suggestion may prove valuable.

Research for better decisions

Do you have any situations that you want more information about before making a decision? Then take a moment to define the situation clearly and list the options you think are feasible. Choosing the most-effective advertising medium, making a more accurate sales projection, or working out what new services your customers want – these situations provide examples of important decisions that research can help you make.

Suppose, for example, that you want to choose between print ads in industry magazines and e-mail advertisements to purchased lists. Figure 4-1 shows what your notes may look like.

Research for your strengths and weaknesses

Perception is everything. What customers think of your product or service is ultimately what determines the success of your business, which is why you should make a habit of asking them, on a regular basis, what they love and what they hate about it.

So how do you find out what customers think? By asking customers to rank you on a list of descriptors for your business/product/service. The scale ranges from 1 to 10 (to get a good spread), with the following labels:

Very bad		Bad		Average		Good		Very good	
1	2	3	4	5	6	7	8	9	10

If you collect a rating of all the descriptive features of your product from customers, many of those ratings will prove quite ordinary. Consider the type of responses you'd get for a bank branch. The list of items to rate in a bank may include current accounts, savings accounts, speed of service, and friendliness of banking staff, along with many other things you'd need to put on the list in order to describe the bank, in detail. You're likely to discover that some items, like current accounts and saving accounts, get average ratings. The reason is that every bank offers those and, in general, handles such accounts in the same way. But a few of the features of a particular bank may be notably exceptional – for better or for worse.

Decision	Information Needs	Possible Sources	Findings
Choose between print ads in industry magazines and e-mail advertisements to purchased lists	How many actual prospects can print ads reach?	Magazines' ad salespeople can tell us.	Three leading magazines in our industry reach 90 per cent of good customers, but half of these are not in our geographic region. May not be worth it?
	What are the comparable costs per prospect reached through these different methods?	Just need to get the budget numbers and number of people reached and divide available money by number of people.	E-mail is a third of the price in our market.
	Can we find out what the average response rates are for both magazine ads and e-mails?	Nobody is willing to tell us, or they don't know. May try calling a friend in a big ad agency; they may have done a study or something.	Friend says response rates vary wildly, and she thinks the most important thing is how relevant the customer finds the ad, not the medium used.
	Have any of our competitors switched from print to e-mail successfully?	Can probably get distributors to tell us this. Will call several and quiz them.	No, but some companies in similar industries have done this successfully.

Conclusions?

Seems like we'll spend less and be more targeted if we design special e-mails and send them only to prospects in our region. Don't buy magazine ad space for now; we can experiment with e-mail, instead. But we need to make sure the ads we send are relevant and seem important, or people just delete them without reading them.

Figure 4-1:
Analysing the information needs of a decision.

Bright spark

Here's a great example of discovering weaknesses through research and turning them into strengths. Comet, the chain of electrical stores, had been losing sales for several years to supermarkets and general retailers as they entered the market. It decided that some flashy destination stores would fix the problem and set about overhauling the layout, product ranges, and signage to differentiate them from Comet's new competitors.

The size and design of the stores was not the main solution to the problem, though. A simple and, at £20,000, inexpensive research programme discovered that Comet's customers felt that its greatest weakness was the quality of its staff – a twofold problem as they also felt that the most important aspect of customer satisfaction was, you guessed it, the quality of the staff. Comet accepted the truth and acted on it by changing its criteria for customer satisfaction. Soon after, it achieved a record trading performance.

Notable negatives, such as long queues at lunchtime when people rush out to do their banking, stand out in customers' minds. They remember those lines and tell others about them. Long queues at lunchtime may lead customers to switch banks and drive away other potential customers through bad word of mouth. Similarly, notable customer service sticks in customers' minds, too. If that same branch has very friendly staff and express queues for more simple transactions during busy periods, this notable warmth and efficiency can build loyalty and encourage current customers to recruit new customers through word of mouth.

With this information, you know what things your customers think you do brilliantly and what features you need to do some work on. You can now improve on the worst-on-the-list features to make them average, at least, and emphasise the high-rated items by talking them up in marketing and investing even more in them to maximise their attractiveness.

Here are a few tips to keep in mind as you gather customer ratings:

✔ Draw a graph of all the features of your product, rated from negative to neutral to positive. A graph will give you a visual image of how your customers perceive your business's strengths and weaknesses. You'll find that most features cluster in the middle of the resulting bell curve, failing to differentiate you from the competition. A few features stick out on the left as notably negative, other features, hopefully, stand out on the right as notably positive.

✔ Offer customers a reward for filling in a survey sheet (that's how important survey sheets are). You can offer a free prize draw from the returned survey sheets, a reduction on current fees, or a discount on future products. Whichever option you choose, let your customers know that their views matter to you – that in itself can improve your customer service scores.

✔ If you want to get fancy, you can also ask some customers to rate the importance of each item on the list to them, personally. If you're lucky, your brilliant areas are important to them and your bad areas aren't.

Planning Your Research

Start research with a careful analysis of the decisions you must make. For example, say you're in charge of a two-year-old software product that small businesses use to manage their invoicing. As the product manager, what key decisions should you be making? The following are the most likely:

✔ Should we launch an upgrade or keep selling the current version?

✔ Is our current marketing plan sufficiently effective, or should we redesign it?

✔ Is the product positioned properly, or do we need to change its image?

So before you do any research, you need to think hard about those decisions. Specifically, you need to

✔ Decide what realistic options you have for each decision.

✔ Assess your level of uncertainty and risk for each decision.

Then, for any uncertain or risky decisions, you need to pose questions whose answers can help you reduce the risk and uncertainty. And now, with these questions in hand, you're ready to begin your research!

When you work through this thinking process, you often find that you don't actually need research. For example, maybe your boss has already decided to invest in an upgrade of the software product you manage, so researching the decision has no point. Right or wrong, you can't realistically change that decision. But some questions make it through the screening process and turn out to be good candidates for research. For these research points, you need to pose a series of questions that have the potential to reduce your decision-making uncertainty or to reveal new and exciting options for you as a decision-maker.

Take the question, 'Is the product positioned properly, or do we need to change its image?' To find out whether repositioning your product makes sense, you may ask how people currently perceive the product's quality and performance, how they view the product compared with the leading competitor's, and what the product's personality is. If you know the answers to all these questions, you're far better able to make a good decision.

You must start by defining your marketing decisions very carefully. Until you know what decisions you must make, market research has little point. See Figure 4-2 for a flowchart of the research process.

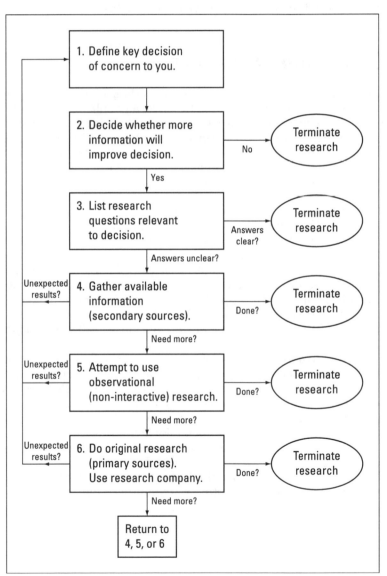

Figure 4-2: Follow this market research process to avoid common errors.

Carrying Out Primary Research

Primary research gathers data from people by observing them to see how they behave or by asking them for verbal or written answers to questions. You can, and should, ask your customers all the time whether they are happy with the service they get from your company, but taking some time out to question your assumptions about how customers view your product or service can yield some of the most valuable insights.

Observing customers

Going 'back to the floor' has become something of a phenomenon of modern business, to the extent that the BBC made a popular TV series of the same name. The experiences of a senior manager who is thrown back into the thick of things can make hilarious viewing – but how and why did they become so disengaged from the basics of their business in the first place? Getting and staying close to your customers, as well as the front-line staff who deal with them every day, is one of the most valuable ways to spend your time.

Consumers are all around you – shopping for, buying, and using products. Observing consumers, and finding something new and of value from doing so, is not hard. And even *business-to-business marketers* (who sell to other businesses instead of end-consumers) can find plenty of evidence about their customers at a glance. The number and direction of a company's lorries on various roads can tell you where their business is heaviest and lightest, for example. Despite all the opportunities to observe, most marketers are guilty of Sherlock Holmes's accusation that 'You have not observed, and yet you have seen.' Observation is the most underrated of all research methods.

Find a way to observe one of your customers as she uses one of your products. Professional research firms can provide a location for customers to come and use your products, or can even put their people into the homes of willing customers. We want you to observe, not just watch. Bring along a pad and pencil, and take care to notice the little things. What does the customer do, in what order, and how long does she spend doing it? What does she say, if anything? Does she look happy? Frustrated? Disinterested? Does anything go wrong? Does anything go right – is she surprised with how well the product performs? Take detailed notes and then think about them. I guarantee that you end up gaining at least one insight into how to improve your product.

Asking questions

Survey research methods are the bread and butter of the market research industry, and for a good reason. You can often gain something of value just by asking people what they think. If your product makes customers happy, those customers come back. If not, adios. And because recruiting new customers costs on average ten times as much as retaining existing ones, you can't afford to lose any. You need to measure and set goals for customer satisfaction.

The survey methods do have their shortcomings. Customers don't always know what they think or how they behave – and even when they do, getting them to tell you can be quite costly. Nonetheless, every marketer finds good uses for survey research on occasion.

Measuring customer satisfaction

Try to design a customer satisfaction measure that portrays your company or product in a realistic light. You can measure customer satisfaction with survey questionnaires or with the rate of customer complaints; the best measures combine multiple sources of data into an overall index.

Your customer satisfaction has to be high, relative to both customer expectations and competitors' ratings, before it has much of an effect on customer retention rates. So make sure that you ask tough questions to find out whether you're below or above customers' current standards. To gauge customer satisfaction, ask your customers revealing questions, similar to the following list:

1. **Which company (or product) is the best at present?**

   (Give a long list with instructions to circle one, and give a final choice, labelled Other, where respondents can write in their own answer.)

2. **Rate [your product] compared with its competitors:**

Far worse			Same			Far better
1	2	3	4	5	6	7

3. **Rate [your product] compared with your expectations for it:**

Far worse			Same			Far better
1	2	3	4	5	6	7

You can get helpful customer responses by breaking down customer satisfaction into its contributing elements. (Focus groups or informal chats with customers can help you come up with your list of contributing elements.) For example, you can ask the following questions about a courier company:

1. **Rate Flash Deliveries compared with its competitors on speed of delivery:**

   Far worse   Same   Far better

   1   2   3   4   5   6   7

2. **Rate Flash Deliveries compared with its competitors on reliability:**

   Far worse   Same   Far better

   1   2   3   4   5   6   7

3. **Rate Flash Deliveries compared with its competitors on ease of use:**

   Far worse   Same   Far better

   1   2   3   4   5   6   7

4. **Rate Flash Deliveries compared with its competitors on friendliness:**

   Far worse   Same   Far better

   1   2   3   4   5   6   7

You can find useful guidelines on how to design a questionnaire on the Web site of the Market Research Society (http://www.mrs.org.uk), under Frequently Asked Questions. The site also includes advice on how to select a research agency and lists sources of free statistical and demographic information.

Customer satisfaction changes with each new interaction between customer and product. Keeping up with customer opinion is a never-ending race, and you must make sure that you're measuring where you stand relative to those shifting customer expectations and competitor performances.

Traps to avoid

As you conduct a customer survey, avoid these all-too-common traps which can render your research practically useless:

- ✔ **Make sure your survey (or surveyor, for that matter) doesn't fluff up customer satisfaction to conceal problems.** In bigger companies, I sometimes see people pressurising customers to give them good ratings because it helps their own prospects. I recently bought car insurance over the phone from an enthusiastic salesperson who unashamedly asked me to give her a high rating on a survey so that she could win the monthly customer service bonus – ten out of ten for effort, but probably not what the company had in mind when it set up the survey. Design your customer service measure to find areas of the business you can improve, which means asking questions that expose any weak spots. The more 'honest' your questions are, the more meaningful the responses will be.

✔ **Watch out for over-general questions or ratings.** Any measure based on a survey that asks customers to 'rate your overall satisfaction with our company on a 1-to-10 scale' isn't much use. What does an average score of 8.76 mean? This number seems high, but are customers satisfied? You didn't really ask customers this question – and even worse, you didn't ask them if they're more satisfied with you than they used to be or if they're less satisfied with competitors than with you. Ask a series of more specific questions, such as 'was it convenient and easy to do business with us?'

✔ **Don't lose sight of the end goal – customer satisfaction.** You may need to find out about a lot of other issues in order to design your marketing plan or diagnose a problem. None of what you find out matters, however, unless it boils down to increased customer satisfaction in the long run. Whatever else you decide to research, make sure you keep one eye on customer satisfaction: It's the ultimate test of whether your marketing is working!

Using the answers

When you have gathered the data, make sure that it gets put to good use, rather than becoming a pile of questionnaires gathering dust in the corner. So which parts of the information you have amassed should you include as an action point in your next marketing plan?

Even the most rudimentary piece of research can throw up a range of different, and sometimes contradictory, findings. One customer may think the most important thing is for you to lower your prices, another may be prepared to pay more for greater staff expertise. You probably can't achieve both of these goals at the same time. Here are a couple of strategies that can help you focus your response:

✔ **Your own instinct should allow you to sort the good research results from the bad.** This doesn't mean you should ignore what you don't want to hear, but it does mean you shouldn't unquestioningly react to everything the research tells you. When Sony asked people whether they would like a portable device so they could listen to music on the move, the company found there was no demand. They went ahead and launched the Walkman anyway, because they felt they had a great product innovation. You shouldn't believe the expression 'the customer is always right' but one that you can heed when doing any research is 'they don't know what they don't know'.

✔ **Concentrate on just one of the strengths and one of the weaknesses.** If you have a quality that's unique in your market in a meaningful way, then you need to exploit it to the full. If you have a real problem that may drive valuable customers away, it needs to be put right fast.

✔ **Pay attention to your most valuable customers.** You can't please all of the people all of the time, so don't try. One of the hidden benefits of observing and asking questions of customers is that it can help distinguish your most valuable customers from those you would be better off without (yes, they really do exist). By looking at survey responses, you will soon be able to spot ideas and customers that generate additional value, and those that simply want more for less. Surveys help you to establish priorities for your business that will keep profitable customers loyal.

The life cycle of any piece of research should last no longer than your next marketing plan – any longer and the market or competition will have moved anyway. (I talk more about rewriting your marketing plan in Chapter 3.)

A Dozen Ideas for Low-Cost Research

You don't have to spend thousands of pounds researching ideas for a new ad campaign (or anything else). Instead, focus on ways of gaining insight or checking your assumptions using free and inexpensive research methods. But how can you do useful research without a lot of time, money, and staff to waste? This section shares a dozen ideas (plus an extra one for free) to get you off on the right foot.

Watching what your competitors do

When you compare your marketing approach to your competitors', you easily find out what customers like best. Make a list of the things that your competitors do differently to you. Does one of them price higher? Does another one give away free samples? Do some of them offer money-back guarantees? How and where do they advertise? Make a list of at least five points of difference. Now ask ten of your best customers to review this list and tell you what they prefer – your way or one of the alternatives. Keep a tally. And ask them why. You may find that all your customers vote in favour of doing something different to the way you do it now.

Creating a customer profile

Take photographs of people you think of as your typical customers. Post these pictures on a bulletin board and add any facts or information you can think of to create profiles of your 'virtual' customers. Whenever you aren't sure what to do about any marketing decision, you can sit down in front of the bulletin board and use it to help you tune into your customers and what they do and don't like. For example, make sure the art and wording you use in a letter or ad is appropriate to the customers on your board. Will these customers like it, or is the style wrong for them?

Entertaining customers to get their input

Invite good customers to a lunch or dinner, or hold a Customer Appreciation event. Entertaining your customers puts you in contact with them in a relaxed setting where they're happy to chat and share their views. Use these occasions to ask them for suggestions and reactions. Bounce a new product idea off of these customers or find out what features they'd most like to see improved. Your customers can provide an expert panel for your informal research, and you just have to provide the food!

Using e-mail for single-question surveys

If you market to businesses, you probably have e-mail addresses for many of your customers. Try e-mailing 20 or more of these customers for a quick opinion on a question. Result? Instant survey! If a clear majority of these customers say they prefer using a corporate credit card to being invoiced because the card is more convenient, well, you've just gained a useful research result that may help you revise your approach.

Watching people use your product

Be nosey. Find ways to observe people as they shop for and consume your product or service. What do they do? What do they like? What, if anything, goes wrong? What do they dislike? You can gain insight into what your consumers care about, how they feel, and what they like by observing them in action. Being a marketing voyeur provides you with a useful and interesting way to do research – at no charge. And if you're in a retail business, be (or ask someone else to be) a *secret shopper* by going in and acting like an ordinary customer to see how you're treated.

Establishing a trend report

E-mail salespeople, distributors, customer service staff, repair staff, or willing customers once a month, asking them for a quick list of any important trends they see in the market. You flatter people by letting them know that you value their opinion, and e-mail makes giving that opinion especially easy for them. A trend report gives you a quick indication of a change in buying patterns, a new competitive move or threat, and any other changes that your marketing may need to respond to. Print out and file these reports from the field and go back over them every now and then for a long-term view of the effectiveness of your marketing strategies, too.

Researching your strengths

Perhaps the most important element of any marketing plan or strategy is clearly recognising what makes you especially good and appealing to customers (I talk more about this in Chapter 1). To research the strengths that set you apart from the competition, find the simplest way to ask ten good customers this simple but powerful question: 'What is the best thing about our [fill in the name of your product or service], from your perspective?' (Or you can do the more detailed survey I describe in the 'Research for your strengths and weaknesses' section earlier in this chapter.)

The answers to this question usually focus on one or, at most, a few features or aspects of your business. Finding out how your customers identify your strengths proves a great help to your marketing strategy. After you know what you do best, you can focus on telling the story about that best whenever you advertise, do publicity, or communicate with your market in any way. Investing in your strengths (versus your competitors' strengths or your weaknesses) tends to grow your sales and profits most quickly and efficiently.

Analysing customer records

Most marketers fail to mine their own databases for all the useful information those databases may contain. A good way to tap into this free data (because you already own it!) is to study your own customers with the goal of identifying three common traits that make them different or special.

A computer shop I'm a customer of went through their records and realised that its customers are

✔ More likely to be self-employed or entrepreneurs than the average person.

✔ More sophisticated users of computers than most people.

✔ Big spenders who care more about quality and service than the absolute cheapest price.

This store revised its marketing goal to find more people who share these three qualities. What qualities do your customers have that make them special, and that would make a good profile for you to use in pursuing more customers like them?

Surveying your own customers

You can gather input from your own customers in a variety of easy ways because your customers interact with your employees or firm. You can put a stamped postcard in shipments, statements, product packages, or other communications with your customers. Include three or fewer simple, non-biased survey questions, such as, 'Are you satisfied with this purchase? no = 1 2 3 4 5 = yes.' Also leave a few lines for comments, in case the customers have something they want to tell you. You generally get low response rates with any such effort, but that's okay. If someone has something to tell you, they let you hear about it, particularly when it's negative. And even a 5 per cent response gives you a steady stream of input you wouldn't otherwise have.

Testing your marketing materials

Whether you're looking at a letter, Web page, press release, or ad, you can improve that material's effectiveness by asking for reviews from a few customers, distributors, or others with knowledge of your business. Do they like the material? Do they like it a lot? If the responses are only lukewarm, then you know you need to edit or improve the material before spending the money to publish and distribute it. Customer reviewers can tell you quickly whether you have real attention-getting wow-power in any marketing communication.

Big companies do elaborate, expensive tests of ads' readability and pulling power, but you can get a pretty good idea for much less money. Just ask a handful of people to review a new marketing material while it's still in draft form.

Interviewing defectors

You can find out far more from an angry customer than you can from ten happy ones. If you have a customer on the phone who wants to complain, then look on it as an opportunity, not a call to be avoided. If you can find out what went wrong and fix it, that customer may well become one of your greatest advocates.

You can easily overlook another gold mine – company records of past customers. Work out what types of customer defect, when, and why. If you can't pinpoint why a customer abandoned ship, try to make contact and ask them directly.

Tracking these lost customers down and getting them on the phone or setting up an appointment may prove difficult. Don't give up! Your lost customers hold the key to a valuable piece of information: What you do wrong that can drive customers away. Talk to enough of these lost customers and you may see a pattern emerge. Probably three-quarters of them left you for the same reason (which can be pricing, poor service, inconvenient hours, and so on – that's for you to find out).

Plug that hole and you lose fewer customers down it. And keeping those customers means you don't have to waste valuable marketing resources replacing them. You can keep the old customers and grow every time you add a new one.

Asking your kids

Seriously! Your children, or any kids on hand that you can get to think about your market for a few minutes, probably have a unique and more contemporary view than you. Ask them simple questions like 'What will the next big thing be in [name your product or service here]?' 'What's cool and what's not this year?' Kids know, and you don't. In any consumer marketing, you need to make sure that you're cool and your competitors aren't. Because kids lead the trends in modern society, why not ask them what those trends are? Even in business-to-business and industrial markets, kids and their sense of what's happening in society can be helpful – often giving you early indicators of shifts in demand that may have an impact all the way up the line, from consumers to the businesses that ultimately serve them.

Finding Free Data

Whatever aspect of marketing you are looking at there is further information available to you – and it won't cost you a penny. Some of that data can give you just what you need to get started on your research project. So before you buy a report or hire a research firm, dig around for some free (or at least cheap) stuff.

There is a world of free data out there, if you know where to look. Also keep in mind that free data generally falls into a category known as *secondary data* – meaning already collected or published by someone else – so you get it second hand. This data is not specific to your company and your competitors can easily access it, too.

Getting info off the Web

Throughout this book, I include numerous Web sites, as these are the quickest and easiest places to find free information. For instance, the Interactive Advertising Bureau (IAB) has more data on how many customers are connected to the Internet and who shop online than I can possibly include here or even in Chapter 10 on E-marketing. Look out for these Web site references, but more importantly remember that Internet search engines, such as Google!, make finding free data simple – and the more you use them, the easier it is to filter out all the sites you're not interested in.

Say you want to set up a Web site where customers can buy your products directly. You want to know how many people have access to the Internet in the UK and how many are prepared to use their credit card details to buy things. You may also want to find a Web site developer that can create a secure and fully transactional site for you. Already you have three questions that need answers and you haven't even started your search.

Go to the Google! search engine (www.google.co.uk), type in the key words 'internet access', and then hit 'Search pages from the UK' – you'll get a list of 17 million sites, most of them trying to sell you something. You can narrow the information down by being more specific. The phrase 'online shoppers' will return 894,000 sites – better, but still too many. Type in 'online shoppers market size', however, and you get just 164,000 suggestions – even better. At the top of the list is that Interactive Advertising Bureau site I just mentioned, which has the answers to all three questions. A bit of practice is all you need to help you find relevant information on the Web quickly and easily.

Hooking up with a librarian

If you don't want to do the search yourself, you can get a professional to search for you, and it will hardly cost you a penny (well, maybe a few pounds). Libraries are an undervalued national treasure, and librarians are trained to archive information as well as know how to access it. Your local library is a good starting place, but you can also get a wealth of market information from university libraries and specialist business libraries.

You can find a lot of what you might need, including industry guides, through the British Library (www.bl.uk/welcome/business.html). You can make enquiries by phone: 020 7412 7454, or by e-mail: business-information@bl.uk.

Tapping into government resources

Often, the best source of free information is national and local government. Many governments collect copious data on economic activity, population size, and trends within their borders. In the UK, the Office of National Statistics (ONS) is the best general source of data on a wide range of demographic and economic topics.

I am always amazed at the sheer range and quantity of information available on the ONS site, and I'm sure you will be too. Of course, I don't know whether you need to know the state of North Sea fish stocks, but if you do, then this is the right place! Described as the 'home of official UK statistics', you can access National Statistics Online at www.statistics.gov.uk.

A lot of the data on the UK population is based on the Census. Although the Census only takes place every ten years, you'll find it's very detailed and, usefully, you can break the data down by neighbourhood. The statistics on inflation and prices, consumer spending, business investment – in fact, anything financial – is more up to date, usually to the last full quarter.

Getting media data

If you're doing any advertising, ask the magazine, newspaper, Web site, or radio station you buy advertising from to give you information about their customer base – snippets about the people exposed to your ads. This information can help you make sure you reach an appropriate audience. You can also use the exposure numbers to calculate the effectiveness of your advertising.

If you've yet to decide where to advertise, or even in which media, then there are some useful media sites you can visit that will give you the numbers on how many and what kind of consumers each title or station will deliver. You can trust these sources, because in most cases they were set up and are supported by the media owners operating in that area to provide an independent verification of sales and audience profiles so that advertisers can see what they're getting – and hopefully buy more. That's why most of the data, for occasional users like you, is free.

The Audit Bureau of Circulations, or ABC as it's more commonly known (www.abc.org), has data on magazines, national and local newspapers, exhibition visitors, and Web sites. You can find out how many people are reading the title, where they live, and what type of consumers they are; for business-to-business magazines, you can find out what sector they work in and what their job titles are. Most of the different media have organisations that provide data like this: For TV it's BARB (www.barb.co.uk), for radio it's RAJAR (www.rajar.co.uk), for outdoor media such as posters it's POSTAR (www.postar.co.uk).

Chapter 5

Harnessing Creativity in Your Business

*O*kay, time to be creative. Ready, set, go. Come up with any good ideas yet? No? Then try again. Now do you have some good ideas? What? No?

If you can't be creative at will, don't be alarmed. Most people face this problem. When there's a need to be creative in marketing, many people find that they require some help. This chapter will help you put the processes in place to generate some unusually creative – and hopefully profitable – ideas.

The Creative Process at a Glance

If you think of creativity as generating wild and crazy ideas, you're right – but only partly right. You have to do some open-minded thinking to come up with creative concepts (I tell you how in the following sections). But to actually make any money from your creativity, you need to have a mix of activities that includes exploring for new ideas and developing the best of them into practical applications in your ads, products, sales presentations, or other marketing activities. Here is a simple four-step process for turning ideas into action:

1. **Initiate.**

   In this step, you recognise a need or opportunity and ask questions that begin the creative process. For example, you may take a look at your delivery vehicle(s) and ask yourself if there isn't some way to make them stand out and communicate what your business is all about. The creative brief that I discuss later on in this chapter is useful at the initiate stage.

2. **Imagine.**

   In this stage of the creative process, you engage in the imaginative, uninhibited thinking that taps into your artistic side. The techniques that I cover in the 'Brainstorming' section later in this chapter are good for this stage; your goal is to see how many wild ideas you can generate.

3. **Invent.**

   Now you need to get more practical. Take a critical look at all those wild ideas and choose one or a few that seem most promising. Work on these ideas to see how to make them more practical and feasible. You can't put flashing lights all over your company vans to catch attention – it's certainly creative but falls foul of road traffic law. Is there another fun, engaging but workable idea from stage 2? A company I know called Innocent Drinks, which makes fresh fruit and yoghurt smoothies, covered its vans in artificial grass and flowers – an eyecatching solution that said a lot about what the company made and even more about its fun approach to business.

4. **Implement.**

   Finally, you need to complete the creative process by pursuing successful adoption or implementation of your new idea or design. You may have a great design for a new company vehicle, but is there a company that can actually transfer your ideas onto the real thing – how, for instance, do you get a phone number and Web address onto fake grass?

Finding Out What You Need to Change

The smartest thing to do when you have a stunning, timeless, classic success in marketing is to leave it alone. But how many of those kinds of concepts can you think of? A tin of Heinz Baked Beans. The Apple computer logo. A Porsche sports car. A Swiss army knife. The Michelin Man. The truth is that even these marketing icons have made many changes over the years – but they're careful to protect the brand heritage they have got. So if you're not changing many of the aspects of your marketing, you should ask yourself why not?

Harnessing creativity in your business allows you to do things differently – differently from before, and differently from your competition. Once you start thinking about creativity and change, you might find yourself surprised by how much of what you do has remained the same. You don't want to allow others to catch up, or for your marketing to become stale, so it's time you started a creative overhaul of your business.

The marketing audit: More fun than it sounds

To find out what your next marketing project should be, do a quick marketing creativity audit right now. Respond to each of the situations in Table 5-1 as honestly as you can, circling 1 if your answer is 'rarely', 5 if your answer is 'frequently', and the numbers in between if your answer is somewhere between 'rarely' and 'frequently'.

Table 5-1	Marketing Creativity Audit				
Marketing Creativity Actions	*Rating* *(1 = rarely; 5 = frequently)*				
We make improvements to the selection, design, packaging, or appearance of our product(s).	1	2	3	4	5
We experiment with prices, discounts, and special offers to achieve our marketing goals.	1	2	3	4	5
We find new ways to bring our product(s) to customers, making buying or using the product(s) more convenient or easier for them.	1	2	3	4	5
We update and improve our brand image or the ways we communicate that brand image.	1	2	3	4	5
We try creative new ways of communicating with customers and prospects.	1	2	3	4	5
We improve the look and feel of our sales or marketing materials.	1	2	3	4	5
We listen to customer complaints or objections, and we find creative ways to turn those complaints into our next business opportunities.	1	2	3	4	5

(continued)

Table 5-1 *(continued)*					
Marketing Creativity Actions	*Rating* *(1 = rarely; 5 = frequently)*				
We change our marketing message.	1	2	3	4	5
We reach out to new types of customers to try to expand or improve our customer base.	1	2	3	4	5
We share creative ideas and have freewheeling discussions with all those people who are involved in marketing our product(s).	1	2	3	4	5

Add up all the numbers you circled to get a score between 10 and 50. See where your score falls in the range following this paragraph to find out what your Marketing Creativity Score means. Depending on your answers, you can rate your marketing creativity as very low, low, medium, or high. You need to be at least in the medium range, if not at the high end, to gain any benefits from creativity.

- 10–19 = very low
- 20–29 = low
- 30–39 = medium
- 40–50 = high

You can't leave anything alone in marketing. This audit reveals aspects of your marketing that nobody has looked at or tried to improve for the past few years. If you can identify any unchanging elements of your sales, service, advertising, mailings, or anything else that touches the customer, you have just found your next marketing project. So jot down three to six things that you tend to take for granted. You've just made your creative to-do list.

Picking your creative role

In marketing (and in business, in general) you have to actually do something with your creative ideas, and make those ideas work, to profit from your imagination. You must make a focused effort to invent practical ways to implement what you imagine.

The creative process includes four steps (see the preceding section) that rely on different types of behaviours. You may be especially suited to one or two of the steps, but probably not to all of them. I recommend you work out which steps you are best and worst at, and then find people to help you fill your creative gaps. Read the following list of styles to see which suits your temperament best:

✔ **Entrepreneur:** The entrepreneur senses a need or problem and asks tough questions to initiate the creative process. ('Why do we do it this way? It seems so inefficient.') This style proves valuable in Step 1 of the creative process, Initiate.

✔ **Artist:** The artist is highly imaginative and a free thinker. When given a focus by the entrepreneur's initiating question, the artist can easily dream up many alternatives and fresh approaches from which to choose. ('We could do this, or this, or this, or . . . ') The artist comes to the fore in Step 2 of the creative process, Imagine.

✔ **Inventor:** The inventor has a more practical sort of imagination and loves to develop and refine a single good idea until he makes it work. ('Let's see. If we adjust this, and add that, it will work much better.') The inventor is most productive in Step 3 of the creative process, Invent.

✔ **Engineer:** The engineer's style is practical and businesslike, and engineers are particularly good at getting closure by taking an untested or rough invention the rest of the way and making it work smoothly and well. ('Great ideas, but let's come up with a firm plan and budget so we can get this thing started.') Engineers make sure the process reaches its essential Step 4, Implement.

Whichever one of these creative roles most closely represents your approach to work, recognise that one role alone can't make good, creative marketing happen. Be prepared to adjust your style by wearing some of the other creative hats at times, or team up with others whose styles differ from your own. That way, you have the range of approaches that you need to combine in order to harness the power of creativity for all your marketing efforts.

Generating Great Ideas

Creativity is the most fundamental and powerful of all the marketing skills. There's always a better way. And if things aren't going your way – sales are slow, the boss rejects your proposals, customers complain about service, or your mailings don't get a good response – then remember to take some time out for creativity. The right creative idea at the right moment can turn the marketing tide your way. But generating that creative spark takes a little time, a little work, and a few strategies.

Finding the time to think

To be creative, you first must give yourself permission to be creative in your work. Creativity requires you to let the mind's engine sit in idle. You can't be creative if you're busy returning e-mails or phone calls, or rushing to finish your paperwork for the day. If the hands are busy, the mind is distracted from creativity, and your imagination may not be able to work. So, for starters, I must ask you to budget time for creativity.

How much time? Well, if creativity is the most powerful and profitable of the marketing skills, how often do you think you should use it? One hour a month? One hour a week? One hour a day? One day a week? You have to decide exactly how much creativity time you need based on what your product or company demands. I don't know how much creativity your business needs or how many opportunities you may capture by being innovative, but I do know that you need to commit some time and effort to using your imagination when you're at work.

I urge you not to think about creativity as something you wheel out from time to time as it's needed, but to make it something you do all the time.

Becoming an ideas factory

Once you've found the time, what do you do with it? You can profitably apply creativity in every aspect of marketing, from finding new customers to developing new products. The important thing is that you have a purpose, but after that the only rule is that there are no rules.

Try soaking up information, questioning the problem, tossing ideas back and forth with an associate, and then setting the whole thing aside to incubate in the back of your mind while you do something else. Plan to work in different ways when you're doing your creativity. Set up a large flip chart and start listing crazy ideas for your next mailing. Ask someone to help you find 20 words that rhyme with your company or brand's name in the hope that this list may lead you to a clever idea for print or radio advertising. Cut out faces from magazines to try to find one that expresses an appealing new personality that can represent your product, and then see how that face might influence everything you then do.

Open yourself up through new and different ways of working, asking questions, and exploring your marketing problems and opportunities.

You can start coming up with more ideas almost straight away, simply by changing the way you approach your work. Here's a list of fundamentals to think about; obsessing about just a few of them will make you a more creative marketer:

- ✔ **Seek ways to simplify.** Can you come up with a simpler way to explain your product or your business and its mission? Life is complicated enough for your customers. Most marketing and advertising is, too. Simplify everything to attract attention and zap the key idea into the customer's mind.

- ✔ **Think like a customer.** This should be easy, shouldn't it – after all, you are a consumer. So why do you change when you go to work? You stop thinking about what you want (like a customer) and start thinking about what you do (like a businessperson). You need to think about what your customers like and might dislike about your business – constantly.

- ✔ **Tinker with everything.** Look at every aspect of what your company does and find a way to change it – for the better, obviously. I explore the idea of change later in this chapter, because it's so important and because so few marketers truly embrace the idea of disrupting what their company does in order to make it do it better.

- ✔ **Try to cut your prices.** If you can't, then it's already the right price – so congratulate yourself and change something else. If you can cut prices, then why haven't you – or put another way, how long will it be before someone else does? You may not think of pricing as creative but, as with all other aspects of your marketing, thinking about how to do it differently can yield startling results –especially if you haven't thought about it at all for a while.

- ✔ **Separate yourself from the competition.** If you are doing things the same as your competitors, why will customers come to you? You need to offer something different, something you will be remembered for. You don't need to spend a lot – what about striking outfits for your customer-facing staff (as long as your staff like the idea, too).

- ✔ **Borrow great ideas from other businesses.** You should show an interest in what other businesses, totally outside your field, do and say. If you can find an idea that is working in another market, but no one is doing in yours, ask yourself how you can apply it to your business.

- ✔ **Find new places to advertise.** Can you think of places to put messages to your customers that nobody in your industry has used before?

- ✔ **Get other people to put the word out for you.** Some people call this public relations and that's what it amounts to. Good marketers are natural publicists – always finding ways to get their business written or talked about by others. I cover this more in Chapter 12.

These activities spur you to engage your imagination in new and unusual ways – it's surprising how often a useful insight comes out of half an hour spent on one of these approaches.

Group creativity

Being creative on your own is hard enough. But often in marketing, and work in general, you have to get a group or team of people to come up with some creative concepts.

Most groups of people, when confined to a conference room for a morning, do little more than argue about stale old ideas. Or even worse, somebody suggests an absolutely terrible new idea, and the rest of the group jumps on it and insists the suggestion is great . . . thus eliminating the need for *them* to think. If you hope to get a group to actually be creative, you need to use structured group processes. That means you have to talk the group into going along with an activity such as brainstorming. Sometimes the group resists at first, but be persistent – ask them what they have to lose by generating ideas for half an hour. I bet that after they try one brainstorming technique, they see how productive the group becomes and want to try more techniques.

I've included some of the best group creativity techniques later in this section. I know that all these techniques work – as editor of *Marketing* magazine I have used them to generate new content and product ideas, and seen other companies use them profitably as well.

 Note that these techniques generally produce a list of ideas. Hopefully a long and varied list. But still, just a list. So be sure to schedule some time for analysing the list in order to identify the most promising ideas, and then develop those ideas into full-blown action plans.

Brainstorming

Brainstorming is a great way to increase the number and variety of ideas. The goal of brainstorming is to get people to generate a very long list of unusual ideas beyond their normal thought patterns – if you push them to use brainstorming this way. To brainstorm, you first state the problem and then ask participants to offer solutions – any solution that comes to mind, the more creative the better. Each solution is written or recorded.

You may need to encourage your group by example. If you've stated the problem as 'Think of new ideas for our exhibition stand', you can brainstorm half a dozen ideas to start with, just to illustrate what you're asking the group to do: A stand shaped like a giant cave, in the form of one of your products, decorated to look like an outdoor space complete with blue sky and white clouds overhead, a stand that revolves slowly, or where you offer tea and strawberries to visitors.

These ideas aren't likely to be adopted by the average company, but they do illustrate the spirit of brainstorming, which is to set aside your criticisms and have some fun generating ideas. The rules (which you must tell the group beforehand) are as follows:

- ✔ **Quantity, not quality, is what matters.** Generate as many ideas as possible.

- ✔ **No member of the group can criticise another member's suggestion.** No idea is too wild to not write down, and you can even go as far as keeping a water gun on hand and squirting the naysayer.

- ✔ **No one person 'owns' any of the ideas.** Everyone builds off of each other's ideas.

Don't let your group just go through the motions of brainstorming. To really get in the spirit of it, they have to *free associate* – to allow their minds to wander from current ideas to whatever new ideas first pop up, no matter what the association between the old and new idea may be.

Question brainstorming

Question brainstorming is another way to generate novel questions that can provoke your group into thinking more creatively. This technique follows the same rules as brainstorming, but you instruct the group to think of questions rather than ideas.

For example, if you need to develop an exhibition stand that draws more prospects, then the group may think of the following kinds of questions:

- ✔ Do bigger stands draw much better than smaller ones?

- ✔ Which stands drew the most people at the last trade show?

- ✔ Are all visitors equal, or do we want to draw only certain types of visitors?

- ✔ Will the offer of a resting place and free coffee do the trick?

After getting these questions from the group, you get the job of answering them and seeing how those answers can help you create a new and successful exhibition stand.

Wishful thinking

Wishful thinking is a technique suggested by Hanley Norins, of ad agency Young and Rubicam, and follows the basic rules of brainstorming, but with the requirement that all statements start with the words *I wish*.

The sort of statements you get from this activity often prove useful for developing advertising or other marketing communications.

If you need to bring some focus to the list to make it more relevant to your marketing, just state a topic for people to make wishes about. For example, you can say, 'Imagine that the Exhibition Fairy told you that all your wishes can come true – as long as they have to do with the company's stand.'

Analogies

Analogies are a great creativity device. You don't think I'm serious, I know, because the idea sounds so trivial. But I define creativity as making unobvious combinations of ideas. A good analogy is just that.

To put analogies to work for you, ask your group to think of things similar to the subject or problem you're thinking about. For example, you may ask a group to brainstorm analogies for your product as a source of inspiration for creating new advertisements about that product. At first, group members come up with conventional ideas – but they soon run out of these obvious answers, and they must create fresh analogies to continue.

Analogies are everywhere in advertising. One of the best examples I've seen is a press ad for the haemorrhoids treatment cream Preparation H. The ad was simply a picture of a bicycle saddle, except it wasn't a saddle, it was a jagged saw blade. The image was so striking, you could almost feel it. Although the ad was from Japan, it could have worked equally well anywhere. That's the trick of a good visual analogy like this – you can communicate your message quickly, cleverly, and effectively. So what is your product or service similar to, or what is the customer need it meets?

Pass-along

Pass-along is a simple party game that can also help a business group break through its mental barriers to reach free association and collaborative thinking.

Say a team of marketing and salespeople meets to generate new product concepts for the product development department of a bank. Now, that sounds like a tough assignment – what can be new under the sun in banking? You may be surprised by what you come up with if you play pass-along:

1. **You, the creative marketer, pick a subject and pass the paper to the first person.**

   Say your subject is how to make your customers' personal finances run better.

2. **This person writes something about the topic in question on the top line of a sheet of paper and passes it to the next person.**

3. **The next person writes a second line beneath the first.**

4. **Go around the table or group as many times as you think necessary. In general, try to fill up a full page of lined paper.**

If people get into the spirit of the game, a line of thought emerges and dances on the page. Each previous phrase suggests something new until you have a lot of good ideas and many ways of thinking about your problem. Players keep revealing new aspects of the subject as they build on or add new dimensions to the lines above. You may end up with a list of ideas similar to those in Figure 5-1.

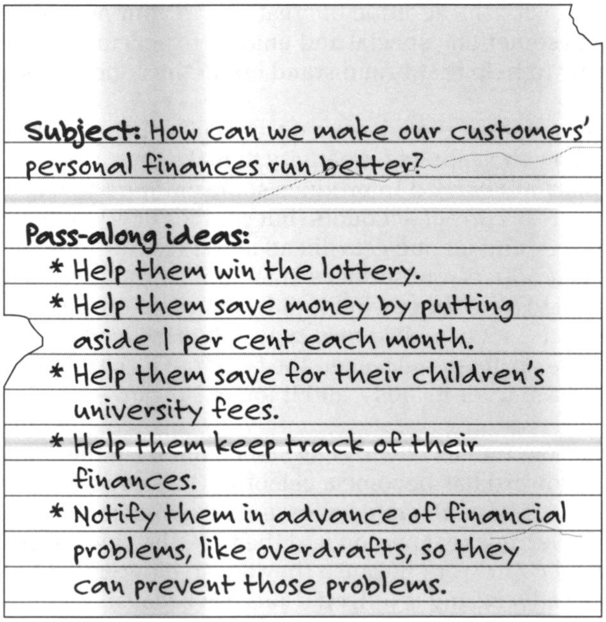

Subject: How can we make our customers' personal finances run better?

Pass-along ideas:
* Help them win the lottery.
* Help them save money by putting aside 1 per cent each month.
* Help them save for their children's university fees.
* Help them keep track of their finances.
* Notify them in advance of financial problems, like overdrafts, so they can prevent those problems.

Figure 5-1:
A list generated by a game of pass-along.

One idea leads to another. So even if the first idea isn't helpful, associating new ideas from the first one can produce useful thoughts. A bank probably can't get into the lottery business (there must be a law against that). But after the members of this group thought along those lines, they came up with some practical ways of increasing their customers' wealth, like plans that can help them transfer money to savings automatically each month.

As this simple example illustrates, generating novel ideas doesn't take long, even in a mature industry like banking – as long as you use creativity techniques.

Applying Your Creativity

Advertising – whether in print, TV, radio, outdoors, at point of purchase, or elsewhere – is a key area of application for creativity. If you work in the advertising industry, or use advertising in your marketing, you're dependent on creativity for your success. Why? Because if your ads just say what you want people to remember, people won't pay any attention to those ads. Too many other ads compete for consumers' attention. Only the most creative ads cut through the clutter, attract attention, and make a permanent mark on consumer attitudes.

Think of the role of creativity in advertising as a vehicle for building relationships between your brand and your prospects. I find this a particularly powerful way to think about advertising's role in marketing – and you can make this role possible with the addition of creativity to your ads. Marketers use creativity to add something special and unique, to accentuate a brand's differences in order to help that brand stand out in the consumers' eyes.

I know you will have seen the advertising for Halifax bank – but have you ever thought about how they applied creativity to make their ads stand out from the crowd. Halifax works hard to produce some unique banking products, such as high interest current accounts, but so does every other major bank on the high street – and no one gets ahead of the rest for long. So how did Halifax make its products and services stand out? It thought creatively. First, the bank decided to sing about what it did, so it came up with new words promoting its products, set to well-known tunes. But Halifax didn't stop there. Instead of hiring a professional singer, the bank ran a competition among its own staff to find a star for its ads – and it found Howard.

Even a few years on, Halifax advertising stands out from the rest of the banking crowd, and Howard has become a celebrity (he's even been animated for one TV ad). The ads have attracted a lot more customers because Howard, as a former bank teller, is a real person and the tunes he sings to are catchy. Mainly, though, the ads work because they are so different and can't be easily copied. Halifax's advertising is judged a success because it

- Attracted attention to itself.
- Was memorable.
- Helped convey a positive perception of the product.

Writing a creative brief

Advertising benefits from the use of a *creative brief,* an information platform on which to do your creative thinking. A creative brief lays out the basic purpose and focus of the ad, and provides some supporting information that provides helpful grist for your creative mill.

Leading advertising agencies design the creative brief with three key components:

- ✔ **Objective statement:** What the advertising is supposed to accomplish. Make the goals or objectives clear and specific – and one objective is easier to accomplish than many. The objective statement also includes a brief description of who the ad is aimed at because this target group's actions determine if you accomplish an objective.

  Think about the task of designing a new pack for one of your product lines. If you write a creative brief first, you have to define what the packaging should accomplish and what sort of customers you want to aim the pack design at. The objective statement demands that you make these decisions.

- ✔ **Support statement:** The product's promise and the supporting evidence to back up that promise. You use this point to build the underlying argument for the persuasive part of your ad. The support statement can be based on logic and fact, or on an intuitive, emotional appeal – either way, you need to include a basis of solid support.

  You have to review (and maybe do some creative thinking about) the evidence available to support your product's claims to fame. What may make you stand out from rival products on the shelves? If you aren't sure, then use the demands of the support statement to do some research and creative thinking. Make sure that you have your evidence at hand so that your ideas for packaging design can communicate this evidence effectively.

- ✔ **Tone or character statement:** A distinct character, feel, or personality for the ad. You choose whether the statement should accentuate the brand's long-term identity or put forth a unique tone for the ad itself that dominates the brand's image. The choice generally flows from your objectives. A local retailer's objective may be to pull in a lot of shoppers for a special Bank Holiday sale. The retailer should give their event a strong identity, so would want to define an appropriate tone for the ad. In contrast, a national marketer of a new health-food line of soft drinks should build brand identity, so the creative brief should focus on defining that brand identity in words (or verbal images).

  Here, you have to define the tone of your packaging, or think about your product's overall image and how the pack can reflect that image in its tone. The tone or character statement requires this step.

The creative brief is useful for any marketing communication, or for any situation in which you must design something creative to communicate and persuade. Figure 5-2 shows an example of a creative brief for a new coffee shop's local advertising.

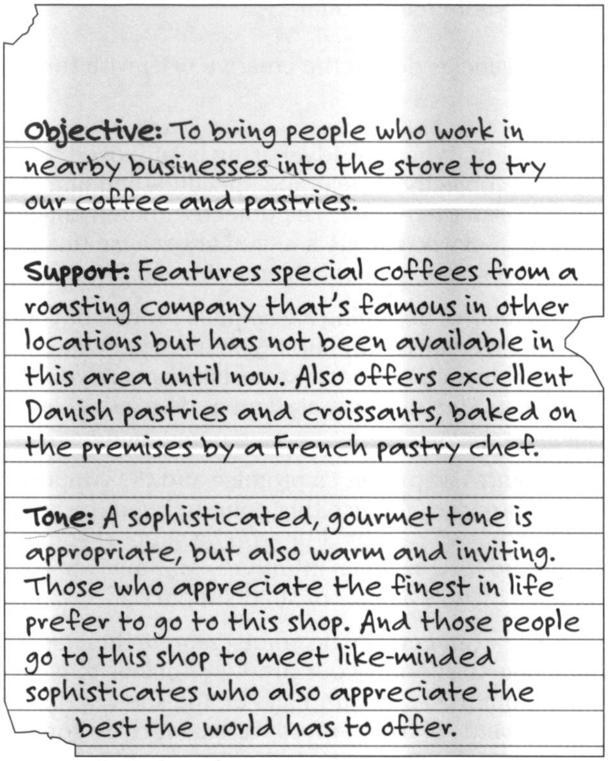

Objective: To bring people who work in nearby businesses into the store to try our coffee and pastries.

Support: Features special coffees from a roasting company that's famous in other locations but has not been available in this area until now. Also offers excellent Danish pastries and croissants, baked on the premises by a French pastry chef.

Tone: A sophisticated, gourmet tone is appropriate, but also warm and inviting. Those who appreciate the finest in life prefer to go to this shop. And those people go to this shop to meet like-minded sophisticates who also appreciate the best the world has to offer.

Figure 5-2:
A sample creative brief.

After you fill in the three sections of the creative brief to your satisfaction, you're ready to start brainstorming or using any other creativity tools you care to try. The creative brief gives you a clear focus and some good working materials as you apply your creativity to developing a great ad or other promotional piece.

Creativity and brand image

One of the most important things you can do in marketing is create a strong, appealing brand image. Creativity is the key to doing just that. As you saw in the section 'Writing a creative brief' earlier in this chapter, advertising

Fresh approach to sandwich-making

There are sandwich bars on every British high street, but on many of them there is one particular sandwich bar – Pret A Manger.

You wouldn't think that getting into a market that is so obviously oversupplied is particularly creative – or clever, for that matter. But Julian Metcalfe and Sinclair Beecham have created a sandwich bar chain that is different and better than the rest, and which has a strong brand identity. For a start, all Pret's sandwiches are freshly prepared on site every day, so the quality is high. The chain also makes sure that the staff treat customers better than an average

sandwich shop, and it makes a difference. They do this by encouraging career development and spending time on keeping staff motivated.

This passion for what they do, and how they treat customers, is evident all over the packaging and on posters inside the outlets. For a company that now has over 100 outlets and has expanded internationally, it still doesn't spend much on advertising. Pret has created a strong brand personality by being creative about the way it runs its business in a fairly ordinary market – and sometimes that's enough.

communicates the all-important brand image or personality to the consumer. Sometimes advertising focuses on that image – and, by doing so, provides a common focus for all other design decisions, from product design to packaging to special events and other marketing communications. A strong brand identity, or personality, can become a living entity, something that the marketer creates and gives to the world. Brand development takes creativity to its farthest extreme by creating new forms of life.

Chapter 6

Making Your Marketing Communications More Powerful

. . . .

. . . .

You communicate constantly in marketing. In fact, most of what marketers do is actually communication of one sort or another. But what's the difference between good and poor marketing communications? The single most important difference is *impact*. Good communications have the *desired* impact; poor communications don't. The key to this idea is the word 'desired'. You can easily make an impact, but for all the wrong reasons. A famous adman once said of his advertising: 'When I want a high recall score all I have to do is show a gorilla in a jockstrap'. He knew that the pursuit of impact for its own sake was a pointless exercise, as it didn't meet any of his client's goals.

In this chapter, we help you make your marketing communications more powerful by showing you some of the best ways to increase the impact of your message. With more effective communication, you can build sales and attract new or better customers.

As you read this chapter, ask yourself this: What goals do you have and how well are you achieving them right now? That will help you decide whether your communications are sending out the right message, and how to change them for the better. This is the sort of continual evaluation of your marketing you should be doing to improve the results in line with your objectives.

Establishing Communications Priorities

Which is more important – getting noticed or getting noticed for the right reason? Of course, the correct answer is both. A powerful ad is nothing if customers don't remember what it was trying to tell them, and about which brand. Equally, a turgid explanation of why your product is worth buying won't grab the customer's attention for long enough to even begin to get that message across. So you need to combine stopping power with persuasion. Customers don't believe you're the best just because you tell them so, you actually have to be the best or find a different message that will sell your product.

Creating an eye-catching and persuasive ad isn't enough. Your ad also has to be clear. Often the most exciting and creative ads fail to actually make the sale because they're not simple and clear enough. A Burger King TV campaign boasted that Burger King's fries had beaten McDonald's fries in a taste test. But consumers didn't pick up the nuances; they just noticed the mention of McDonald's, and rumour has it that sales went up at McDonald's instead of Burger King. Oops.

Clarity is the first job of the marketer. Creativity, excitement, and persuasion are actually secondary to clarity. Is that clear? Good! The following sections tell you what you need to know to make your marketing endeavours successful.

If you can communicate more effectively and persuasively than your competitors, then consider your marketing communications a success; if not, then you're throwing precious marketing pounds away, and you probably can't convince many people to buy your product.

Strengthening your marketing communications

Communication goes on in many ways, at many points of influence – wherever you have some exposure to your markets. You need to craft a compelling message to send out through all influence points, from advertising to packaging and point-of-sale. But how do you create a compelling marketing message? By following these steps:

1. **Position the product in your customers' minds.**

   You need the right positioning strategy as a foundation – along with products that follow through on the promises you make. A *positioning strategy* is a detailed (but readable) statement of how you want customers to think and feel about your product (or service). Your customers don't need to see your strategy, but you and everyone who works in your organisation should know what it is. You can describe your positioning with attributes and adjectives (such as 'fast', 'helpful', or 'sexy'). You can also describe your positioning with comparisons to competitors ('faster than a BMW') or with metaphorical comparisons ('faster than a speeding bullet'). See Chapter 2 for details if you don't already have a clear positioning strategy taped to the wall above your desk.

2. **Craft a *basic appeal*, some motivating message that gets that positioning across.**

Here is where you need to work out what you can say that clearly conveys the positioning strategy. Take the basic statement of how you want people to think of your product and convert it into a message that may actually convince them. For example, if you want to introduce a new, healthier kind of pizza made only of organic and low-fat ingredients, your positioning statement may be, 'healthier pizza that doesn't sacrifice taste'. Okay, now craft the basic appeal that may convince others to see the pizza that way. Here's a possibility with appeal: 'Instead of fighting to keep your kids from eating the unhealthy junk-food pizzas they love, why not give them healthy pizzas that are actually better tasting, too?'

3. **Find a creative big idea – something that packages your appeal in a message so compelling that people stop in their tracks.**

The message should persuade people of your point or convince them to give your product or service a try – and it should do so creatively or else it will be boring and nobody will pay attention. For example, suppose you're doing marketing for a pizza restaurant chain whose basic positioning is 'organic and low-fat, so it's healthy and it also tastes good'. A basic appeal you want to use now to convince people of that positioning strategy is to tell parents, 'Instead of fighting to keep your kids from eating the unhealthy junk-food pizzas they love, why not give them healthy pizzas that are actually better tasting, too?' Now, what creative idea can you come up with to turn this appeal into a compelling communication? Here are some options:

- Mother goes to chemist's shop to get prescription for child and is shocked when the pharmacist reads the doctor's note, and then pulls a freshly-baked pizza out of a big oven, boxes it, hands it over the counter, and says, 'Give him as many pieces as he wants, day or night.'

- Kids stare longingly through the glass-fronted case of sweet shop, in such a crowd that it's hard to even see what has drawn their attention – it turns out to be the newest flavour of the low-fat, organic pizza.

- A journalist is interviewing swimmers on a remote tropical island where the average age is higher than anywhere else in the world. In response to the question, 'What is the secret of your amazing health and longevity?' a tanned and fit grandmother says, 'We don't do anything special, we just order pizza every night.' She then dives off a cliff into a tropical pool of water. The pizza, of course, is from a little old hut with the logo of our brand over its door and a crowd of village children in the door, hands out, happily receiving slices of the magical pizza.

4. **Develop, edit, and simplify your creative idea until it's transparently clear and fits the medium you want to communicate it in.**

   Note that your choice of medium is partially determined by your message – and by the creative idea you select to get it across. To tell a story, you may choose television advertising if your budget is large. A streaming video version for your Web site or a radio ad version of the story will cut your costs compared to TV advertising (see Chapter 9). And to give you really low-cost options, you can commission a cartoonist to do a series of drawings in comic-strip format and then turn them into a print ad, flier, or place them on your Web site.

These steps, when done well, create a compelling marketing message and communicate that message persuasively. The task is a challenging but a vital one – crafting the compelling message you need for all your marketing communications.

Deciding whether to appeal to logic or emotions

You face a choice in many marketing communications: Should you build your appeal and communication strategy around a strong claim, backed by irrefutable evidence? Or, in contrast, should you make an emotional appeal that feels right to the customer but lacks hard evidence?

You have to make this choice based on what you're marketing and who you're marketing it to because everyone makes decisions in both ways, depending on the situation. People usually make an emotional decision about who they want to marry, but they usually make rational decisions about what jobs to search for and which employment offers to accept. Similarly, in purchase decisions, sometimes the emotions prevail and sometimes the logical parts of our minds dominate.

To complicate matters even further, people are inconsistent about when they use which mode. Some people make highly emotional decisions about major purchases like cars and houses; others approach the decision carefully and rationally, comparing statistics and running the numbers. Which camp do you fall into? If you've ever bought a car, try to recall why you bought it. If you say, 'Because I liked it' or 'Because I felt good about being seen driving it' or something similar, your emotions probably dominated your purchase decision. If, however, you say things like 'Because it has a higher resale value and *What Car?* rated it highly on reliability and running costs', then you made a logical or rational decision.

Each person tends toward one end or the other of this range – and makes decisions more rationally or more emotionally. And so you can pitch your marketing communications at the rational buyer or at the emotional buyer. You can even segment your market based on this difference, and design separate marketing campaigns for each!

When you design your communications, emphasise strongly one or the other way of thinking. When you waffle, trying to appeal to both sides of the brain at once, your message usually ends up weaker. Your job, as the communicator, is to get into the customer's head and sense which is the hotter button – the emotional or rational one.

So, which camp do your customers and prospects fall into? You probably know already, but it is worth asking your customers or carrying out some ad hoc research (See Researching Your Customers, Chapter 4).

Have you heard the one about the Skoda?

Have you seen any of the recent advertisng for Skoda cars? You will almost certainly remember the jokes: What do you call a Skoda with no roof? A skip. Why do Skodas have heated rear windows? To keep your hands warm when you're pushing them.

The jokes play on the perception that Skoda cars are poorly made. Such jokes are still relevant today because, even though the East European car manufacturer was bought by Volkswagen in the early 1990s and the product began to get much, much better – it even won 'Car of the Year' awards from *What Car?* magazine – the old image problems were slow to go away. and Skoda's UK marketers knew it.

Instead of relying on a message that told consumers how good the cars now were (the rational message), the marketers took the very brave, but very original step of confronting people's prejudices head on. The 'It's a Skoda. Honest' ads included one featuring a confused car park attendant apologising to a driver whose car had been 'vandalised' with a Skoda badge. Perception of the brand and sales shot up in the UK – and rumour has it that there was some jealousy among marketers in other European countries who had stuck with the old style product-benefit ads.

Four Easy Strategies to Strengthen Your Appeal

You want to help people see what makes your product great. You want to get these people to come into a shop, send an e-mail, or make a phone call to buy it. But you can't just tell potential customers that your product is great because they won't pay any attention: They've heard that one before. To start with, you need an appealing message. The message must sell itself!

What can you communicate that appeals to the consumer's basic motives and desires – and does so with enough strength to move them to action? You can use one or more of the strategies listed in the following sections to improve the impact of your appeal.

Most appeals are ineffective. It is difficult to achieve the kind of impact you want as a marketer.

Image strategy

An *image strategy* shows people your product and its personality – it presents a good image of your brand, product, service, or business. For example, a health spa may develop a sophisticated logo and colour scheme and work sophistication into everything, from its print ads and Web site to its decor, towels, robes, and bottled water. What's your image? And do you communicate that image in an appealing way through all points of contact with your customers and prospects?

Information strategy

An *information strategy* communicates facts that make your business appealing. For example, a van hire company may want to let prospects know how many of what kind of vans it has available, in what good condition it keeps those vans, and how reasonable it makes its terms of rental. The facts should make the sale. And if you know you're particularly strong in a certain area, then communicate the facts of your brilliance instead of wasting effort on more ordinary information. What information can you communicate that will appeal to customers and prospects?

Motivational strategy

A motivational strategy builds a compelling argument or feeling that should inspire prospects to take action and make a purchase.

An advertising campaign for the Weightwatchers clubs ran over the post-Christmas period and featured real customers telling viewers how much weight they had lost, how easy it was, and how great they felt as a result. Prospects often experience strong emotional responses to these stories, so this approach should lead to new sales. What motivation can you provide that can move prospective customers to make a purchase now?

Demonstration strategy

A *demonstration strategy* leverages the fundamental appeal of the product itself by simply making that product available to prospects. Sampling is when you get handed a product to taste or try as you're walking through a shopping centre, or when a sachet of coffee gets posted through your door. Sometimes marketing really is as easy as making the product available to people – like when a car dealership offers free test-drives of an exciting new model. Does your product have fundamental appeal that you can take advantage of by making it more accessible to prospects?

Catching Your Customers' Eyes and Pulling Them In

Stopping power is the ability of an advertisement or other marketing communication to stop people in their tracks, to make them sit up and take notice. Communications with stopping power generate 'What did you say?' or 'Did you see that?' responses. These communications generate a high level of attention.

Pulling power is the ability of a marketing communication to draw people to a place or event. Pull power is the primary goal of all local advertising. (By local advertising, I mean advertising focused on a specific town or city.) Marketers use publicity, personal selling, direct mail, price-based promotions, and point-of-purchase spending to try to exercise effective pull power.

Stopping power

The high level of clutter in the marketing environment means that most efforts to communicate fail. Most ads go unnoticed by most of the people they target.

To see for yourself how 'blind' people are to ads, ask a friend to recall five ads they saw on television last night (and they probably saw dozens). Watch their reaction. A puzzled look may cross your friend's face as they try desperately to remember what they know they must have seen. Then they may say, 'Oh, yeah. I saw that funny ad where this bloke . . .' Your friend may come up with several ads that way, if last night's crop of advertising was fairly good; and of these, they may remember the brand names of one or two – but rarely all.

And if you do the same exercise, but ask your friend about print ads in magazines or newspapers or brochures or junk mail letters, you may well draw a complete blank. Many people don't recall even one ad in a magazine they read yesterday unless you actively prompt them. Or try asking about radio ads. Same problem.

Sex, anyone?

Advertising research reveals another secret of stopping power: Sex. As the header for this section illustrates, even the word catches your eye. So to give an ad stopping power, just give it some sex appeal.

However, there's a hitch. The same research that shows sex-based ads have stopping power also shows that these same ads don't prove very effective by other measures. Brand recall – the ability of viewers to remember what product the ad advertised – is usually lower for sex-orientated ads than other ads. So although these ads do have stopping power, they don't seem to have any other benefits – they fail to turn that high initial attention into awareness or interest. Sex-based ads don't change attitudes about the product: In short, they sacrifice good communication for raw stopping power.

The only exception to the rule that sexy ads are bad communicators is when sex is relevant to the product. If you're marketing a lingerie shop, running some print ads of scantily clad, attractive female models in the Sunday newspaper certainly makes sense. But I'd leave sexy models out of ads for hardware shops, lawn-care services, or office supplies, because they have no obvious relevance.

David Ogilvy, the adman who founded Ogilvy and Mather, found out that sex doesn't always sell well the hard way. The first advertisement he produced featured an attractive, naked woman next to an oven. Ogilvy later admitted that the ad failed because the sexy woman had nothing to do with the appeal of the oven – he should have included a beautiful cake or a golden roast chicken because they are actually relevant to the product.

This simple activity puts the importance of stopping power into perspective. You can be sure that thousands of other marketing messages bombard your customer, along with your own. For that reason, your ads need to have much more stopping power than most if you hope to get a significant number of people to remember and think about your product!

According to Hanley Norins, who spent a lot of time training the staff at advertising agency Young and Rubicam to make better ads, seven principles apply in making an ad or any marketing communication a real stopper. I've modified those principles through my own experience, coming up with the following list. Your ad must do the following:

- **Have intrinsic drama that appeals to everyone.** The ad should attract many people outside of the target audience. If kids like an ad aimed at adults or vice versa, that ad fulfils this principle.

- **Demand participation from the audience.** The ad needs to draw people into some action, whether that action is calling a number, going to a shop, laughing out loud, or just thinking about something. A stopper of an ad should never permit the audience to play a passive role.

- **Force an emotional response.** This principle should hold true, even if you're making a rational appeal. The heart of the ad must still contain some basic human need, something about which people feel passionate.

- **Stimulate curiosity.** The audience should want to know more. This desire gets them to stop and study the ad – and follow up with further information searches afterward.

- **Surprise its audience.** A startling headline, an unexpected visual image, an unusual opening gambit in a sales presentation, or a weird shop window display – all have the power to stop people by surprising them.

- **Communicate expected information – in an *detcepxenu* way.** (*Hint:* Try reading that mystery word backward.) A creative twist, or a fresh way of saying or looking at something, makes the expected unexpected. You have to get the obvious information in: What the brand is, who it benefits, and how. But don't provide the information in an obvious way, or the communication doesn't reach out and grab attention and the audience just ignores your ad.

- **Occasionally violate the rules and personality of the product category.** The product has to stand out. People notice things that violate expected patterns (and patterns certainly exist in marketing). So one way to do this is to make your ad distinctly different from what consumers have come to expect in your product's category. If you market office-cleaning services, for example, you no doubt buy *Yellow Pages* ads and make up fliers with your price list and a few client testimonials. Yawn! To complement these ordinary marketing efforts, send a sponge in the mail to prospective clients with your name and phone number on one side and, on the other, the message, 'Just in case you still insist on doing the cleaning without our help'.

Although the preceding list was inspired by Hanley Norins, his book, *The Young and Rubicam Traveling Creative Workshop* (Prentice Hall), has a great deal more in it that you may find inspiring, too.

Pulling power: Building customer traffic

Smaller or local marketers usually concern themselves with pulling power. After all, somebody has to actually sell a product at the ground level – in the local market, and customer by customer. And so, at this level, you just need to draw in those customers. Pulling power is everything.

Because of this pull orientation, local marketing communications are unique:

- ✔ Local communications tend to be part of a short-term, tactical effort, rather than a long-term campaign. Don't feel you have to do anything permanent. Short, powerful bursts usually have more pull power.

- ✔ You can do local communications on a shoestring budget – far smaller than the millions spent by national or multinational advertisers. Keep it simple!

- ✔ Local communications should get customers into the shop, make the phone ring, attract more people to your Web site, or accomplish some other pull-orientated tactical goal. If your marketing communication isn't pulling, then pull it.

For maximum pulling power, give people a strong reason to act. Tell consumers your location and that you have what they need. Ask potential customers to visit, call, return a coupon, or visit your Web site. And keep inviting these people, always in new and creative ways, so they never forget you.

Part III
Advertising Everyone Can Do

"You're not quite what I expected."

In this part . . .

Advertising can be fun and we're going to ask you to have some serious fun. Advertising needs to be creative and have that special spark to work really well.

In Part III, we outline the essentials of effective, eye-catching, mind-altering communications that can build your brand or reputation, attract great leads, or actually make a sale. The essence of great advertising communications remains the same across all the dozens of possible media – from the lowly business card or the simple brochure to the sophisticated print ad or local television spot ad.

And you have a lot of media choices – probably more than you realise – because you can always advertise in alternative ways, and advertising doesn't have to be as expensive as most people assume.

So, read on to find out how you can pump up your marketing communications and put advertising to better effect in your business. (By the way, this last sentence is a *call to action*, to use an ad copywriter's term that we discuss in Chapter 13. You always want to tell people what you expect them to do when you write an ad. Do you include a call to action in all your marketing communications?)

Chapter 7

Brochures, Press Ads, and Print

. . . .

In This Chapter

▶ Recognising the elements of printed advertising

▶ Understanding design and layout issues

▶ Designing with type

▶ Designing the simplest print product of all – brochures

▶ Placing and testing your print ad

. . . .

*M*ost marketers budget more for print advertising than any other type – the exception being the major national or multinational brands that market largely on television. But for most local and regional advertising, print probably provides the most flexible and effective all-around advertising medium.

Print advertising also integrates well with many other marketing media. You can use written brochures and other sales support materials (which have many design elements in common with print advertising) to support personal selling (see Chapter 13) or telemarketing (see Chapter 14). Similarly, a print ad in a magazine can generate leads for direct marketing (see Chapter 11). Print ads also work well to announce sales promotions or distribute coupons. (We cover the use of print ads for promotions in Chapter 15.)

And anyone with a basic computer and inkjet printer can now set up shop and create his or her own fliers, brochures, business cards, and ad layouts. In fact, Microsoft Word includes a number of excellent templates that simplify layout and allow you to bang out a new brochure or other printed marketing piece in as little as an hour. Print advertising and print-based marketing are the backbone of most marketing campaigns, even today in this high-tech world.

Designing Printed Marketing Materials

Many marketers start with their printed marketing materials (such as ads, brochures, or downloadable PDF-format product literature on their Web sites), and then work outward from there to incorporate the appeal and design concepts from their printed materials or ads into other forms of marketing. (A common look and feel should unite your print ads, brochures, and Web site, for example.)

Brochures, *tear sheets* (one-page, catalogue-style descriptions of products), posters for outdoor advertising, direct mail letters, and catalogues all share the basic elements of good print advertising: Good copy and visuals, plus eye-catching headlines. Therefore, all good marketers need mastery of print advertising as an essential part of their knowledge base. This section covers the essentials.

When designing anything in print, remember this: Your ad's purpose is to stimulate a sale. Think ahead to that goal. What will people see when they make that purchase? If your product sells in shops, create signs, packaging, displays, or coupons that echo the ad's theme and remind the buyer of that theme. If the sale occurs on your Web site, adjust the appearance of the site to be consistent with the ad. And if you make the sale in person, supply the salespeople or distributors with catalogues, order forms, PowerPoint presentations, or brochures (see the 'Producing Brochures, Fliers, and More' section later in this chapter) that are consistent with your design, to remind them of the ad that began the sales process. Roll the ad's design forward to the point of purchase and beyond if you plan follow-up mailings, a reply-paid warranty card, or other post-purchase contacts.

Dissecting the anatomy of printed materials

Before you can create great printed marketing materials, you need to dissect an ad, brochure, tear sheet, or similar printed marketing matter and identify its parts. Inside most printed marketing materials you'll find parts and each part has a special name:

- **Headline:** The large-print words that first attract the eye, usually at the top of the page.

- **Subhead:** The optional addition to the headline to provide more detail, also in large (but not quite as large) print.

✔ **Copy or body copy:** The main text, set in a readable size.

✔ **Visual:** An illustration that makes a visual statement. This image may be the main focus of the ad or other printed material (especially when you've designed an ad to show readers your product), or it may be secondary to the copy. Such an image is also optional. After all, most classified ads use no visuals at all, yet classifieds are generally more effective than display ads for the simple reason that people make a point to look for classified ads (instead of making a point to avoid them, as many people do with displays!).

✔ **Caption:** Copy attached to the visual to explain or discuss that visual. You usually place a caption beneath the visual, but you can put it on any side or even within or on the visual.

✔ **Logo:** A unique design that represents the brand or company (like Nike's swoosh). Register logos as trademarks.

✔ **Signature:** The company's trademarked version of its name. Often, advertisers use a logo design that features a brand name in a distinctive font and style. The signature is a written equivalent to the logo's visual identity. Here's how a furniture maker called Heritage Colonial Furniture may do it:

HERITAGE
Colonial Furniture®

✔ **Slogan:** An optional element consisting of a (hopefully) short phrase evoking the spirit or personality of the brand. In all its print ads, Renault uses the slogan 'Createur D'Automobiles'. Of course, everyone knows that Renault creates automobiles, but this slogan, which emphasises the company's Frenchness, works in tandem with the advertising theme for all its cars and is as much a part of Renault's identity as the diamond logo and the signature. As another example, a furniture maker called Heritage Colonial may use as its slogan, 'Bringing the elegance and quality of early antiques to the modern home.'

Figure 7-1 shows each of these elements in a rough design for a print ad (a brochure's layout is a bit more complicated and is covered at the end of this chapter). We use generic terms in place of actual parts of an ad ('headline' for the headline, for example) so that you can easily see all the elements in action. This fairly simple palette for a print ad design allows you endless variation and creativity. You can say or show anything, and you can do so in many different ways. (And you can use this layout for a one-page marketing sheet to include in folders or as handouts at trade shows even if you aren't buying space to run the ad in a magazine or newspaper.)

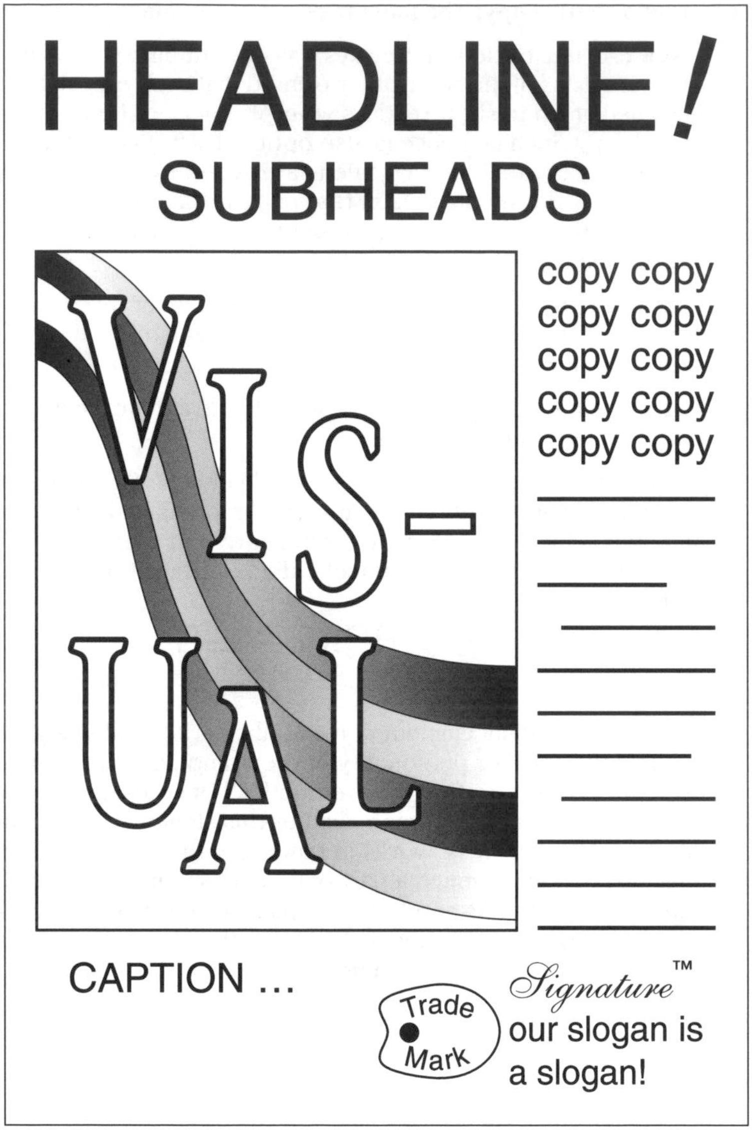

Figure 7-1:
The elements of a print ad.

Putting the parts together: Design and layout

Design refers to the look, feel, and style of your ad or other printed marketing materials. Design is an aesthetic concept and, thus, hard to put into precise terms. But design is vitally important: It has to take the basic appeal of your product and make that appeal work visually on paper (see Chapter 6 for details of how to develop appeal). Specifically, the design needs to overcome the marketer's constant problem: Nobody cares about your advertising. So the design must somehow reach out to readers, grab their attention, and hold it long enough to communicate the appeal of the product you're advertising and attach that appeal to the brand name in the readers' memories.

A memorable photograph is often the easiest way to grab the reader. And if you don't have a better idea, use a photo of an interesting face or of a child, as long as you can make the image relevant in some way to your product. Beautiful nature scenes are also good eye-catchers.

Great advertising has to rise off the page, reach out, and grab you by the eyeballs. In the cluttered world of modern print-based marketing, this design goal is the only one that really works. So we want you to tape up a selection of ads from the same publication(s) yours will go in (or use samples of competitor brochures or catalogue sheets or whatever exactly it is you will be designing in print). Put a draft of your design up along with these benchmarks. Step back – a long way back. Now, does your ad grab the eye more than all the others? If not . . . back to the drawing board!

Understanding the stages in design

Designers often experiment with numerous layouts for their print ads or other printed materials before selecting one for formal development. We strongly recommend that you do the same – or insist that your designer or agency do the same. The more layouts you look at, the more likely you are to get an original idea that has eye-grabbing power. But whether you design your own print materials or have experts do the work for you, you want to be familiar with the design stages.

- ✔ **Step 1. Thumbnails:** The rough sketches designers use to describe layout concepts are called *thumbnails*. They're usually small, quick sketches in pen or pencil. You can also use professional design and layout packages like Quark XPress or InDesign to create thumbnails.

- ✔ **Step 2. Roughs:** Designers then develop thumbnails with promise into *roughs,* full-size sketches with headlines and subheads drawn carefully enough to give the feel of a particular font and *style* (the appearance of the printed letters). Roughs also have sketches for the illustrations. The designers suggest body copy using lines (or nonsense characters, if the designer does the rough using a computer).

Are you using an ad agency or design firm to develop your print ads or other printed marketing materials? Sometimes clients of ad agencies insist on seeing designs in the rough stage, to avoid the expense of having those designs developed more fully before presentation. We recommend that you ask to see rough versions of your designs, too, even if your agency hesitates to show you its work in unfinished form. After the agency realises that you appreciate the design process and don't criticise the roughs simply because they're rough, you can give the agency more guidance and help during the design process.

✔ **Step 3. Comprehensive layout:** After a rough passes muster, designers develop that rough into a *comp* (short for *comprehensive layout*). A comp should look pretty much like a final version of the design, although designers produce a comp on a one-time basis, so the comp may use paste-ups in place of the intended photos, colour photocopies, typeset copy, and headlines. Designers used to assemble comps by hand, but now many designers and agencies do their comps on computer. A high-end PC and colour printer can produce something that looks almost like the final printed version of a four-colour ad or other printed marketing material. Designers refer to a computer-made comp as a *full-colour proof.*

✔ **Step 4. Dummy:** A *dummy* is a form of comp that simulates the feel – as well as the look – of the final design. (Every design should have a feel or personality of its own, just as products should have a personality. Often you can create the best personality by simply carrying over the personality you've created for the product. Consistency helps.) Dummies are especially important for brochures or special inserts to magazines, where the designer often specifies special paper and folds. By doing a dummy comp, you can evaluate the feel of the design while you're evaluating its appearance.

Designing and submitting your ads the old-fashioned way

The traditional way to submit a design to a printing firm is to generate what printers call *camera-ready artwork*, a version of the design suitable for the printer to photograph with a large-scale production camera in order to generate *colour keys* (to convert colours to specific inks) and *films*, clear sheets for each layer of colour to be printed. You (or the designer) produce this camera-ready art by making a *mechanical* or *paste-up*, in which you paste typeset copy, visuals, and all the other elements of the design onto a foam-core board, using a hot wax machine.

A hot wax machine heats wax and spreads it on a roller so that you can roll a thin layer of warm wax onto the back of each element. The wax sticks each piece neatly to the board, allowing those pieces to be peeled off easily, in case you want to reposition anything. When you have everything the way you want it, you send the artwork off to your printer.

Designing and submitting your ads on a computer

You can still work with a glue stick or hot wax and scissors to do rough layouts if you want to, but the modern, and more popular, way to design and submit your ad to a printer is to do so electronically. If you're quick and able on a computer and like to work in design and layout programs (such as Adobe InDesign or Quark XPress), you can do the same kind of creative rough designing simply by searching for images on the Web. (To find an image, try specifying an image search in Google, but remember not to use copyrighted images in your final design without permission or payment.) Copy the images onto your computer, and you can click and drag them into different programs and pages.

We recommend that you invest a bit of time and effort in honing these computer-based design techniques. Look up the latest *For Dummies* books on how to use Quark XPress, Microsoft Publisher, or any other design and layout program of your choice, or just work in Word, which is pretty impressive in its latest incarnations as a basic design program itself. Also take a look at the growing number of great-looking ad templates you can purchase on CD or via e-mail, and then adapt them in any of the common graphic design programs. As an example, see many options at www.stocklayouts.com.

When your preliminary design is ready for the printer, you (or the ad agency) can send the design over the Web using desktop publishing software that the printing firm accepts. You can even do the colour separations for four-colour work on your PC and send those colour separations, too. (Ask the printer for instructions to make sure that you submit the design in a format that the printer's system can use.) The printer then makes plates for printing the design straight from the file that you've e-mailed to them. *(Plates* are metal or plastic sheets with your design on them – the printer applies the ink to the plates when the printing press does its thing.)

Until recently, electronic submission to printing firms generally had to be done from a professional software package like Quark XPress, but increasingly, printers are accepting Word files or PDF files generated by Acrobat (we prefer this route, because it reduces the chances of incompatibility problems). And if you're designing in a recent version of Word, you'll find that creating a PDF file can be done right out of your program, because Acrobat is now built in.

Finding your font

A *font* is a particular design's attributes for the *characters* (letters, numbers, and symbols) used in printing your design. *Typeface* refers only to the distinctive design of the letters (Times New Roman, for example). Font, on the other hand, actually refers to one particular size and style of a typeface design (such as 10-point, bold, Times New Roman).

The right font for any job is the one that makes your text easily readable and that harmonises with the overall design most effectively. For a headline, the font also needs to grab the reader's attention. The body copy doesn't have to grab attention in the same way – in fact, if it does, the copy often loses readability. For example, a *reverse font* (light or white on dark) may be just the thing for a bold headline, but if you use it in the body copy, too, nobody reads your copy because it's just too hard on the eye to read.

Choosing a typeface

What sort of typeface do you want? You have an amazing number of choices because designers have been developing typefaces for as long as printing presses have existed. (Just click Format⇨Font in Microsoft Word to see an assortment of the more popular typefaces.)

A clean, sparse design, with a lot of white space on the page and stark contrasts in the artwork, deserves the clean lines of a *sans serif typeface* – meaning one that doesn't have any decorative *serifs* (those little bars or flourishes at the ends of the main lines in a character). The most popular body-copy fonts without serifs are Helvetica, Arial, Univers, and Avant Garde. Figure 7-2 shows some fonts with and without serifs.

Figure 7-2:
Fonts with and without serifs.

But a richly decorative, old-fashioned sort of design needs a more decorative and traditional serif typeface, like Century or Times New Roman. The most popular body-copy fonts with serifs include Garamond, Melior, Century, Times New Roman, and Caledonia.

Table 7-1 shows an assortment of typeface choices, in which you can compare the clean lines of Helvetica, Avant Garde, and Arial with the more decorative designs of Century, Garamond, and Times New Roman.

Table 7-1	Popular Fonts for Ads	
Sans Serif	*Serif*	
Helvetica	Century	
Arial	Garamond	
Univers	Melior	
Avant Garde	Times New Roman	

In tests, Helvetica and Century generally top the lists as most readable, so start with one of these typefaces for your body copy; only change the font if it doesn't seem to work. Also, research shows that people read lowercase letters about 13 per cent faster than uppercase letters, so avoid long stretches of copy set in all capital letters. People also read most easily when letters are dark and contrast strongly with their background. Thus, black 14-point Helvetica on white is probably the most readable font specification for the body copy of an ad (or other printed marketing materials), even if the combination does seem dull to a sophisticated designer.

Generalising about the best kind of headline typeface is no easy task because designers play around with headlines to a greater extent than they do with body copy. But as a general rule, you can use Helvetica for the headline when you use Century for the body, and vice versa. Or you can just use a bolder, larger version of the body copy font for your headline. You can also reverse a larger, bold version of your type onto a black background for the headline. Use anything to make the headline grab the reader's attention, stand out from the body copy, and ultimately lead vision and curiosity into the body copy's text. (Remember to keep the headline readable. Nothing too fancy, please.)

Sometimes the designer combines body copy of a decorative typeface, one with serifs, like Times New Roman, with headers of a sans serif typeface, like Helvetica. The contrast between the clean lines of the large-sized header and the more decorative characters of the smaller body copy pleases the eye and tends to draw the reader from header to body copy. This book uses that technique. Compare the sans serif bold characters of this chapter's title with the more delicate and decorative characters in which the publishers set the text for a good example of this design concept in action.

Making style choices within the typeface

Any typeface gives the user many choices, and so selecting the typeface is just the beginning of the project when you design your print. How big should the characters be? Do you want to use the standard version of the typeface, a lighter version, a **bold** (or darker) version, or an *italic* version (one that leans to the right, like the letters spelling *italic*)? The process is easier than it sounds. Really! Just look at samples of some standard point sizes (12- and 14-point text for the body copy, for example, and 24-, 36-, and 48-point for the headlines). Many designers make their choice by eye, looking for an easy-to-read size that isn't so large that it causes the words or sentences to break up into too many fragments across the page – but not so small that it gives the reader too many words per line. Keep readability in mind as the goal.

Figure 7-3 shows a variety of size and style choices for the Helvetica typeface. As you can see, you have access to a wonderful range of options, even within this one popular design.

Figure 7-3:
Some of the many choices that the Helvetica typeface offers designers.

Helvetica Light 14 point

Helvetica Italic 14 point

Helvetica Bold 14 point

Helvetica Regular 14 point

Helvetica Regular 24 point

Helvetica Regular Condensed 14 point

Helvetica Bold Outline 24 point

Keep in mind that you can change just about any aspect of type. You can alter the distance between lines – called the *leading* – or you can squeeze characters together or stretch them apart to make a word fit a space. Assume that anything is possible, and ask your printer, or consult the manual of your desktop publishing or word-processing software, to find out how to make a change.

While anything is possible, be warned that your customers' eyes read type quite conservatively. Although most of us know little about the design of typefaces, we find traditional designs instinctively appealing. The spacing of characters and lines, the balance and flow of individual characters – all these familiar typeface considerations please the eye and make reading easy and pleasurable. So, although you should know that you can change anything and everything, you must also know that too many changes may reduce your design's readability. Figure 7-4 shows the same ad laid out twice – once in an eye-pleasing way and once in a disastrous way.

<table>
<tr><td>

WHEN LIFE GIVES YOU LEMONS...

What should you do? Juggle them? Make lemonade? Open a farm stand? Or give up and go home to Momma?

WHO KNOWS? It's often hard to come to grips with pressing personal or career problems. Sometimes it's hardest to see your **own** problems clearly. Fortunately, JEN KNOWS. Jen Fredrics has twenty years of counseling experience, a master's in social work, and a busy practice in personal problem solving. Call her today to find out how to turn your problems into opportunities.

And next time, when life gives you lemons, you'll know just what to make. An appointment.

</td><td>

WHEN LIFE GIVES YOU LEMONS...

What should you do? Juggle them? Make lemonade? Open a farm stand? Or give up and go home to Momma?

WHO KNOWS? It's often hard to come to grips with pressing personal or career problems. Sometimes it's hardest to see your own problems clearly. Fortunately, JEN KNOWS. Jen Fredrics has twenty years of counseling experience, a master's in social work, and a busy practice in personal problem solving. Call her today to find out how to turn your problems into opportunities.

And next time, when life gives you lemons, you'll know just what to make. An appointment.

</td></tr>
</table>

Figure 7-4:
Which copy would you rather read?

Don't just play with type for the sake of playing (as the designer did in the left-hand version of the classified ad in Figure 7-4). Stick with popular fonts, in popular sizes, except where you have to solve a problem or you want to make a special point. The advent of desktop publishing has led to a horrifying generation of advertisements in which dozens of fonts dance across the page, bolds and italics fight each other for attention, and the design of the words becomes a barrier to reading, rather than an aid.

Choosing a point size

When designers and printers talk about *point sizes*, they're referring to a traditional measure of the height of the letters (based on the highest and lowest parts of the biggest letters). One *point* equals about $\frac{1}{72}$ of an inch, so a 10-point type is $\frac{10}{72}$ of an inch high, at the most.

Personally, we don't really care – we've never measured a character with a ruler. We just know that if the letters seem too small for easy reading, then we need to bump the typeface up a couple of points. Ten-point type is too small for most body copy, but you may want to use that size if you have to squeeze several words into a small space. (But why do that? You're usually better off editing your body copy and then bumping up the font size to make it more readable!) Your eye can't distinguish easily between fonts that are only one or two sizes apart, so specify a larger jump than that to distinguish between body copy and subhead, or subhead and headline.

Producing Brochures, Fliers, and More

You can get your print design out to the public in an easy and inexpensive way, using brochures, fliers, posters, and many other forms – your imagination is the only limit to what you can do with a good design for all your printed materials. Your word-processing or graphics software, a good inkjet or laser printer, and the help of your local photocopy or print shop (which also has folding machines) allows you to design and produce brochures quite easily, and also come up with many other forms of printed marketing materials. In this section, however, we focus largely on a basic brochure, because it's easy, a business staple, and effective at marketing your company.

You can also do small runs (100 or less) straight from a colour printer. Buy matte or glossy brochure paper designed for your brand of printer, and simply select the appropriate paper type in the print dialog box. Today's inexpensive inkjet printers can produce stunning brochures. But you have to fold these brochures yourself, and the ink cartridges aren't cheap. So print as needed rather than inventory a large number of brochures. Or try contacting your local copy shop. Kall Kwik and many other copy shops now accept e-mailed copies of files, and can produce short runs of your brochures, pamphlets, catalogue sheets, or other printed materials on their colour copiers directly from your file.

Many brochures foolishly waste money because they don't accomplish any specific marketing goals; they just look pretty, at best. To avoid a pretty, but pointless, brochure that doesn't achieve a sales goal, make sure that you know:

- ✔ Who will read the brochure
- ✔ How they will get the brochure
- ✔ What they should discover and do from reading the brochure

These three questions focus your brochure design and make it useful to your marketing.

Marketers often order a brochure without a clear idea of what purpose the brochure should serve. They just think a brochure is a good idea: 'Oh, we need them to, you know, put in the envelope along with a letter, or, um, for our salespeople to keep in the boots of their cars, or maybe we'll send some out to our mailing list, or give them away at the next trade show.'

With this many possibilities, the brochure can't be properly suited to any single use. The brochure becomes a dull, vague scrap of paper that just talks about the company or product but doesn't hit readers over the head with any particular appeal and call to action.

Listing your top three uses

Define up to three specific uses for the brochure. No more than three, though, because your design can't accomplish more than three purposes effectively. The most common and appropriate uses for a brochure are:

- ✔ To act as a reference on the product, or technical details of the product, for prospects
- ✔ To support a personal selling effort by lending credibility and helping overcome objections (to find out more about sales, read Chapter 17)
- ✔ To generate leads through a direct-mail campaign (we talk about direct-mail campaigns in Chapter 11)

Say you want to design a brochure that does all three of these tasks well. Start by designing the contents. What product and technical information must be included? Write the information down, or collect necessary illustrations, so that you have the *fact base* (the essential information to communicate) in front of you. You will include in your brochure copy (and perhaps illustrations) designed specifically for each of these three purposes.

Writing about strengths and weaknesses

After you create your fact base (see the preceding section), organise these points in such a way that they highlight your product's (or service's) greatest strengths and overcome its biggest challenges. Don't know what your product's strengths and weaknesses are? List the following, as they relate to sales:

- ✔ The common sales objections or reasons prospects give for why they don't want to buy your product
- ✔ Customers' favourite reasons for buying, or aspects of your product or business that customers like most

With your fact base organised accordingly, you're ready to begin writing. Your copy should read as if you're listening to customers' concerns and answering each concern with an appropriate response. You can write subheads like 'Our Product Doesn't Need Service' so that salespeople or prospects can easily see how your facts (in copy and/or illustrations) overcome each specific objection and highlight all the major benefits.

Incorporating a clear, compelling appeal

Add some basic appeal (see Chapter 6), communicated in a punchy headline and a few dozen words of copy, along with an appropriate and eye-catching illustration. You need to include this appeal to help the brochure stand on its own as a marketing tool when the brochure is sent out to leads by post or passed on from a prospect or customer to one of his or her professional contacts.

The appeal needs to project a winning personality. Your brochure can be fun or serious, emotional or factual – but it must be appealing. The appeal is the bait that draws the prospect to your hook. Make sure your hook is well baited!

Putting it all together

When you have all the parts – the appeal, the fact base, and so on – you're ready to put your brochure together. The appeal, with its enticing headline and compelling copy and visual, goes on the front of the brochure – or the outside when you fold it for mailing, or the central panel out of three if you fold a sheet twice. The subheads that structure the main copy respond to objections and highlight strengths on the inside pages. And you organise the fact base, needed for reference use, in the copy and illustrations beneath these subheads.

Although you can design a brochure in many ways, we often prefer the format (along with dimensions for text blocks or illustrations) in Figure 7-5. This format is simple and inexpensive because you print the brochure on a single sheet of 490mm x 210mm paper that you then fold three times. The brochure fits in a standard DL (110mm x 220mm) envelope, or you can tape it together along the open fold and mail it on its own. This layout allows for some detail, but not enough to get you into any real trouble. (Larger formats and multi-page pieces tend to fill up with the worst, wordiest copy, and nobody ever reads those pieces.)

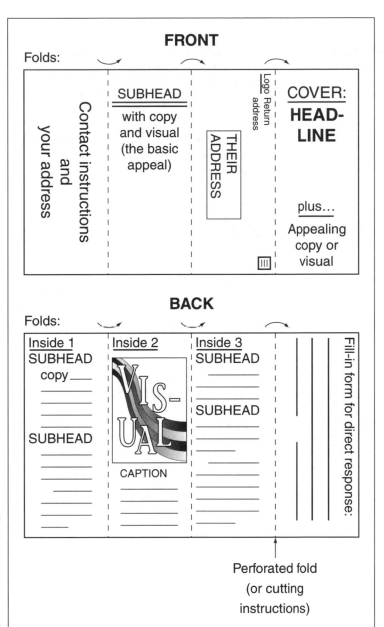

Figure 7-5:
A simple, multi-purpose brochure layout.

You can use the design shown in Figure 7-5 for direct mailings to generate sales leads, and you can also hand the brochure out or use it for reference in direct-selling situations. You can produce this brochure, using any popular desktop publishing software, and you can even print and fold it at the local photocopy shop (if you don't need the thousands of copies that make off-set printing cost-effective). To convert this design to an even simpler, cheaper format, use A4 paper and eliminate the *return mailer* (the left-hand page on the front, the right-hand on the back, which can be returned with the blanks filled in to request information or accept a special offer). If you do remove the return mailer, however, be sure to include follow-up instructions and contact information on one of the inside pages!

Placing a Print Ad

This section covers a marketing speciality called *media buying*, with an emphasis on buying print ad space. Media agencies and the marketing departments of big companies have specialists who do nothing but buy media, and some brokers specialise in it for mid-sized or smaller marketers. But if you're a smaller-scale marketer, you can easily work out how to buy media space on your own.

Can you afford to advertise?

If you're marketing a small business, start by buying magazines or newspapers that you're sure your prospective customers read. Then look for the information in them that identifies the publisher and gives a phone number for advertisers to call. Call and request a *rate card* (a table listing the prices of ads by size of ad and also showing the discount rate per ad if you buy multiple ads instead of just a single one). With a magazine, also ask for the *schedule,* which tells you when ads for each issue need to be placed and what the topics of future issues will be. Alternatively, you can get information for advertisers on the Web sites of many publications.

After you've collected a selection of rate cards from magazines or newspapers, take a hard look at the pricing. How expensive is the average ad (in the middle of the size range for each publication)? This may be a broad number.

If a single ad costs 5 per cent or more of your marketing budget for the entire year, throw the rate sheets away and forget about advertising in those publications. Your business is not currently operating on a large enough scale to be able to do this kind of advertising. You need dozens of ad placements at a minimum to make a good print ad campaign, so don't begin unless you can easily afford to keep going.

Instead of blowing that much money on a single ad, spread it over more economical forms of advertising and marketing, like brochures, mailings, and e-mails. If you operate on too small a scale or budget to afford advertising, try turning that ad design into a good flier and mailing it, instead. You can send the flier to 200 names and see what happens – that's a lot less risky and expensive than buying space in a magazine that goes to 200,000 names. Or you can search for smaller-circulation publications with a more local or specialist readership, where the rates may be much cheaper.

Finding inexpensive places to advertise

Many local businesses buy ad space in theatre programmes. What does this cost? Less than £70 for many programmes. Compare that price to an ad in a major magazine, which can cost £15,000. That's a big difference! If buying ads in the best publications to reach your market is too expensive, you can always find smaller-circulation publications that charge less.

One great way to advertise for less is to take advantage of the tens of thousands of newsletters published by professional groups and interest groups. You can buy ad space in 10 or 20 such newsletters for far less money than buying one ad insertion in a national daily newspaper. But you may have to be creative and persistent, because opportunities to advertise in newsletters aren't as obvious as with larger and more professional publications.

Professional associations' monthly newsletters provide an excellent opportunity for small-budget advertising. Professionals are people who have buying power, so even if you don't sell a product aimed at the people the newsletter is written for, they may still respond to your ad. Some insurance agents have advertised successfully in newsletters that go to doctors, for example. And increasingly, such newsletters are published in Web versions in addition to – or even instead of – print versions. With a Web publication, you can take advantage of the larger reach of the Web with the lower price of a small publication.

Also explore local newspapers. You can find hundreds of newspapers and weeklies with *circulation* (readership) only in the tens of thousands, which means their rates for ads are one-fifth to one-tenth the price of a national newspaper. Of course, you don't reach as many people, either – advertising tends to be priced on a *cost per thousand readers* basis (the cost of buying that ad divided by the number of readers who read the publication, then multiplied by 1,000), so you generally get as much exposure as you're willing to pay for. But by buying ads in small-circulation publications, you avoid taking huge risks, and you minimise your investment. If an ad pays off, you can try running it in additional publications. But if the ad doesn't produce the results you want, you can afford to write off the cost without feeling too much pain.

Keep the scale of your print advertising (and indeed any advertising) at a level such that you can afford to run an ad that may produce zero sales. Although that's certainly not your goal, zero sales are always a possibility, and you want to base your buying decision on that possibility.

Selecting the ad size

What size ad should you buy? The answer depends in part on the design of your ad. Does the ad have a strong, simple visual or headline that catches the eye, even if it's only a third of a page in size? Or does the ad need to be displayed in a larger format to work well?

In addition to your (or your designer's) judgement about the specifics of your ad, also take into account some general statistics on what percentage of readers *notice* an ad based on its size. As you may expect, the rate goes up with size – bigger ads get more notice (all other things being equal), according to a study by Media Dynamics (see Table 7-2).

Table 7-2	Selecting the Right Size
Size of Ad	*Index (recall scores)*
Page, colour	100
2-page spread, colour	130
⅔-page vertical, colour	81
½-page horizontal, colour	72

The bigger the ad, the bigger the impact. But also consider the fact that the percentage of readers noticing your ad doesn't go up *in proportion* to the increase in size. Doubling the size of your ad gives you something like a quarter more viewers, not twice as many – that's partly why the cost of a full-page ad isn't twice the cost of a half-page ad.

If you're watching your pennies, a full-page ad is often your best choice. Even though a large ad costs more, it is sufficiently more noticeable than smaller sizes, which means you'll reach more readers and, thus, bring the cost per exposure down a bit. However, remember that while a full-page ad is more economical, it's also more risky, because you will have blown more money if the ad doesn't work. You may want to try testing a new design with a quarter-page, inexpensive ad, and if that pays off, buy a full-page ad the next time.

Testing and improving your print ad

Is anybody actually reading your ad? A *direct-response* ad, one that asks readers to take a measurable action like call, fax, or go to a shop, gives you a clear indication of that ad's effectiveness within days of its first appearance. Say you expect to receive a lot of enquiries and orders over the telephone during the week the issue with your ad goes on sale. If you don't receive those calls, you know you have a problem. Now what?

Troubleshooting your ad

What if you want to know more about why that direct-response ad didn't get the desired level of response? Or what if you want to study an *indirect-response ad* – one that creates or strengthens an image or position in order to encourage sales? Much brand advertising is indirect, leaving it to the retailer or local office to close the sale. No phones ring, whether consumers liked the ad or not, so how do you know whether the ad worked?

To get this sort of information, you can go to a market research firm and have your ad tested for effectiveness. In fact, if you plan to spend more than £100,000 on print ads, you can probably consider the £12,000 or so needed to hire a research firm to pretest the ad money well spent. *Pretesting* means exposing people to the ad in a controlled setting and measuring their reactions to it.

To test an ad and see whether it's effective, use one of the free techniques in Chapter 4: You can assemble your own panel of customers and ask them to rate your ad and give you feedback about why they do or don't find that ad appealing. This feedback can give you good ideas for a new, improved version next time. You can also tap into the large-scale studies of ad readership done routinely by some research firms. Just subscribe to the study, and the firm feeds you detailed data about how well each ad you publish works.

A number of commercial media research services can give you additional information about how and to what extent people read your ad, as well as telling you what your competitors are up to and how much they're spending. Roper Starch Worldwide (www.roper.com) may be the best known of these services. If you sign up for its Starch Ad Readership service, you can find out how your ad performs compared with the industry norm. Starch surveys 75,000 consumers each year, asking them about specific ads to find out to what extent consumers notice and read an ad, and to measure the level of interest the ad generated.

Say that the Starch data shows that readership of your ad falls a little lower than average and that, although many people note the ad, few read enough to get the point or even the brand name. Should you kill this ad and start over?

The answer depends on what's wrong with the ad. Starch data (or data from similar services or even a volunteer consumer panel) can help you find out because the Starch survey looks at individual elements of the ad, as well as the overall ad. You can find out how many people read the headline (or even the first versus second line of a two-line headline). Then you can see how many continued on to the first paragraph of the body copy, the photograph, or the logo and signature.

Sometimes you find a problem that can be fixed without starting from scratch. Maybe your headline and photo get high Starch scores, but the body copy flunks. You can try rewriting and shortening the copy, and you may also try changing the layout or your choice of fonts. Perhaps the body copy is in reverse font, which consumers find hard to read. Often, switching the text to dark letters on a white or light background raises the Starch score, without any other changes!

Or maybe you need to switch from a black-and-white or two-colour visual to a four-colour one. Sure, you have to pay more, but if the Starch scores go up enough, the resulting ad may yield a better return, despite its higher price. Studies show that full-colour ads are recalled better than two-colour ads, which in turn outperform mono ads. So, as with size, more is better when it comes to colours. However, you need to run the numbers to see how the extra costs and extra readers affect your cost per thousand figure. As with all print ad decisions, you should be able to reduce the options to reasonable estimates of costs and returns and then pick the highest-yielding option.

Ad analysis for free?

Maybe you don't really need to spend good money on a research service to find out if your ads are working. Here are some alternatives:

- Run three variations on the ad and see which one generates the most calls or Web site visits (offering a discount based on a code number tells you which responses come from which ad).

- Do your own ad tests. Ask people to look at your ads for 20 seconds, and then quiz them about what they remember. If they missed much of the ad, you probably need to rewrite it.

- Run the same ad (or very similar ones) in large and small formats and see which pulls in the largest number of consumers.

Any experiments you can run as you do your marketing give you useful feedback about what's working and what isn't. Always think of ways to compare different options and see how those options perform when you advertise, giving you useful insight into ad effectiveness.

Some brilliant examples

Marketers generally assume that they have to work hard with colours and text to make their ads noticeable and persuasive. Statistically, they're right. But don't discount the power of imaginative design to simplify the task. You can do a simple two-colour ad that actually works better than other, more elaborate ads.

Two recent press campaigns prove that simple can be best. One from *The Economist* uses the same white and red design that the magazine has been using in its poster advertising for the past few years. The press ad consists of a black-and-white Albert Einstein mask with a dotted line around it – the idea being that readers can cut out and wear the mask to look intelligent, or they can buy the magazine. There are only two colours and only two words on the page – '*The Economist*'.

Another ad, this one from Volkswagen, uses more words but even less colour. Their full-page 'Word Search' ad plays on the simple puzzle idea but with a twist. The design is the shape of a car (the Golf) created from black letters on the white page, while in the top left-hand corner is a list of phrases, such as 'power-assisted steering' and 'engine immobiliser'. The strapline says, 'Full of hidden extras', inviting the reader to look for the hidden words inside the car. Great print advertising doesn't have to be expensive, it just has to be clever.

Chapter 8

Signs, Posters, and More

• •

In This Chapter

▶ Finding successful signs for your business

▶ Using flags, banners, and awnings

▶ Designing billboards and other large signs

▶ Utilising transport advertising

▶ Opting for bumper stickers, umbrellas, and shopping bags

• •

*O*utdoor advertising refers to a wide variety of advertising. The most obvious (but not necessarily most important for you) are large (to very large!) signs and posters, including roadside billboards, but we also include signs, flags, and banners in this medium. *Outdoor advertising* also includes what the experts call *ambient advertising*, which means putting an ad in any unexpected place to catch people by surprise.

All these methods try to communicate your message through public display of a poster, sign, or something of similar design requirements. That's why we incorporate signs, flags, banners, bumper stickers, transit advertising, and even T-shirts in this chapter, along with the traditional poster formats. These media are more powerful than many marketers realise – some businesses succeed by using no other advertising, in fact. In this chapter, you find out how to design for and use *outdoor advertising* (the term we use to indicate outdoor signs and banners, plus related displays like posters and signs, which, just to keep you on your toes, can be displayed indoors as well as out).

Whenever you review your marketing, do an audit of your signs, posters, T-shirts, and other outdoor ads. How many do you have displayed? Are they visible? Clear and appealing? Clean and in good repair? And then ask if you can find an easy way to increase the number and impact of these signs. When you need to make your brand identity and marketing messages visible, you can never do too much. The more the merrier!

The Essential Sign

Signs (small, informational outdoor ads or notices) don't show up in the index or table of contents of most books on marketing. *Signs* are displays with brand or company names on them and sometimes a short marketing message or useful information for the customer, too. In my experience, every marketer needs to make good use of signs.

Signs are all over – if you're in an office right now, look out of the nearest window and you can probably see a handful with ease. And signs are undeniably important. Even if signs serve only to locate a shop or office, they do a job that marketers need done. If your customers can't find you, you're out of business. So why do marketers – or at least those marketing experts who write the books – tend to ignore signs so completely?

You can't find a national or international set of standards for signs. You also can't find a major association to promote standards and champion best practices. When evaluating signs, we can't send you to the experts easily as we can with radio, TV, print, or other outdoor media. You'll probably end up working with a local sign manufacturer, and you and your designer have to specify size, materials, copy, and art. Fortunately, you're not all on your own; you can find some guidance and help. Following are a few things to remember:

✔ There is some information on the use of signs in the UK, but it's more about what you are allowed and not allowed to display. The Office of the Deputy Prime Minister (at www.odpm.gov.uk) has a document called 'Outdoor advertisements and signs: A guide for advertisers' under its 'Planning, Guidance and Advice' section. Many basic signs will normally be permitted, while others will require planning application consent from your local authority.

✔ If you rent retail or office space, your landlord may have put some restrictions regarding signs into your lease. Research these possible constraints and talk to those who feel they have authority over your sign and seek their approval based on a sketch and plan before you spend any money having signs made or installed.

✔ Consult your local or regional business telephone listings when you need to have a sign made. You should find several options. You may want to talk to a good design firm or experienced designer for a personal reference, too. And modern high street copy shops now provide cheap high-tech solutions for smaller or temporary signs.

✔ To stand out next to those shiny, high-tech signs and project a quality image, have your sign designed and painted by an artist or consider hiring a cabinet-maker, stained glass artist, oil painter, or other arts and crafts professional. Most signs have little real art about them. Unusual and beautiful signs tell the world that your company is special. In fact, a really special sign, well displayed in a high-traffic area, has more power to build an image or pull in prospects than any other form of local advertising.

What your sign can do

Signs have limited ability to accomplish marketing goals – but perhaps not as limited as you think. As well as displaying the name of your business, you can include a phone number or email address so that even when your premises are closed, potential customers know how to get in touch with you. And you can say what your business does – a butcher doesn't have to be just a 'butcher', he can be a 'family-owned free range butcher'. With signs, as with all marketing communications, it's the way that you say it that counts!

Every morning on my way to work I pass Munson's coffee shop. I couldn't begin to tell you how many other shops I must pass or what they are called, but I remember Munson's (and go in occasionally) because of the chalk board they put on the pavement outside the shop. No matter how early I am, there is always a new piece of homespun philosophy written on the board, enticing customers in for a drink or snack. It's cheap, easy and effective marketing – and it's a sign!

Aside from their practical value (letting people know where you are), signs can and should promote your image and brand name. An attractive sign on your building or vehicle can spread the good word about your business or brand to all who pass by. Don't miss this brilliant opportunity to put your best foot forward in public.

You will see many commercial signs that are in poor condition. Signs sit out in the weather, and when they fade, peel, or fall over, they give negative advertising for your business. Don't let your sign give the public the impression that you don't care enough to maintain your signs (they may even think you're going out of business!). Renew and religiously maintain your signs to get the maximum benefit from them.

Writing good signs

As a marketer, you need to master the strange art of writing for signs. Too often, the language marketers use on signs is ambiguous. The sign just doesn't say anything with enough precision to make its point clear. Keep in mind the suggestions outlined in the following sections.

Make sure your sign says what you want it to

One of my favourite stories about how to easily turn a bad sign into a good sign comes from the marketing consultant Doug Hall. A friend of his put up a sign that read 'Seasons in Thyme – EPICUREAN FOOD & WINE'. Do you have any idea what that company does? Doug changed his friend's sign to 'Seasons in Thyme RESTAURANT. Casual, Elegant, Island Dining'. For the first time in all his years in business the owner received some customers who said they came in because they had seen the sign.

Before you approve any design, review the copy to make sure that the writing provides a model of clarity! Try misinterpreting the wording. Can you read the sign in a way that makes it seem to mean something you don't intend to say? And try thinking of questions the sign doesn't answer that seem obvious to you – remember that the consumer may not know the answers. For example, some people have a terrible sense of direction, so a sign on the side of a shop leaves them confused about how to enter that shop. Solution? Put an arrow and the instructions 'Enter from Front' on the sign.

Use a header to catch your customer's eye

Marketers design some signs to convey substantial information – directions, for example, or details of a shop's merchandise mix. Informational signs are often too brief or too lengthy. Divide the copy and design into two sections, each with a separate purpose, as follows:

- ✔ **Have a header.** The first section is like the header in a print ad (see Chapter 7), and you design it to catch attention from afar and draw people to the sign. Given this purpose, brevity is key – and don't forget the essential large, catchy type and/or visuals.

- ✔ **Communicate essential information.** The second section of the sign needs to communicate the essential information accurately and in full. If the first section does its job, viewers walk right up to the sign to read the informational part, so you don't need to make that type as large and catchy. The consumer should be able to easily read and interpret the wording and type of the information, and this section needs to answer all likely viewer questions.

Most signs don't have these two distinct sections, and so they fail to accomplish either purpose very well – they neither draw people very strongly nor inform them fully. Unfortunately, most sign makers have a strong urge to make all the copy the same size. When pressed, the sign makers sometimes make the header twice as big as the rest of the copy; but going further than that seems to upset them. Well, to get a good sign, you may have to upset some people. As in many aspects of marketing, if you want above-average performance, you have to swim against the current.

You may have to make your sign bigger to fit the necessary words on it in a readable font. So be it. The form of the sign must follow its function.

Be creative!

Speaking of being unconventional, what about adding a beautiful photograph to your sign to give it more of the eye-catching appeal of a good print ad? Most sign printers/makers can include photographs now, but few marketers take advantage of this option.

Another problem – marketers write the copy on most signs in the most tired and obvious manner. Tradition says that a sign, unlike any other marketing communication, must simply state the facts in a direct, unimaginative way. One reason you don't see much creativity in signs? Most marketers assume people *read* signs. That's the conventional wisdom – that your customers and prospects automatically find and read your signs.

Try walking down an average high street and then listing all the signs you remember seeing. Some stand out, but most go unseen. And I bet you can't re-create the text of very many of those signs your eye bothered to linger on long enough to read. To avoid having your sign being lost in this sea of similar signs, you have to make yours stand out!

Whenever you find other marketers making silly mistakes, you can turn their errors into your opportunities. And signs permit innovation in two interesting areas. You can innovate in the copy and artwork, just as you can in any print medium – from a magazine ad to a roadside billboard. But you can also innovate in the form of the sign itself. Experiment with materials, shapes, lighting, location, and ways of displaying signs to come up with some novel ideas that give your sign drawing power. Signs should be creative and fun. (So should all marketing, for that matter.)

Here are some of the many variations in form that you can take advantage of when designing a creative sign:

- ✔ Vinyl graphics and lettering (quick and inexpensive but accurate to your design)

- ✔ Hand-painted (personal look and feel)

- ✔ Wood (traditional look; routing or hand carving enhances the appeal)

- ✔ Metal (durable and accurate screening of art and copy, but not very pretty)

- ✔ Window lettering (hand-painted or with vinyl letters/graphics)

- ✔ Lighted boxes (in which lettering is back-lit; highly visible at night)

- ✔ Neon signs (high impact)

- ✔ Magnetic signs (for your vehicles)

- ✔ Signs printed from an inkjet printer output, sent out from a local frame shop to be laminated on a display board with a plastic coating (this new form of framing is intended for indoor use, but I've seen some companies use it out of doors and it holds up surprisingly well. With it, you can make your own signs on your own printer)

- Electronic displays (also known as *electronic message repeaters*; movement and longer messages, plus a high-tech feel, make these displays appropriate in some situations)

- Flat-panel TV screens (with shifting sign content and images or video; the price of these TVs has been coming down)

- Pavement projection (a unit in the shop window moves and spins a logo or message at the feet of passers-by at night)

Discovering Flags, Banners, and Awnings

Movement is eyecatching, so t hink of flags as more dynamic kinds of sign, and try to find ways to use them to build brand awareness, to make your location(s) more visible, or to get a marketing message displayed in more forms and places than you could otherwise. Also note that the costs of cloth-based forms of advertising can be surprisingly reasonable – that's why outdoor messages on canvas or synthetic cloth make up an important part of many marketing campaigns.

Flagging down your customers

Did you know that Shakespeare used flags to advertise? In Elizabethan times the Globe Theatre in London had a small tower with a flagpole that advertised the next play to be shown – they were even colour coded, black for a tragedy and white for a comedy. Today you'll find that theatres, galleries, and museums are still some of the biggest users of flags and banners because they can adorn their buildings with colourful banners that promote forthcoming performances – the temporary nature of the medium suits the rotation of the plays and exhibitions. Do you have a similar short-term message that you could get across on a flag or banner?

A number of companies specialise in making custom-designed flags and banners. Of course, you see tacky paper banners – often produced by the local copy shop – hanging in the windows of retail shops on occasion. But I'm not talking about those banners (because they probably don't help your image). I mean a huge, beautiful cloth flag flapping in the breeze. Or a bold 3-x-5-foot screen-printed flag suspended like a banner on an office or trade-show wall. Or a nylon table banner that turns the front and sides of a table into space for your marketing message.

Consider using a flag or banner as a sign for your shop or business. So few marketers take advantage of this way to use a banner that it can help you stand out. A flag or banner is less static and dull than the typical metal or wood sign. Cloth moves, and even when it isn't moving, you know it has the potential for movement – giving the banner a bit of excitement. Also, flags or banners often seem decorative and festive. People associate flags and banners with special events because these decorations are traditionally used in that context, instead of for permanent display.

Flag companies give you all these options and more. These businesses regularly sew and screen large pieces of fabric, and they can also supply you with cables, poles, and other fittings you need to display flags and banners. In recent years, silk-screening technology and strong synthetic fibres have made flags and banners brighter and more permanent, expanding their uses in marketing.

You can find suppliers of a full line of stock and custom products by searching online, looking in your local Yellow Pages or in the services section directories of trade magazines such as *Marketing*. Whoever you contact, ask to see their custom flag and banner price list, which includes a lot of design ideas and specs, and also ask to see photos of effective banners from previous clients.

The only limits to how big or how imaginative you can get with a banner are the size of the building you can hang it from and, of course, the size of your budget. Recent years have seen many big organisations commission temporary *building wraps*, which cover the whole or a large part of their premises. As I was writing this chapter, London 2012, the group leading the bid to host the Olympics, revealed the biggest building wrap in Europe – two banners covering the roof of the Millennium Dome, which can be seen from planes as they fly into London. You may not be able to do anything on this scale, but it does show that you don't have to stick to stock formats.

Canopies and awnings

If appropriate for your business, consider using an awning and canopy. For retailers, awnings and canopies often provide the boldest and most attractive form of roadside sign. Office sites may also find awnings and canopies valuable.

Awnings combine structural value with marketing value by shading the interior and can even extend the floor space of your store by capturing some of the sidewalk as transition space. An awning can perform all the functions a sign can, and more, and it can do so in a way that's highly visible but not intrusive. Even a row of awnings does not look as crass and commercial as huge signs because your eye accepts them as a structural part of the building. So you get the same amount of advertising as with a big sign without looking pushy.

Posters: Why Size Matters

If you are planning to use posters to advertise, one of the first things to think about is how long customers will have to read your ad and from how far away. This will help you decide how much you can say in your ad, and how to say it.

Here's a simple exercise to help you understand the design requirements for a large-format poster. Draw a rectangular box on a sheet of blank paper, using a ruler as your guide. Make the box 12 cm wide and 6 cm high. That's the proportion of a standard *48-sheet* poster (I talk more about poster formats later in this chapter). Although a poster is large (over 6 metres wide in this instance), from a distance it will look as small as that box on your sheet. (See Figure 8-1.) Now hold your paper (or Figure 8-1) at arm's length and think about what copy and artwork can fit in this space, while remaining readable to passers-by at this distance. Not much, right? Now imagine they are driving past it in a car. Next imagine them staring at it for minutes while waiting for the 8.30am train from Dorking to Waterloo. Sometimes you have to take care to limit your message to a few, bold words and images, or your poster becomes a mess that no one can read. At other times you can afford to include more detail – the people waiting for that train may even be grateful for the distraction!

Figure 8-1:
From a distance, a large roadside poster looks no bigger than this image.

CAN YOU READ THIS
CAN YOU READ THIS
CAN YOU READ THIS
CAN YOU READ THIS
CAN YOU READ THIS
CAN YOU READ THIS

That's the problem with outdoor advertising, in general – viewers have to read the ad in a hurry, and often from a considerable distance. So the ad has to be simple. Yet people who walk or drive the same route view the same ad daily. So that ad has to combine lasting interest with great simplicity.

With all these constraints, you see the difficulty of designing effective outdoor ads. Make your message fun, beautiful, or at least important and clear, so that people don't resent having to see it often.

Deciding on outdoor ad formats

The Outdoor Advertising Association (www.oaa.org.uk) describes four different sectors in the outdoor market: Roadside, transport, retail, and non-traditional & ambient:

- ✔ **Roadside.** You can choose anything from phone kiosks to 96-sheet ads, which at 40-feet wide by 10-feet high are the largest of the standard poster formats. Special builds, such as a real car stuck to a billboard, and banners count as roadside ads, too.

- ✔ **Transport.** While it includes standard poster sites in stations, airports, and on trains and tubes, transport is a wide-ranging outdoor sector that covers (literally) bus-sides, taxis, and trucks. For that reason, it has its own lexicon of jargon – from *L-Sides* to *T-Sides* and the enticingly named *Super Rears*. All that really matters is that they're ways of advertising on the outside of buses, which I cover later in this chapter.

- ✔ **Retail.** If you have a product that is sold through retailers then outdoor ads near those outlets can make a lot of sense. As well as poster sites at supermarkets, the retail sector includes shopping centres, cinemas, gyms, and petrol stations – and can include ads on trolleys and screens.

- ✔ **Non-traditional formats & ambient.** They couldn't even come up with a straightforward name for this sector, which just proves how diverse it is. Think petrol pump nozzles, takeaway lids, ticket backs, beermats, floor stickers – in fact, think anything at all. I talk about some of the more popular ambient formats, as well as the truly outlandish, later in the chapter.

Figure 8-2 shows the proportions and relative sizes of the standard *roadside* outdoor formats.

You can also explore the growing number of variations on these standards. Want your message displayed on the floor of a building lobby, on a shopping trolley, or alongside the notice boards at leisure centres? Or how about on signs surrounding the arenas and courts of athletic events? You can use all these options and more, by directly contacting the businesses that control such spaces or using one of a host of ad agencies and poster contractors that can give you larger-scale access.

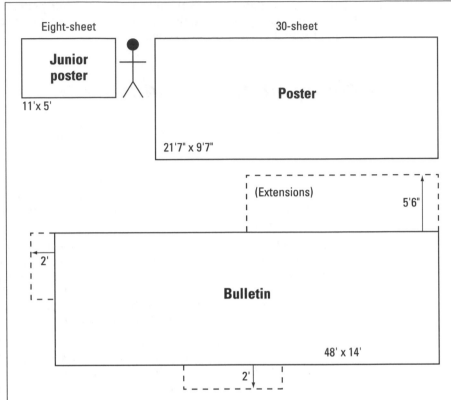

Figure 8-2:
Three standard sizes for outdoor advertising in the UK.

Maximising your returns

The costs of outdoor advertising vary widely. But to give you some idea of what's involved, a 48-sheet poster at a roadside in the North West region (Manchester and Liverpool) will cost you around £300 for a two-week period – the standard time for an outdoor campaign. You are unlikely to buy just one poster site, and even more unlikely to find an outdoor advertising company that will sell you one. The typical way poster space is sold is by a pre-determined group of panels in one area, or a national campaign. So, if you wanted to advertise on 25 of the best 48-sheet sites in Manchester and Liverpool for two weeks it would cost you approximately £7,500. Or 70 sites giving coverage across the North West region would cost £19,250.

The money is one thing, but who is seeing your posters is quite another. The audience for poster campaigns is measured in several ways, broadly how many of the local or national population will see it, how often, and how clearly. For example, you can buy 100 48-sheet posters in London for £42,000, which will be seen by 2 million Londoners over a two-week period. That's around 26 per cent of the area's population, so you achieve a *cover* of 26 per cent. Your *frequency* is the number of times a person sees your ad over the period, in this case 8.1 times. And your *Visibility Adjusted Impacts (VAIs)* for each panel is a score telling you who actually looks at each panel. VAI is a measure of the quality or location of your panels – basically the higher the score, the more effective the campaign (but also the higher the cost). Your 100 48-sheets in London have a VAI of 100, but if you were to splash out £105,000 on the 50 best 96-sheets in the capital you would get a VAI of 205.

You can get measurements on outdoor advertising effectiveness from Postar (www.postar.co.uk), but as you have to pay a subscription fee I suggest that you go direct to the outdoor advertising companies for ratecards and data. You can find the main poster companies through the Outdoor Advertising Association Web site (www.oaa.org.uk).

Messages on the Move: Transport Advertising

Transport advertising is any advertising in or on railway or underground systems, airports, buses, taxis, on the sides of vans or lorries, and more. Although transport advertising is a form of outdoor advertising, this is misleading because you set up some transit ads indoors: Ads at airport terminals, ads displayed within tube carriages, and so on.

Transport ads work well if you get the people in transit to take an interest in your product, from consumer products to business services. I've seen transit ads generate sales leads for local estate agents and for international consulting firms. Yet few marketers make use of them. Consider being an innovator and trying transit ads, even if your competitors don't.

Standard options – the ones most easily available through media buying firms and ad agencies – include bus shelter panels, and bus and taxi exterior signs, and posters and back-lit signs in airports.

You find one definite advantage in transport advertising – it typically delivers high frequency of viewer impacts in a short period of time. Public transport vehicles generally travel the same routes over and over, and so almost everyone along the route sees an ad multiple times.

Bus shelter panels

Shelter panels are 6-sheet (120 cm x 180 cm) posters. These ads appear at bus-stop shelters. You can mount them behind a Lucite sheet to minimise the graffiti problem. In many cities, the site owners have back-lit some of the shelter panels for night-time display. A two-week showing typically costs anywhere from £120 to £280, depending upon the area, or up to £550 per panel for the busiest London sites.

Bus advertising comes with well-accepted standards in the UK, largely due to the fixed available space on any single- or double-decker bus – although some companies now offer the option of full-bus branding, as well. Figure 8-3 shows the standard bus ad sizes, but you should contact a poster contractor who specialises in this kind of advertising (such as Viacom Outdoor `www.viacom-outdoor.co.uk`) before producing any posters.

Sometimes advertisers combine an L-Side with a Superside and rear panels to maximise impact on pedestrians and drivers as they watch the bus go by. Add a shelter poster to the mix, and you have incredibly good coverage! Such combinations can be effective, especially if you think your ad may be challenging to read or you want to display two or three complementary ads to the same viewer. You can brand a double-decker London bus like this for around £2,500 for a month, while a single side will cost around £900.

Taxi advertising

Taxi advertising provides you with a route to target local customers and high-value businesspeople. You can advertise on the outside, inside, cover the whole cab, or on the back of receipts – there's even a company called Cabvision that sells ads on its in-taxi TV channel! You can expect to pay £5,000 for 40 side panels for a month in a city such as Bristol or Newcastle, or up to £75,000 for 600 panels in London. Liveried taxis, where the entire vehicle is wrapped in your ad or identity for maximum standout, will cost around £38,500 for ten over six months in cities such as Liverpool, Leeds, or Glasgow. Again, contact a company that specialises in this form of advertising, such as Taxi Media (`www.clearchannel.co.uk/taximedia`).

Airport advertising

Airport advertising is a comparatively new option but is taking off fast. If you want a relatively well-to-do audience with a rich mix of tourists and professional travellers, enquire about airport advertising options with international site owners and domestic specialists such as JCDecaux (`www.jcdecauxairport.co.uk`) or Airport Advertising (`www.airport-advertising.co.uk`).

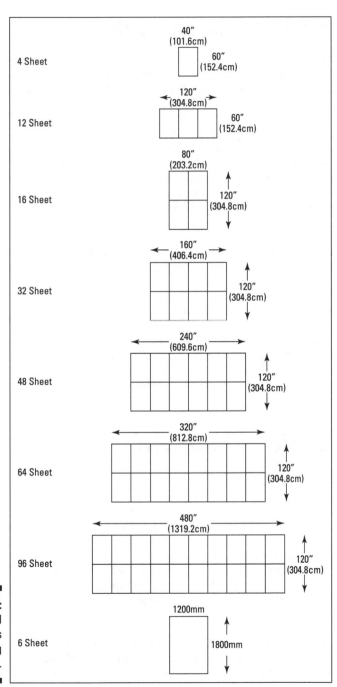

Figure 8-3:
Standard
sizes for bus
advertising
in the UK.

A note about your own vehicles

Does your company have its own vehicles on the road? If so, are you using them for outdoor advertising? Most marketers say either 'no' or 'sort of' when I ask them this question. Small, cheap, magnetic signs on the doors don't count. Nor does just a painted name on the door or side panel of a van or lorry. If you pay for as much display space as even a standard-sized van offers, you would probably hire a designer or agency and put great care into your message. And, in fact, you are paying for the exterior space on your vehicles; the cost just doesn't show up in the marketing budget. So why not cash in on this investment more fully by treating that lorry or van as a serious advertising medium? Mount frames for bus-sized posters and display a professionally designed ad that you change monthly or weekly. Or hire a competent airbrush painter to do a more permanent, custom job on each vehicle.

The freight company Eddie Stobart is one business that uses branded vehicles to great effect. You will have seen the dark green lorries with yellow and red lettering on the motorway, but did you know that each one carries a different woman's name. Its branding is so good that there is an Eddie Stobart fan club, with 25,000 members, and many more people are secret Eddie 'Spotters'. A different company, coincidentally using similar colours, is the Foxtons chain of estate agents. Since 2001, Foxtons has branded its entire fleet of company cars in striking limited edition liveries, from 'Italian Job' to 'Urban Graffiti'. You can use your vehicles as more than just a form of transport, too – all it requires is a little imagination.

Ambient Media – Your Ad in Unusual Places

Ambient or *non-traditional advertising* does exactly what it says on the tin – or takeaway lid, or egg, or petrol pump nozzle. In fact, I can't really tell you what ambient media is, as it covers so much and changes so rapidly. I can tell you what it isn't, which is any of the traditional outdoor advertising opportunities. Ambient is one of the fastest-growing sectors within outdoor advertising, because you can create a lot of impact for relatively little outlay. The nature of ambient advertising also means it can offer you precise targeting by area or by audience type.

I like to divide ambient advertising into two parts: The *uncontroversial* and the *unconventional*. *Uncontroversial* includes all forms of outdoor advertising that are really just poster ads in disguise, and which are in almost constant use by some fairly major advertisers. These ads appear on petrol pump nozzles, floor stickers in supermarkets and train stations, and posters in public conveniences. *Unconventional* includes everything else. In my time I have heard about ads that appear on pretty much everything you can imagine – and a lot of what you probably wouldn't. These unconventional places include tube maps and tickets, urinal stickers, and even on cows standing by the side of major roads.

Just because it's different doesn't mean ambient advertising is a great idea for your product or service. You should only use ambient advertising when you know that the idea is a good fit for your brand or you're prepared to take a gamble with the investment (most of the wilder ideas have pretty poor audience measurement, so it's more about whether it feels right to you).

Here are some of the most interesting ambient media ideas I've heard of – and some of the companies that have used them effectively:

- ✔ **Rubbish skips.** Directory enquiries service 118 118 used skips to communicate the idea of people throwing away their old telephone directories.

- ✔ **Petrol pump nozzles.** Good for targeting drivers with impulse buys, and used by food and drink brands such as Polo and Red Bull.

- ✔ **Takeaway lids.** Full-colour Adlids have been used by a host of organisations, from Blockbuster Video ('Here's just four of our new takeaways', plus a money-off coupon) to the Inland Revenue.

- ✔ **Chalk ads.** Sometimes known as vandaltising, chalk-drawn ads on pavements have been used by companies such as Gossard to advertise a new range of underwear. Be careful, though, this idea is less popular with local councils, despite the fact that the ads eventually wash away.

- ✔ **Car park tickets.** A great way to reach people just before they go shopping. This method has been used by retailers such as Sainsbury's and Specsavers.

- ✔ **Shopping trolleys and floor posters.** I group these together as they offer the same great benefits to you if your products are found on supermarket shelves. Did you know that 75 per cent of purchasing decisions are made in-store and over 90 per cent of advertising budget is spent out of store? Trolleys and floor posters act as reminders to shoppers that your product exists, and can even direct them to the right shelf.

- ✔ **ForeheADS.** Why use your head when you can use someone else's? This is a wacky idea, which involves renting out the foreheads of cash-strapped students, who must be seen out in public for at least three hours a day to earn their fee. Companies including *FHM* magazine and CNX have used ForeheADS to carry their logos as a temporary tattoo.

Small but Effective – from T-shirts to Shopping Bags

A broad definition of a sign may include any public display of your brand or marketing message. To me, a message on a T-shirt is just as legitimate as a message on a poster. And it is often a lot easier and cheaper to make. The following sections share simple, small-scale ways to get your message across.

T-shirts, umbrellas, and bumper stickers, anyone?

Don't forget that you can sometimes get people to advertise your company on their vehicles or bodies for free. (we cover T-shirts in the 'Praising T-shirts' sidebar.) Your customers may think of a nice T-shirt as a premium item or gift for them, but you can see that T-shirt as a body billboard! It's nice that people are willing to go around with your advertising messages on their clothes (or even on their bodies – temporary tattoos are also a marketing option). Don't overlook this concept as a form of outdoor advertising. In fact, use it as much as you can. People happily display marketing messages if they like them.

Praising T-shirts

Sometimes you just need a cheap T-shirt. I have a drawer stuffed full of them, and many of those shirts have artwork that promotes a company or brand name. If you can make a T-shirt appropriate to your brand, then by all means use T-shirts as a premium item!

You can find even a good-quality T-shirt pretty cheaply, so you can easily implement the quality premium strategy with T-shirts. You achieve quality by making sure your T-shirts use a heavy, all-cotton fabric and sport a compelling design developed by a real designer.

Oh, and you need to use an experienced, quality-conscious silk-screener to put that fine design on those good T-shirts.

The poor selection of shirts available to T-shirt buyers from shops and other sources frustrates those buyers. A lack of exciting new designs, not a lack of drawer space, holds these customers back. So you just need to put a cool design on your T-shirt to get your target audience to want it. Customers can't get enough of this premium item – provided your design is fresh and good. No, I don't really want another cheap pen with some company's name on it. But I'm happy to get another good T-shirt. I may even pay you for it.

To find companies that provide customised T-shirts, try your local Yellow Pages for listings of silk-screening shops near you (generally listed under 'Printing') or take a look at the back of a trade magazine such as *Marketing*.

Similarly, umbrellas (also available from premium companies – see Chapter 13) can broadcast your logo and name and a short slogan or headline – although only in especially wet or overly sunny weather.

Don't overlook bumper stickers and car-window stickers. If you make them clever or unique enough, people eagerly seek those stickers out. Don't ask me why. But because people do, and because the cost of producing bumper stickers is cheap, why not come up with an appealing design and make stickers available in target markets as giveaways on shop counters or at outdoor events?

Commercial or brand-orientated bumper stickers are used by people who think the brand is so cool that it enhances the car – and this is a hard thing to achieve for some marketers. An alternative is to keep your brand identity small, and star an appealing message, instead. A clever joke, an inspiring quote, or something similar is appealing enough to get your message displayed. And for mugs, window stickers, and other premium items, the secret is to have a great visual design or other picture that people enjoy, or to offer a humorous cartoon.

You can even include a nice sticker in a direct-mail piece, where that sticker can do double duty – acting as an incentive to get people to retain and read the mailing and giving you cheap outdoor advertising when they display the sticker on their vehicles. (Contact local print shops, sign makers, or T-shirt silk-screeners; any of these businesses sometimes produce bumper stickers, too.)

It's in the bag

The big department stores believe in the importance of shopping bags as an advertising medium. But many other businesses fail to take advantage of the fact that shoppers carry bags around busy shopping centres and high streets, and also on trains and buses, giving any messages on the bags high exposure.

To use bags effectively, you need to make them far easier to read and far more interesting than the average brown paper or white plastic shopping bag. Remember, you're not just designing a bag – you're designing a form of outdoor advertising. So apply the same design principles. Come up with a *hook* – a striking image or attention-getting word or phrase that gets everyone looking at that bag. And try alternative colours or shapes. (By the way, most bag suppliers can customise their bags – check with suppliers in your local area. If no suppliers around you can customise bags, contact printers and silk-screeners, they can always handle bag orders for you, too.)

If you offer the biggest, strongest bag in a shopping area, you can be sure that shoppers stuff everyone else's bags into yours, giving your advertising message the maximum exposure. Of course, bigger, stronger bags cost more, which is why most shops offer wimpy bags that hurt your hands or rip open and spill their contents in the mud. But if you have an ad message you can get across with a bag, compare the cost of a better bag to other media. Pretty cheap, right? So why not go for it?

If you aren't in the retail business, you may think that this idea doesn't apply to you. Wrong! Plenty of store managers view bags as an irritating expense, rather than a marketing medium. Offer to supply them with better bags for free, in exchange for the right to print your message on the bags. Voilà! A new marketing medium for your campaign. A specialist such as Bag Media (www.bagmedia.co.uk) can design and distribute bags for you to pre-selected groups of retailers, from veterinary practices to garden centres and sandwich bags to pizza boxes.

A Few Commonsense Rules for Outdoor Advertising

Depending on whether you're advertising on roadside or transport sites, follow these commonsense rules when designing your poster to make sure that it catches and holds customers' attention:

- ✔ If your poster site is by the side of a main road, people will have just a few seconds to see and understand your ad. Keep the image simple and use as few, large words as possible. Make sure that you use colours that contrast, so they can be seen from a good distance.

- ✔ Think like a bored passenger. When you advertise on interior tube panels, inside taxis or on train platform posters you can afford to use more complex visuals and a greater number of words.

- ✔ Can you layer the message, so that you provide a clear, large-scale, simple message for first-time viewers, but also a more detailed design and message for repeat viewers to find within the poster?

- ✔ Humour and wordplay work well for posters. Try to use them in your ad to build involvement from the viewer.

- ✔ Show your logo. Whether you're just using posters or are including other media in your marketing campaign, don't forget the logo! You will get improved recognition for your business, and better results from your advertising, if you use your logo consistently across everything you do.

Chapter 9

TV and Radio Ads (Or Your Own Show!)

In This Chapter

▶ Designing ads for radio

▶ Creating great video ads for little cash

▶ Using the emotional power of television

*R*adio and television are well-established, extremely powerful marketing media, while video (especially if shot in digital format) is a hot new item for streaming-video messages on your Web site. Video also offers marketing messages on television screens and computers on your stand at a trade show.

The problem, traditionally, with radio and TV is that the costs associated with producing and broadcasting ads have been quite high, making these media too expensive for smaller marketers. We want to encourage you to be open-minded about radio, video, and TV, because new and easier ways to produce in these media are emerging all the time, along with a growing number of low-cost ways to broadcast your ads. Every year brings more radio and television stations, including cable and satellite TV channels, and digital radio that you can 'listen' to through a digital set, digital TV, or through your PC.

And even if you don't use these commercial media, you can quite possibly find more limited ways to share your ads with prospects. In fact, more and more marketers use CDs or Web sites that communicate in digital video, or with PowerPoint-type slides and radio-style voice-overs. Modern technology is making these media more flexible and affordable for all marketers.

Creating Ads for Radio

Conventional wisdom says you have only three elements to work with when you design for radio: Words, sound effects, and music. In a literal sense that's true, but you can't create a great radio ad unless you remember that you want to use those elements to generate *mental images* for the listener. And that means you can often perform the same basic plot on radio as on TV. Radio isn't really as limited as people think – it's just rarely used to full advantage anymore. Society's love affair with radio has been eclipsed by its love of TV and films.

Favour direct over indirect action goals for radio ads. Sometimes you want to use radio just to create brand awareness *(indirect-action advertising)*, But in general, the most effective radio ads call for direct action. Give out a Web address (if the listener can remember that address easily) or a freefone number in the ad.

Put your brand name into your radio ad early and often, regardless of the story line. If you fail to generate the desired direct action, at least you build awareness and interest for the brand, which supports other points of contact in your marketing campaign. Radio is a great support medium, and not enough marketers use it that way. You may as well fill the vacuum with *your* marketing message!

Here's a simple rule that can help you avoid confusion in your radio ad: Ensure that your script identifies all sound effects. Sound effects are wonderful and evocative, but in truth, many sound very similar. Without context, rain on the roof can sound like bacon sizzling in a pan, a blowtorch cutting through the metal door of a bank vault, or even an alien spaceship starting up. So the script must identify that sound, either through direct reference or through context. You can provide context with the script, the plot, or simply by other sound effects. The sounds of eggs cracking and hitting a hot pan, coffee percolating, and someone yawning all help to identify that sizzle as the breakfast bacon, rather than rain on the roof or that blowtorch.

Buying airtime on radio

We often find ourselves urging marketers to try radio in place of their standard media choices. Why? Because, although local retailers frequently use radio for pull-orientated advertising, many other marketers overlook radio as a viable medium. Those advertisers don't realise how powerful radio can be – and they may not be aware of its incredible reach. In the UK, around 66 per cent of the adult population tune into radio every week and over 80 per cent each month, and from early morning until mid-afternoon there are more people listening to radio than are watching TV (according to RAJAR). We bet your target audience is in there somewhere! (Also consider radio for all your publicity needs. You can find a lot of radio talk shows willing to invite you on as a guest if you pitch your expertise well and have a unique angle to discuss.)

RAJAR (or Radio Joint Audience Research, as it's less commonly called) is the UK's single audience measurement system for commercial radio stations and the BBC. Every quarter RAJAR releases detailed listening figures for all the UK's national and local radio stations, which you can access for free at www.rajar.co.uk. You can also get in touch with the Radio Advertising Bureau (or RAB), which does a good job of promoting radio as an advertising medium and is a great source of advertiser data and ideas for creative radio advertising (www.rab.co.uk).

Radio is the second biggest medium, after TV, in terms of time spent with it (see Figure 9-1). And while people are spending less time watching TV and DVDs, radio is growing owing to the fact that people can listen to it while doing other things – like cleaning, driving, or more likely being stuck in a traffic jam! Those people can only welcome the distraction of your well-crafted radio ad.

You can also target radio advertising quite narrowly – both by type of audience and by geographic area. This fact helps make radio a very good buy. The general lack of appreciation for this medium also helps by keeping ad prices artificially low.

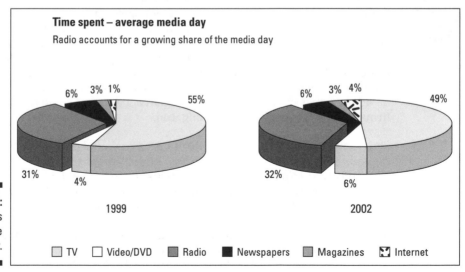

Figure 9-1: Radio's share of the media day.

Radio airtime is cheaper and more cost-effective than TV airtime, but you need to use the figure we're about to give you with caution – the price of both media can vary widely by region and audience, and, for the biggest advertisers, you can reach a larger total audience by using TV than by using radio. So here goes. Studies have shown that radio airtime is a seventh of the price of TV and that radio offers three-fifths of the advertising awareness effect of TV. If you divide effectiveness by cost, you can see that radio is around four times as cost-effective as TV.

Targeted advertising via radio

We like the fact that radio stations make a real effort to target specific audiences – after all, most advertisers try to do the same thing. You can get good data, both demographic and lifestyle- or attitude-orientated information, on radio audiences. And you can often find radio stations (or specific programmes on those stations) that reach a well-defined audience, rich in those people you want to target, making radio an even better buy.

You can get details of radio station formats and audience characteristics for all UK commercial radio stations from the communications regulator Ofcom, just by looking at the UK Radio Licensees section of its Web site, at www.ofcom.org.uk.

And here's another option for radio advertising that you may not have considered. How about running ads over the internal broadcasting systems used in many shops? This opportunity gives you another great way to target a particular audience going about a particular task – for instance, you could advertise your brand of tiles to DIY shoppers using Tiles FM. *In-store radio* is an entirely different medium from a buying perspective because the shop, or more usually a specialist media owner, develops and controls the programming. As a result, most marketers don't know how to use in-store radio. But an ad agency may be able to help you gain access, and some media-buying firms handle this kind of advertising, too.

So remember: Don't overlook radio! It can give you better reach, better focus on your target market, and greater cost-effectiveness than other media. Like TV, radio can *show* as well as tell – you just have to use the listener's imagination to create visual images. And if you manage to create a really good script, we guarantee you can catch and hold audience attention.

If you're planning to make radio a big part of your marketing plan, then we can recommend a book dedicated to telling you how to do it better – *An Advertiser's Guide to Better Radio Advertising*, by Andrew Ingram and Mark Barber from the RAB, also published by Wiley.

Cheaper Ways to Use the Power of Video

If you're thinking of skipping this section, consider this: Video can cost £1,000 per minute to produce – or even £10,000 if you're making a sophisticated national TV ad. But video can also cost £50 a minute or less.

Do you have access to a high-quality hand-held digital video camera? Well, that camera (when combined with a good microphone) is actually capable of producing effective video for your marketing, especially for use on the Web, where low-resolution video files are usually used, making camera quality less important. Many marketers don't realise that the limiting factor in inexpensive or homemade video is usually the sound quality, not the picture quality. So as long as you plug in a remote microphone and put it near anyone who is speaking, you can probably make usable video yourself.

Here are some tips if you decide to shoot video yourself:

✔ Write a simple, clear script, and time it before you bother to shoot any video.

✔ Clean up the background. Most amateur efforts to shoot video presentations or ads for marketing are plagued by stuff that shows up in the background. Eliminate rubbish bins, competitors' signs, and anything else unsightly.

✔ Use enough light, and try to have multiple light sources. A digital video camera is just a fancy camera, and it needs light to work. Normal indoor lighting is too dim for quality video. Instead, add more lights, including bright floodlights and open windows. And make sure light shines from both sides so that you fill the shadows. (Shadowed areas get darker in the video.)

✔ Shoot everything more than once. Editing is easy (well, easier) as a result of the many software programs you can use on your own PC to edit video. But editing is much easier if you have lots of footage to select from. Always repeat each short section several times, then, in editing, choose the version that came out best. That's how they make films stars look good, and it can work well for you, too!

✔ You can produce radio ads or sound-only messages for your Web site using the same digital recording and editing capabilities as you use to do homemade digital video. The key is a quiet environment and a good microphone for recording. Or you can go into a production studio's sound booth and let the technicians there worry about the technical aspects.

✔ If you want actors, consider recruiting them locally and even asking people to volunteer. We hate to promote this idea, but if you can avoid paying Equity rates for your actors, you're better off. Paying union rates and residuals is appropriate for major or national campaigns but can be prohibitive for small marketers.

For information on editing and production, check out the many *For Dummies* books that help you better understand what's involved. Or hire a media production firm that can do high-quality work at moderate rates. With plenty of smaller production firms around, try interviewing some in your area and getting samples of their work plus price quotes – you may find that by the time you master the software and come up to speed, you're spending as much doing your own work!

Designing Ads for TV

Television is much like theatre. TV combines visual and verbal channels in real-time action, making it a remarkably rich medium. Yes, you have to make the writing as tight and compelling as good print copy, but the words must also sound good and must flow with the visuals to create drama or comedy.

TV ads must use great drama (whether funny or serious), condensed to a few seconds of memorable action. These few seconds of drama must etch themselves into the memory of anyone who watches your ad. In terms of a great film, you can't reduce it to a formula. A good script with just the right touch of just the right emotion. Great acting. Good camera work and a good set. The suspense of a developing relationship between two interesting characters. You don't need to achieve this level of artistry to make a good TV ad, but you certainly need to achieve a higher-than-average level to stand out. And if you can create truly great TV, your ad pays off in gold.

TV looks simple when you see it, but don't be fooled – it's not simple at all. Hire an experienced production company to help you do the ad, or do what many marketers do and hire a big ad agency (at big ad agency prices) to design and supervise the production of it. This choice costs you, but at least you get quality work. Just remember that *you* ultimately decide whether the script has that star potential or is just another forgettable ad. Don't let the production company shoot until they have something as memorable as a classic film (or at least close).

If you work for a smaller business and are used to shoestring marketing budgets, you may be shaking your head at my advice. You think you can do it yourself. But why waste even a little money on ads that don't work? If you're going to do TV, do it right. Either become expert yourself or hire an expert. Without high-quality production, even the best design doesn't work. Why? Because people watch so much TV that they know the difference between good and bad ads – and they don't bother to watch anything but the best.

If you're on a shoestring budget and can't afford to hire an expert or don't have the time to become one yourself, consider the following bits of advice:

✔ **Forgo TV ads and put your video to work in more forgiving venues.** Simple video can look great in other contexts, like your Web site or a stand at a trade show, even if it would look out of place on television. (See the 'Cheaper Ways to Use the Power of Video' section earlier in this chapter.)

✔ **Consider doing a self-made *spoof ad*.** Make fun of one of the silly TV ad genres, like the one where a man dressed in black scales mountain peaks and jumps over waterfalls to deliver a box of chocolates to a beautiful woman. Because the whole point is to make a campy spoof, you don't want high production value. You can do this strategy on your own pretty easily, but you still need help from someone with experience in setting up shots and handling camera and lights.

✔ **Find a film student at a nearby college who is eager to help you produce your ad.** To budding film-makers, your video is an opportunity to show they can do professional work. For you, using a student may be an opportunity to get near-professional work at a very low price. But make sure the terms are clear upfront. Both the student and their tutor need to clarify (in writing) that you will own the resulting work and can use it in your marketing.

Getting emotional

TV differs from other media in the obvious way – by combining action, audio, and video – but these features make TV different in less obvious ways, as well. It is especially easy to evoke emotions in TV and video, just like traditional theatre. When you plan to use TV as your marketing tool, always think about what emotion you want your audience to feel.

Select an emotional state that fits best with your appeal and the creative concept behind your ad. Then use the power of imagery to evoke that emotion. This strategy works whether your appeal is emotional or rational. Always use the emotional power of TV to prepare your audience to receive that appeal. Surprise. Excitement. Empathy. Anxiety. Scepticism. Thirst. Hunger. Protective instincts of the parent. You can create all these emotional states and more in your audience with a few seconds of TV. A good ad generates the right emotion to prime viewers for your appeal. The classic Hamlet cigar ad is a strictly emotional appeal ('Happiness is a cigar called Hamlet' – we bet you can even hear the music as you read that line).

Some marketers measure their TV ads based on warmth. Research firms generally define warmth as the good feelings generated from thinking about love, family, or friendship. Although you may not need to go into the details of how researchers measure warmth, noting *why* people measure warmth can help you. Emotions, especially positive ones, make TV ad messages far more memorable. Many marketers don't realise the strength of this emotional effect because you can't pick the effect up in the standard measures of ad recall. In day-after recall tests, viewers recall emotional-appeal TV ads about as easily as rational-appeal ads. But in-depth studies of the effectiveness of each kind of ad tend to show that the more emotionally charged ads do a better job of etching the message and branding identity in viewers' minds.

So when you think TV advertising, think emotion. Evoking emotion is what TV can do – often better than any other media, because it can showcase the expressiveness of actors and faces – and emotion makes for highly effective advertising.

Look, Mum . . .

Be sure to take full advantage of TV's other great strength: Its ability to show. You can demonstrate a product feature, show a product in use, and do a thousand other things just with your visuals.

Actually, in any ad medium, you want to show as well as tell. (Even in radio, you can create mental images to show the audience what you want them to see, see 'Creating Ads for Radio' earlier in this chapter.) The visual and verbal modes reinforce each other. And some people in your audience think visually, although others favour a verbal message, so you have to cover both bases by using words and images in your advertising. But in TV, you have to adapt this rule: The TV ad should *show* and tell (note the emphasis on showing). Compare this scenario with radio, where you show by telling; or print, where the two modes balance each other out, so the rule becomes simply to show and tell.

Because of this emphasis on showing, TV ad designers rough out their ideas in a visually-orientated script, using quick sketches to indicate how the ad will look. You – or preferably the competent agency or scriptwriter you hire – need to prepare rough storyboards as you think through and discuss various ad concepts. A *storyboard* is an easy way to show the key visual images of film, using pictures in sequence. The sketches run down the centre of a sheet of paper or poster board in most standard storyboard layouts. On the left, you write notes about how to shoot each image, how to use music and sound effects, and whether to superimpose text on the screen. On the right, you include a rough version of the *script* (the words actors in the scenes or in a voice-over say). See Figure 9-2 for an example storyboard.

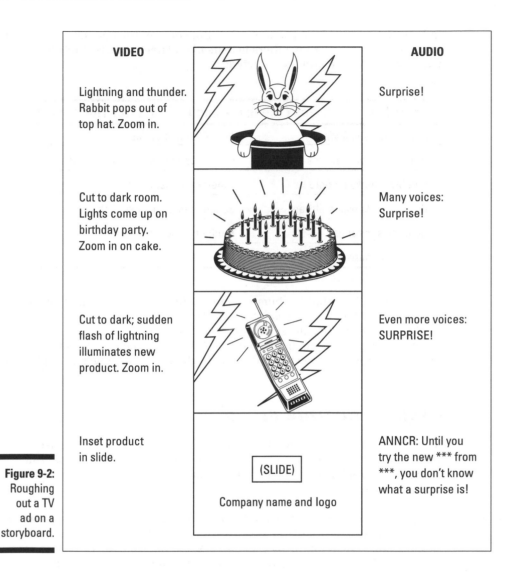

VIDEO		AUDIO
Lightning and thunder. Rabbit pops out of top hat. Zoom in.		Surprise!
Cut to dark room. Lights come up on birthday party. Zoom in on cake.		Many voices: Surprise!
Cut to dark; sudden flash of lightning illuminates new product. Zoom in.		Even more voices: SURPRISE!
Inset product in slide.	(SLIDE) Company name and logo	ANNCR: Until you try the new *** from ***, you don't know what a surprise is!

Figure 9-2: Roughing out a TV ad on a storyboard.

A question of style

You can use a great variety of styles in TV advertising. A celebrity can endorse the product. Fruit modelled from clay (claymation) can sing and dance about it. Animated animals can chase a user through the jungle in a fanciful exaggeration of a real-life situation. Imagination and videotape know no limits, especially with the recent growing availability of high-quality computerised animation and special effects at a reasonable cost. But some of the common styles work better – on average – than others in tests of ad effectiveness. Table 9-1 shows styles that are more and less effective.

Table 9-1	It Don't Mean a Thing If It Ain't Got That Swing
More Effective Styles	*Less Effective Styles*
Humorous commercials	Candid-camera style testimonials
Celebrity spokespeople	Expert endorsements
Commercials with children	Song/dance and musical themes
Real-life scenarios	Product demonstrations
Brand comparisons	

Most studies show that the humour and celebrity endorsement styles work best. So try to find ways to use these styles to communicate your message. On the other hand, making ads that are the exception to the rule may give you an edge, so don't give up hope on other styles. Just make sure that your ad lands well above average if you don't want the rule of averages to apply to it.

Buying airtime on TV

Which television stations work best for your ad? Should you advertise on a national (*terrestrial*) channel or on a digital channel? Should the ad run in prime time, evening, or late night-time slots? What programmes provide the best audience for your ad?

The UK's main provider of TV audience measurement is BARB (Broadcasters' Audience Research Board), at www.barb.co.uk. BARB is a not-for-profit organisation owned jointly by the BBC, ITV, Channel 4, Five, BSkyB, and the Institute of Practitioners in Advertising (IPA). You can get television audience data minute by minute through BARB, which keeps track of how many people are watching which channel (and TV programme) by installing homes around the country with a little black box that sits on top of the TV set. Although BARB is not for profit, you can't get this data for free. An annual subscription will cost you upwards of £3,850, so it's worth considering whether you really need that depth of data. For instance, if you're trying to selling gardening products to amateur gardeners and know that you're only interested in home-improvement TV programmes, the channels themselves can give you the viewing figures you need.

Some of BARB's biggest customers are research firms such as AC Nielsen (www.nielsenmedia.co.uk), Thomson Intermedia (www.thomson-intermedia.com), TNS (www.tns-global.com), and Mediatel (www.mediatel.co.uk), through which you can get comparative media data, including TV coverage. These companies are also able to overlay the BARB data with more comprehensive demographic and lifestyle data. In turn, these companies' customers include the ad agencies and media-buying agencies, so if you're using an agency to buy your airtime or create your ad, it's worth asking them for media data before getting out your own credit card.

Working out the cost of a TV ad

There are several different factors that affect how much you will pay for a TV advertising campaign.

The first, and most important, bit of jargon you need to know is *TVRs*, which means television ratings. Audience delivery is measured in TVRs, which can be confusing but has the merit of giving you an idea of how many people in a particular target audience will see your ad – and target audiences are important because it means you're not wasting money advertising to people who are unlikely to buy your product. A TVR is defined as the percentage of a particular audience that has seen an advertising break (it's worth remembering that they may have spent the ad break talking to their partner or making the tea, so it's always an approximation). So, 10 adult TVRs = 10 per cent of all adults saw the ad break.

You can actually get a TVR that is higher than 100 per cent, which means that a viewer may see your ad more than once, and is counted separately each time. The actual number of times viewers are exposed to a commercial break is called *impacts*. If you think that repeat viewing is important to your campaign, these can be useful programmes or times of the day to target.

The target audience

You can choose to target any of the 13 target audiences, shown in the following list, that are commonly sold by broadcasters. Heavy TV viewers such as housewives or general audiences are usually cheaper to buy because they are easier to reach than audiences such as upmarket men.

> Adults
>
> 16- to 34-year-old adults
>
> ABC1 (upmarket) adults

Men

16- to 34-year-old men

ABC1 Men

Women

16- to 34-year-old women

ABC1 women

Housewives

Housewives & children

ABC1 Housewives

Children

Time of the broadcast

The size and type of audience likely to see your ad is governed by the time of day it appears – so that's another factor that will affect how much you pay. Broadcasters call these *dayparts*, and they're timed as follows:

Daytime 6am–5.29pm

Early peak 5.30pm–7.29pm

Late peak 7.30pm–11pm

Night-time 11.01pm–5.59am

The highest price you will usually pay is for the highest audience – in peak time, between 5.30pm and 11pm.

Other factors

You also need to factor in a few other variables to the cost of your ad:

- **The length of your commercial.** Airtime is sold in multiples of 10 seconds, with the most common ad length at 30 seconds.

- **What time of year you need to advertise.** If you're in the business of selling Christmas gifts, you will pay considerably more for airtime than if you can advertise in the cheaper months of January, February, March, and August.

- **Size of the region you advertise in.** Prices also vary by *macro region*, which reflects the size of the local population and relative demand. The highest advertiser demand is for London, which is why it is the most expensive to buy. If you operate in the Border region, Tyne Tees, or

Yorkshire, however, you can expect to pay the lowest prices for TV airtime. Some TV macro regions can even be split into *micro regions*. So if your business is in the East Anglia area, for instance, you can buy just that part of the larger Anglia macro region, giving you tighter targeting and better value for money.

Because of the complexity of some of these calculations, think hard about using a media agency to plan and buy the airtime. You can let a media agency know what you're trying to achieve with your ad, and what type of people you need to target and let their experts do the rest. Many of these agencies buy up chunks of airtime in advance, so you benefit from an agency-wide deal and don't have to negotiate individually with the TV sales houses. Media agencies can also advise you on TV opportunities you may not have previously considered.

Making your own TV (or radio) programme

There are a lot of TV and radio ads out there, and there is a constant danger of your ad becoming just one of the many that people are exposed to, and increasingly, trying to avoid. You don't want your ad to be the one that makes the viewer leave the room to make the tea. The following sections give you a few alternative strategies to consider.

Advertiser-funded programming (AFP)

The experts have come up with a new term, *branded content*, to describe something that is not quite an ad, but which can be used to communicate a commercial message. In TV and radio, that means creating your own show (or at least, segment of a show) – the official term for this is *advertiser-funded programming* or *AFP*. This type of communication is still in its early days, and there are a lot of restrictions in place about what you can or cannot say about your product. But it's worth asking your agency, or the radio stations and channels themselves, about these opportunities, because they allow your message to stand out from the clutter of all the other ads.

B&Q's *Real DIY Show*, Heinz's *Dinner Doctors*, and Renault's *Scenic Days Out* are some of the earliest examples of AFP. There is a lot of excitement around this type of communication because it allows advertisers to give viewers something they want (entertainment) rather than something many of them don't (ads). Now look at those programme names again. The real benefit of AFP is that you can give viewers *relevant content*, or information that is close to your product or service. Don't get too close, though. Heinz nearly got fined by the TV regulators for showing recipes that used baked beans and spaghetti hoops. As we say, it's early days, but AFP will become a popular route for advertisers and you should look out for likely opportunities.

Sponsoring a TV or radio programme

If AFP is still waiting in the wings, then sponsorship must be centre stage. Alright, you don't quite get your own TV or radio programme, but if you find a show that is a good fit with your product, then it's almost as good (and with a lot of the risk taken out).

TV and radio sponsorship is growing fast in the UK as advertisers try to avoid the dual issues of ad clutter and digital personal video recorders (PVRs) such as Sky+ and TiVo, which allow viewers to skip through the ad break. You don't need us to tell you that TV and radio sponsorship (together worth nearly £215 million, and representing a quarter of all sponsorship spend) is growing – you'll have seen it for yourself. Ford and Sky's football coverage, Talk Talk and *Big Brother*, Pizza Hut and *The Simpsons* are all good examples of current sponsorship deals because you can see the relevance between the brand and the programme.

You don't need to pay anything like the £10 million for three years that Cadbury pays to sponsor *Coronation Street*. You can find relevant programmes at less popular times of the day, or on digital channels, for a sponsorship price of around £150,000.

Interactive TV advertising

Interactive TV advertising has more in common with traditional spot TV advertising, but we include it here because, if you can get viewers to press the red button, you can take them away from the mainstream TV environment and into your own dedicated space. Interactive TV advertising gives you a lot of opportunities to do things a traditional 30-second spot would not. You can give additional product information, issue a call to action (such as requesting a brochure), and you can capture your prospective customers' data. It is even possible to fulfil a transaction entirely using interactive TV ads. There is an additional cost for constructing the microsite and capturing the data (upward of £100,000), on top of the cost of the airtime for the ad itself. The benefit of interactive TV ads is that you get real, measurable customer transactions from your investment – and that's something traditional TV advertising can't always deliver.

Part IV
Powerful Alternatives To Advertising

"We're looking for a salesperson who can get his foot in the door – Are you that person, Mr Snartley?"

In this part . . .

In marketing, the goals never really change. We're no more nor less eager to find new customers and grow our revenues than were last year's or last decade's crop of eager marketers.

But the means of achieving these goals can and do change. We should always look for alternatives and fresh approaches. You especially have to stay on top of your game in today's advertising because entirely new ways of communicating with customers and prospects have emerged in the last couple of decades, and marketers no longer need to feel confined to traditional advertising. Telemarketing, fax machines, direct mail, and now e-mail, Web pages, paid listings on search engines, and many more innovations are transforming marketing.

In addition, I highly recommend that you explore the power of publicity and of events in your marketing area. Sometimes, these approaches can be more effective than anything else in the entire field of marketing, yet marketers traditionally give them little thought and funding in most businesses.

You can, in fact, design for any business an effective marketing program that completely skips conventional advertising and substitutes one or more of the many alternative media instead.

Chapter 10

E-Marketing

*W*hat does e-marketing make you think of? Web sites, yes. But e-marketing includes online advertising and e-mail as well as using text, pictures, or even video to reach customers through their mobile phones. These digital tools have opened up lots of new ways to help you sell your products or services. Even better, a lot of these tools are cheaper and certainly more cost effective than traditional advertising using press or TV.

It seems that nearly every month there is a new way to communicate with customers using digital media. The principle of rapid evolution is a good one, but in practice it can be safe to wait a while before jumping in to the newest techniques, as they can be costly, untried and worse, aggravating to the very people you were trying to win over. We encourage our readers to watch and wait before trying out techniques such as blogging (personal diary-type Web sites by an independent author, which some companies have tried to mimic for commercial gain and been damagingly exposed for it) or blue-jacking (sending unsolicited messages to Bluetooth-enabled portable devices and mobile phones). There are plenty of more traditional techniques that work and which have sufficient numbers of the public using them to make them an essential part of any company's marketing activity.

Over half the UK population is now online, and mobile phone usage is above 80 per cent – meaning that however much or little you spend on e-marketing, you should definitely find a line for it in your marketing budget. For that reason, this chapter covers just what you need to know to begin your foray into e-marketing.

Reaching Out with a Web Site

E-marketing changes fast and changes often, and the best way to use it is to change with it. And that means creating a Web site for your business.

Consider this: People spend more time using the Internet than they do with any other media apart from TV. We bet you're surprised by that fact, but it's true. A Europe-wide survey of Web users by Forrester Research found that people spent eight hours and 20 minutes a week online compared with 11 hours watching TV and just under seven hours listening to the radio. You would advertise on TV if your budget stretched to it (and few people use the TV to do their shopping), so you should have a presence on the second-most used medium because you can afford to. In fact, you can't afford not to!

Getting a Web presence is relatively easy. Sometimes this can be as simple as getting a listing on an online business directory covering your area, so that when consumers key in your business name or search for the type of services you offer using a search engine such as Google or MSN they can find your address and phone number. We strongly believe that every business – including yours – should have a Web site, even if all it does is provide your contact details and opening hours. You can think of your Web site as a shop window, where potential customers from all over the world can look at the products or services you offer. You can even turn this site into an actual shop. Having a transactional Web site can be one of the lowest cost ways to expand geographically without having to move out of your neighbourhood (it's not called the World Wide Web for nothing, you know!).

A good Web site can bring in customers who would never have found your product or service were it not for the Internet. So it's worth spending some time and money creating a decent Web site to attract them.

You need a unique and memorable Web site address, and an easy to use and appealing design (doubly so, if it's going to be a *transactional site* where customers can buy using a credit or debit card). The following sections tell you what you need to know. Of course, you also need to think about how customers will find your site out of the millions out there. Head to the section 'Getting Your Site Noticed' later in this chapter for that info.

Choosing a Web address

First you must find and register a Web address (also known as a *domain name* or *URL*). Unless you are starting a business from scratch, you probably already have a Web address in mind that you would like to use. Your Web address should be as close as you can possibly get to the name of your business, or, if you need a site for each of your products and services, then it should relate closely to them. You may think this sounds obvious, but we see too many Web addresses that fall into the trap of having little to do with the parent business (usually because the most obvious name is being used by someone else, which we cover later in this chapter).

Totally Thomas is a small independent toy shop based in a small town in West Yorkshire. I (first/second author) live at the opposite end of the country and would never have found it if the owners hadn't picked a good name (and made sure it could be found through the Google search engine). My son is obsessed by Thomas the Tank Engine and this shop is dedicated to Thomas products. The Web address is www.totallythomas.net, although the owner also uses the address www.totallythomas.co.uk to redirect users to the Web site. We think this is a good example of Web address choice because the owner hasn't been put off by the fact that www.totallythomas.com belongs to a company in San Diego that also sells Thomas merchandise. Instead of going for a unique but obscure name, the owner has registered both the .net and .co.uk extensions to make sure UK customers are likely to end up at his online store.

As you search for potential Web addresses, keep the following points in mind to make sure you end up with the best name for your site:

- ✔ **A good address relates to your business or product.** The Web address www.streetspavedwithgold.com is available to register, along with all of the other main name extensions. It's catchy. It's amusing. Should you rush off and register it? Not if it fails this first test: Does the name relate to your product or service? Remember, it's better to be relevant than to be clever.

- ✔ **A good name is memorable.** Customers should be able to remember your Web address easily. That doesn't mean you have to register anything stunningly cool or clever – and besides, if the Web address is obscure people are less likely to remember it. Using your company name makes the site memorable to anyone who knows the name of your business. You can easily remember that IKEA's global Web address is www.ikea.com and it's www.ikea.co.uk in the UK. But you can just as easily combine two or three easy words and make a string into a memorable address. An online competitor to IKEA in the UK is the very simply named www.thisisfurniture.com.

- ✔ **A good name is not easily confused with other addresses.** If consumers can easily mix up your site with similar addresses, some will go to the wrong site by accident. If your company name is a common word or is similar to others, add an extra term or word to your Web address to distinguish it. For example, Triumph is a brand name that both the lingerie maker and the motorcycle manufacturer have equal claim to. Although customers are unlikely to mistake one brand for the other, they could easily find themselves on the wrong Web site. As a result, the motorbike brand trades from `www.triumphmotorcycles.com` while Triumph International uses `www.triumph.com`.

✔ **A good name doesn't violate trademarks.** You don't want to bump into someone's trademark by accident. Legal rights now favour the trademark holder rather than the domain name holder – putting an end to the ugly practice of 'cyber-squatting' that existed a few years ago. To be sure that you don't inadvertently step on someone else's toes, check any Web address against a database of trademarks. The Patent Office provides a searchable database at `www.patent.gov.uk` but if you think you may run into an issue you should ask a lawyer to do a more detailed analysis. We cover trademark law in Chapter 14.

Checking your name's availability

Picking a name is the easy part. The trickier part is finding out whether that name is available, and getting creative if you find out it's not.

Any good provider of Web services will have its own site that allows you to check on the availability of a Web address. Just go to a search engine like Google, type in 'domain names' and use one of the many registrant sites that come up. At this stage, it doesn't matter which site you choose as you're not committing any money. Just be sure that your Internet service provider (ISP) checks your name against all of the main *extensions* – `.com`, `.co.uk`, `.net`, or `.org` are among the most desirable, as people remember them first.

In the best of all possible worlds, your Web name search will reveal that your name is free and clear. If that's the case, thank your lucky stars, jump up and down, and make a few happy noises. Then register your name. The section 'Registering your site name' tells you how. But, as few of us live in the best of all possible worlds, you're more likely to find that your name is already taken. In that case, don't despair. You still have options and, depending on which avenue you take, you may still get to use your name.

If someone has registered the name you want with one or most of the main extensions, but left the more obscure `.biz`, `.org.uk`, or even `.me.uk` extensions, you're wisest seeking another name because customers could forget your extension and go to someone else's site instead.

When the Web is an important sales route for your business, a simple rule to follow is that it is best to own most or all of the possible extensions and versions of your Web address.

If the person who owns the rights to your Web address isn't willing to sell it to you, you may want to go back to the drawing board and find another name that isn't being held hostage. Many online operators are looking to make easy money by buying up Web addresses for the purpose of selling them at a profit.

Other routes can help you secure the name you want. Many sites that were registered in the frenzy of the dotcom boom eventually come back on to the open market because they were never used or because the original registrar forgot to re-register. When this happens the Web address becomes *detagged*. Alternatively, if you believe you have a stronger or more legitimate claim to a Web address than someone else, you can use a disputes resolution service, or even legal action, to make them give the name up. For information on detagging and disputes, visit Nominet at `www.nominet.org.uk`, which is officially recognised as the `.uk` name registry by the industry and government.

Registering your site name

After you ensure that your Web address is available, you're ready to register your name. Doing so is inexpensive, and the process is simple. The example we give here is based on the provider `easily.co.uk`, which charges £35 to register a `.com`, `.org`, or `.net` address for two years, or £9.99 to register a `.uk` address. All you need to do is type in the domain name you want, and the easily site will tell you which extensions are available (if any are not available you can also see who owns them). Highlight all the extensions you want and then get out your credit card. The process is as easy as that – and easily will even e-mail you a reminder when the address needs to be renewed.

You can use any provider to register your Web address, and some are half as cheap as the example we give here. The only thing to stop you going for the cheapest price is to consider whether you also want the provider to *host* the site (meaning to provide the server space where your site resides on the Web). You can transfer Web addresses to another provider after the event, but it is simpler (and sometimes cheaper) to find the right provider for your needs in the first place.

If consumers may get confused by alternate spellings or mis-spellings of your domain name, register them, too. Registering a name is cheap, so you shouldn't lose a prospective customer just because they can't spell your name.

Creating a Compelling Web Site

Designing good Web pages is a key marketing skill, because your Web site is at the centre of all you do to market on the Web. Also, increasingly, Web sites are at the heart of companies' marketing – businesses put their Web addresses on every marketing communication, from premium items (like company pens) to letterheads and business cards, and also in ads, brochures, and catalogues. Serious shoppers will visit your Web site to find out more about what you offer, so make sure your site is ready to close the sale. Include excellent, clear design, along with plenty of information to answer likely questions and move visitors toward a purchase. Web sites have earned their place in the core of any marketing activity. If you're a consumer-orientated marketer, you want your Web site to be friendly and easily navigated as well as to do the following:

- ✔ Engage existing customers, giving them reasons to feel good about their past purchases and connect with your company and other consumers (at least to connect emotionally, if not in actual fact).

- ✔ Share interesting and frequently updated information about your products or services and organisation on the site, so the consumer can gain useful knowledge by visiting it.

- ✔ Maintain a section of the site or a dedicated site for business-to-business (BtoB) relationships that matter to your marketing (such as distributors, stores, and sales reps). Almost all consumer marketers also work as business-to-business marketers, and the same advice we gave on BtoB at the beginning of this section should apply to this aspect of consumer marketing, too.

Finding resources to help with design

You can easily create a basic Web site – one that includes your contact details plus a few pages showing what your business does – on your own. This is the simplest and cheapest route to create a web presence, if all you need is to let customers know where to find you and why they should get in touch. If your needs are more advanced – you want customers to be able to buy direct from your site, for example, you should skip down to the section on 'Hiring a professional designer'. This section doesn't tell you how to use authoring languages or how to do any of the programming. That would fill an entire book, not a chapter, let alone a section. If you decide to do it yourself, you can find excellent books that do go into all the details.

If you want to create your own Web pages, we recommend, in particular, *Creating Web Pages All-in-One Desk Reference For Dummies* by Emily A. Vander Veer (Wiley). It goes a bit deeper than the also good *Creating Web Pages For Dummies* by Bud E. Smith (also by Wiley). Or, if you really want the light version, check out *Cliffs Notes' Creating Your First Web Page* by Alan Simpson (Wiley). These three titles cover the range in both price and detail, so take your pick. If you like tinkering, you can certainly build your own Web pages using Web authoring software like FrontPage or Dreamweaver and contract with a Web provider to put them up on the Web.

You can find a provider to host your site quite easily – and searching the Web is the best place to start. Just pick one that offers the fee structure, services, and flexibility you want at the right price – and change providers if they don't satisfy.

Consider using your domain name and provider to create your own e-mail addresses, too. An example is `craig@craigsmith.co.uk`. Having your e-mail done through your own domain looks so much more professional and gives you more control over the parameters than going through Yahoo!, AOL, or some other public domain does.

Hiring a professional designer

If you aren't a do-it-yourselfer, you have a very easy way to create good Web pages: Find an expert who can do it for you under contract.

Good Web site design is harder than it looks and you should probably go to a reputable design firm and ask them to do it for you. We recommend a business relationship (spelled out on paper in advance) that specifies that you, not they, own all content at the end (so that you can switch to another vendor if it doesn't work out) and also specifies an hourly bill rate and an estimate of the site's size and complexity with a cap on the number of billable hours needed to design it.

You can expect to pay anything from £750 for a basic brochure-style Web site of ten pages to upwards of £10,000 for a Flash-animated fully transactional (or e-commerce) Web site. That's quite a range, even for custom-designed pages, so here's a basic list of what you can expect to get, and for what price:

- You can get a simple template-style Web site for as little as £50 from some of the Web providers that register domain names and host Web sites, or with Web authoring software programs like FrontPage and Dreamweaver. Some programs are quite good, but people often recognise these one-size-fits-all designs, which may lower viewers' opinions of your site design.

- For a basic, custom-designed site (around five to ten pages), where the client provides a company logo, images, and copy, you should plan to spend around £750 to £1,500. You can get a Web designer to arrange Web hosting set up, too. A basic hosting plan costs around £50 to £100 per year, which includes domain name registration.

- A more advanced site of up to 20 pages with a custom look built around your logo, and which contains navigation suited to the service or product that you're offering will cost between £1,500 and £3,500 (although here the price starts climbing depending on what bells and whistles you want to add on). The customised graphics and stock photography necessary for these sites can also drive up your costs, but if your online presence needs this unique, professional look to set you apart from your competitors, then the money may well be worth it.

Beyond the cost of the site, you also need to be aware of additional costs that you may incur – or that you should budget for – in order to enhance the professional appearance and functionality of your Web site:

- ✔ Consider an online shopping trolley, for an extra £300 to £500 on top of your bespoke site design. Many basic hosting plans include a shopping trolley, so you can implement this feature fairly easily by using theirs (but you lose out on the custom-look Web site). Assume that you will be adding products over time, so select a shopping trolley that gives you room to grow.

- ✔ Consider streaming video, animation, and database management. You can use these technologies as important delivery methods, like showing a speaker in action, demonstrating a new product or providing services, and supporting the consumer online.

- ✔ Build some room for stock photography into your budget because sites with relevant images – especially of real people – are graphically more appealing and hold the visitor's attention longer. We highly recommend using photographs in most sites. If you use high-resolution files of the photos, they may be slow to load, which means you could lose some impatient viewers or the few who are still on low-speed phone lines. But stock photography houses sell (at a lower price) low-resolution images that are optimal for the Web and load quickly. These won't slow your site down.

- ✔ You should also have your contractor update your site monthly (Web designers will charge around £70 per hour) because these updates give customers good reasons to keep coming back to the site. Special promotions or some other monthly feature will add to this evolving appeal.

- ✔ Plan to spend more for search engine submission, a service which automatically submits your Web site to all the major search engines so that traffic goes up. This will cost around £100 per year for monthly submissions. We cover the details of how to do this in the 'Getting Your Site Noticed' section later in this chapter because, even if you hire someone to do it, you ought to be involved in the strategising.

Developing a registration-based site

If you visit the Interactive Investor Web site at www.iii.co.uk you can get access to a host of financial news and share price information. When you try to access the interactive information, however, you get redirected to the registration page, where you can create your own share portfolio to track the performance of your investments, and can contribute to the discussion boards.

Registering costs you nothing, and you have much to gain, because of the many extra options and prize competitions that Interactive Investor offers. Why do they give extra content to registered users, and why give away this valuable content? They want to find out who their customers are. The registered users stay in touch and may choose to trade shares directly over the site. Interactive Investor uses its Web site to develop direct marketing relationships with registered users and it's a very savvy way to use the Web site as a major marketing tool. You may want to consider this option, too.

Getting Your Site Noticed

Search engines *locate* (or index) billions of sites from user queries each day. Google alone indexes more than 3.3 billion Web site pages. A lot of prospective customers are in that statistic somewhere. Research shows that 70 per cent of all Internet users go to one of the main search engines to research the options before making an online purchase. In other words, if your site isn't at or near the top of the list of relevant sites, you lose customers to the sites that are. So how can relevant queries find their way to your pages rather than to all the others? You're a needle in an immense haystack.

 Search engine marketing can be a financial black hole. Search engines have become so sophisticated and complex in such a short space of time that the rules have changed fundamentally in the space of just a few years, and the techniques needed to get to the top of search pages have become more complex, too. Some Web providers and consultants will try to convince you that search engines can be fooled into giving your site an artificially high ranking. Others will make out that it's rocket science and can be done at the right price. The truth lies somewhere in between. We can tell you that you do need help in getting to the top or close to the top of any list. Trust us, paying for good advice is well worth it. You may have the ability, but certainly don't have the time to spend trying to beat highly complex search systems. In the following sections we explain some of the basics so you know what a good search marketing company can do for you.

Buying visibility on search engines

Because the search engines look at traffic when ranking pages, anything you do through direct communication with your customers to build traffic can help. Also, you should use a link to related sites to improve your ranking. You can use the simple but powerful strategy of doing a search, like one your customers may do, and see what sites appear in the top ten listings. Then visit each of these sites and see if you can find appropriate places and ways to link from your site to theirs (and vice versa, if possible). For example, a company that distributes products for you or vice versa is a natural to link to your site. Also, a professional association in your industry may be a good fit for you to link to, although it may be harder to talk into linking back to your site. Build such links and the higher-ranked sites tend to draw yours up toward them. But make sure that you have great, useful content to justify those links.

Next, to make your site visible to anyone searching for it, optimise your listing by spending some money on it. Sorry, but there's no such thing as a free lunch on the Internet any more!

We advise you to forget anything you might have heard about *meta tags*. Things have changed so quickly in search marketing that these tags, which used to influence where and how your Web site appeared in search engines, are now largely ignored by the major search engines. They can have an effect on how your Web site is described on a search engine, but these days the *title tag* is the only tag worth worrying about. Title tags determine what words appear in the little blue bar at the top of a user's Web browser (and the same words would appear if they chose to save the Web site in their 'Favourites' file. We consider this a technicality best left to your Web site designer. The Internet Web world has moved on, and so should you.

DIY search marketing with Google

If you do want to have a go at search marketing yourself, then here's an example of how to begin with *pay-per-click* advertising. But bear in mind that a good search marketing consultant can work with you to identify the key words that will generate the best returns for your business, not just for Google but for all the top search engines.

Go to www.google.com and click the Advertising Programmes link. They lay out the most recent offerings for us marketers here. We specifically recommend that you look (by clicking on another link) at Google AdWords, a facility allowing you to pay per click when people click through to your site. To use this option, do the following:

1. **Designate a short list of highly specific and appropriate key terms that customers may use to search for you.**

2. **Bid by saying how much you'd pay for a click. You can get in to the game for just a few pence per click. Web advertisers call this offer your *per-click bid.***

   Google allows you to track your results day by day, see your ranking, and see what results (clicks and costs) you get.

3. **If you want more clicks, raise your bid for a higher listing or improve your use of terms or descriptive sentences, and watch to see if your results improve. Google will also recommend a maximum cost per click (CPC), based on estimated clicks per day – matching the amount will give you the highest exposure and number of clicks.**

We're not going to tell you more about it because Google presents your advertising options well and simply. Just go and have a look at the options – and pick any that seem to fit your site and budget. You don't need to make a long-term commitment; you can experiment at low cost until you find a mix that works.

Yahoo! advertising

Yahoo! (as well as MSN, Wanadoo, AltaVista, and Lycos) uses Overture as its service for buying search engine visibility. Overture uses a bidding system based on the number of clicks your site gets, much like Google's AdWords (see the preceding section for more on Google). You can find Overture by going to `www.content.overture.com`. This link takes you to areas where you can research the Overture options we describe in this book and, if you want, actually make purchases and begin to do your marketing on Yahoo! A Nielsen audit found that Yahoo! search engine listings reached more than 80 per cent of active Internet users. We don't know if that percentage is really true, but Yahoo! certainly has an extensive reach. You may want to buy some visibility in Yahoo! searches, as well as Google. Often, you can use the same key terms in both, which simplifies your work as a marketer. However, you may need to adjust your per-click bids (see the preceding section) differently to get good visibility on Yahoo! Depending on your industry, one or the other search engine may tend to be more expensive. You just have to see and make appropriate adjustments as you go.

Content as a traffic driver

Most Web sites are really just huge, interactive advertisements or sales promotions. After a while, even the most cleverly designed ad gets boring. To increase the length of time users spend with your materials, and to ensure high involvement and return visits, you need to think like a publisher, not just an advertiser. For this reason, we consider Web content to be the hidden factor for increasing site traffic. Unless you have valuable and appealing content, you may have difficulty building up traffic on your site.

✔ **Offer information and entertainment:** People like to use the Web for research. Often, that research relates to a purchase decision. To be part of that research and purchase process, put useful, noncommercial information on your site. B&Q, the home improvement retailer, strikes a nice balance between online sales and DIY adviser. Its site, at `www.diy.com`, lists all its major product lines as you would expect, but there is also a useful 'How To...' area that provides step-by-step instructions on everything from building a barbeque to tiling a wall. Professional services firms can get in on the act, too. The law firm Lewis Silkin keeps its Web site, at www.lewissilkin.com, regularly updated with articles and opinions on the latest legislation that may affect its clients, or more importantly, prospective clients. 'Newsnotes' on topics such as age discrimination in the workplace provide a taster of the advice the firm can offer, without giving too much valuable consultancy away.

Tracking Your Site's Traffic

The Web offers an unmatched ability to evaluate how effectively your online marketing is working and to capture information on the people who are visiting your site. Compared with other media, digital marketing is entirely transparent – meaning you can see how many visitors you get and, if they register on your site, who they are. You should make the most of this rare opportunity to measure the impact of your expenditure.

Interpreting click statistics

You may find click-through statistics a useful and easy-to-get indicator of how well an ad or search-engine placement is performing. If you get a lot of people clicking through to your site from an ad or placement, that ad is clearly doing its job of attracting traffic for you. So, all else being equal, more clicks are better. However, all else isn't equal all the time. Here are a few wrinkles to keep in mind when interpreting click rates:

- When a pop-up ad pops up, the companies you buy the ad space through usually report it as a click. But don't believe the numbers because you have no indication that someone actually read or acted on that pop-up – they may have just closed it without looking. Dig deeper into the statistics from whoever sold you that pop-up ad to find out how it actually performed. You can probably get some more detailed data if you ask, but you need more than the simple click count.

- Some ads have multiple elements that load in sequence, creating a countable click with each loading so that one ad may generate several click-through counts. This counting method may lead you to think that the more complex ad is better, but the higher number can be an artifact of the way those who sell ad space on the Web count the clicks. (Ask your provider if it can sell Web ad space to you, or visit any really popular site and look for the section in it that's for advertisers if you want to buy ad space.)

✔ Quality is more important than quantity. Who are these people who clicked to your site? That information is harder to know but more important. If you get ten thousand clicks in a week, that's nice – but do they include relevant and active prospects or not? Only by digging into detailed reports on who goes where and looks at what on your Web site, plus information on what types of e-mailed questions you get and the average order size in that week, can you really begin to evaluate the quality of those clicks. See the following section 'Paying attention to your site's visitors' for details on how to find out who's visiting your site.

If you're getting poor quality of traffic clicking through, experiment with putting ads in other places or redesign your ads to specifically focus on your desired target. Keep working on it until you have not the most click-throughs, but the best.

You can evaluate performance of Web advertising every day or week, and you can get statistics on each and every ad that you run. So use this data intelligently to experiment and adjust your approach. Aim to increase both the quantity and the quality of clicks week by week throughout your marketing campaign and track the impact on enquiries and sales.

Paying attention to your site's visitors

Each time someone visits your Web site, they are exhibiting interest in you and your products (or they're lost – which is less likely if your site is aptly named and clearly designed so that no one can confuse it with unrelated types of businesses). And when someone exhibits interest, that makes them interesting to you. So whatever you do, however you go about setting up a site, make sure that you capture information about your visitors in a useful form that gets sent to you regularly.

Ask your Web provider what kinds of reports they can offer you – probably more than you imagined possible. With these reports in hand, you can track traffic to your site. You probably notice that you, unlike the giants of the Web, don't have as much traffic as you may want. Sure, millions of people use Google to do searches or go to eBay to bid on auctioned products. But the average Web site only has a few dozen visitors a day. For an effective site, you need to build up this traffic at least into the thousands of visitors per day. How? By making sure it gets noticed in search engines.

Designing and Placing a Banner Ad

A lot has changed in just a few years in Internet advertising. You can see how quickly things have moved on just by looking at what has happened to the most common form of online advertising – the *banner ad*. A banner used to be the only format for online advertising. That traditional format still exists, but for many marketers 'banner' has become a generic term for a whole host of different online ad formats.

We've jumped from one-size-fits-all banners, through as many different types of ad formats as you could wish for, and have come out at the other end with a selection of standard sizes that fit the needs of most advertisers (see Figure 10-1). The *Universal Advertising Package* (UAP), as its creators at the Internet Advertising Bureau (IAB) call it, comprises a superbanner (running across the top of a Web page), skyscraper, large rectangle, and a regular rectangle. The UAP formats are much larger than existing online formats, meaning your ad will stand out better. You can find out all about the technical specifications for UAP formats at the IAB's Web site (www.IABuk.net).

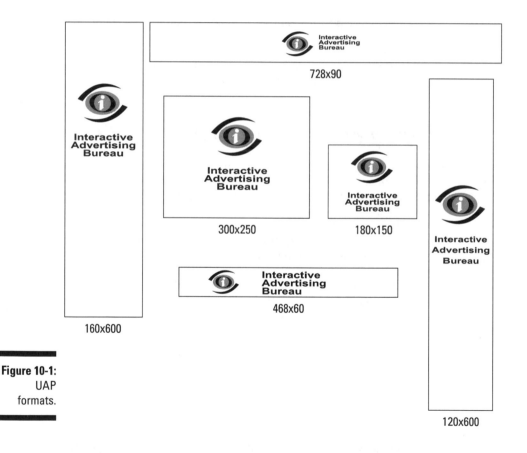

Figure 10-1:
UAP
formats.

The most important advantage of the UAP formats is that they can make the whole process of buying online advertising much more cost-effective. You should pay less for the production of an online campaign if you're not having to re-create your ad for each Web site you advertise on, and you can compare costs of online ad space more easily if you're comparing like with like – rather than apples with oranges, as was the case before.

Hiring a Web media service

Companies that provide *Web media services* (meaning Web page design) can also design and place banner ads and pop-up ads for you. The search for agencies or individuals to do this work for you can be a long and random one. If you're lucky enough to know a competent Web designer or programmer, seriously consider using their services – they can create custom banners to your specification quite easily because it's such a small ad format.

If you have more ambitious plans for rich media online ads, however, you will need to study the extensive field. To make it easier, we recommend you go straight to the Internet Advertising Bureau Web site at www.iabuk.net and visit the membership directory section. In this section, you will find companies offering every kind of Web media service, from ad server and counting providers (online campaign analysis) to Web site design. In the 'creative agencies' list alone there are 50 suppliers, from Advertising.com to Zenith Optimedia.

We have to point out that the larger (and more expensive) agencies are well represented in the IAB membership, so you can find cheaper, local assistance if you're prepared to put in the leg work.

Creating your own banner ad

Creating your own banner ads is a relatively easy process, particularly if you have designed your own Web site and are familiar with HTML coding. Basic banner ads can be created using off-the-shelf design software such as Photoshop or Paint Shop Pro. Not surprisingly, the Web is a good starting point for finding templates for banner ads. Because the format is now so common, a lot of sites allow you to use their standard designs for free. One of the best known is AdDesigner.com (you can guess the Web address), which makes it easy to design a professional looking animated banner ad within minutes. We can't seen why any marketer planning a small-scale online campaign would take anything other than the DIY route, given the high standards of these templates, but if you're really not keen on having a go, it is just as simple to search for one of the many factory-orientated banner ad designers that can make you an ad quickly and for less than £50.

Focusing on a simple design

We think the best design for starters is a banner that flashes a simple one-line offer or headline statement, shows an image of your logo or product, and then switches to a couple more lines of text explaining what to do and why to do it ('Click here to take advantage of our introductory offer for small business owners and get 20 per cent off your first order of . . . ').

You want your ad to be simple and bold – able to attract the viewer's attention from desired information elsewhere on the screen for long enough to make a simple point.

This ad style delivers a clear marketing message using both print and illustration. Make sure that if prospects click on the banner, they go directly to a page on your Web site that supports the product or service with more information and with several easy purchase options.

Being positively creative with your ad

Online advertising that's well done can do many more tasks for you than a TV ad, press ad, or poster. For a start, users who click on your ad can be delivered directly to your transactional Web site. Job done (well, almost – see 'Creating a Compelling Web Site' earlier in this chapter). An online ad can be tactical, by alerting customers to a special offer for instance, or brand-building, by raising awareness of your product or service without a clear call to action. And unlike TV or press ads, you (or the size of your budget) control how intrusive your ad becomes.

Why would you want any Web user to miss an ad you're paying good money for? Obviously, you wouldn't. So be careful about the gimmicks your ad uses. Case in point: Bells-and-whistles online advertising gimmickry (or *rich media*, as the experts call it). With this type of media, you can buy an ad that totally obscures a page someone is trying to view, that chases their cursor around the screen, and basically forces them either to pay attention or close it. That technology runs contrary to every other trend in the advertiser–customer relationship, which is why we don't believe it will be around for long. In the meantime, you can create some eye-catching online ad designs that integrate with the Web page they appear on – and don't irritate potential customers.

Placing your banner ads

Designing the banner is just the beginning because you have to buy space to display it from publishers. If you poke around on large sites like www. yahoo.com, you can find sections devoted to advertisers like you, where you can explore ad buying options and rates and ask for help from a salesperson. Alternatively, you can go to an online media-buying agency and hire them to do the placement. These agencies take a small commission but probably more than make up for this loss by knowing where to place the ads to target your core customer base, negotiating better rates and avoiding some of the inflation of exposure numbers that can happen when you have to rely on the publisher's accounting.

What can it cost you to place a banner ad? Typically between £5 and £10 per thousand viewers – not bad if you have an ad that actually generates some responses. But watch the banner ad closely and pull or modify it, or try running it elsewhere, if the click rate is too low to justify the cost. You may have to make a few tries to get it right, but with the rapid feedback possible on the Web, this experimentation can take place fairly quickly and inexpensively.

Using E-Mail for Marketing

You can create, or hire your Web site designer to create, an e-mail that looks like a well-designed Web page, with animation and clickable buttons linking to your site. Now, all you have to do is blast it out to millions of e-mail addresses and surely you can make millions overnight.

Not so fast! Okay, so you have this great marketing message or sales pitch, and you want to send it to everyone in the world who has an e-mail address. You can actually do that, but we don't advise it. The more specific and narrow your use of e-mail for marketing, the better. And since the introduction of legislation in the UK, Europe, and the US, marketers must be careful to avoid violating all sorts of restrictions on *spam*, or junk e-mails. We help you stay on the sunny side of the law in this section.

The only e-mail to send: Good e-mail

The best e-mail is a personal communication with a customer you know (and who wants to hear from you), sent individually from you with an accurate e-mail return address as well as your name, title, company name, full mailing address, and phone number. The e-mail may read as follows:

Dear so-and-so

I wanted to follow up after your purchase of (your product) on (date) to see how it's working out for you and to thank you for your continuing business. If you have any concerns or questions, please let me know by return e-mail, or feel free to call me directly on 0123 123 1234.

Best wishes

Your Name

Your customer is going to receive, open, read, and appreciate an e-mail like this one. She may even respond to it, especially if the customer has any current concerns or questions or has another order on its way. Even if she doesn't reply to it, however, she appreciates that e-mail. And that message doesn't irritate anyone or look like spam.

Use e-mail as much as you can for legitimate, helpful one-to-one contact and support of customers or prospects.

Sometimes, you can also send out an e-mail to a list rather than an individual, but please make sure that you have a clear purpose that benefits those people on the list. And ensure that your list only includes people who have indicated they are happy to be communicated with – to stay within the law and, more importantly, to avoid angering people.

Understanding e-mail etiquette

Good will is a valuable asset, and you don't want to destroy it with your e-mail! The following list has some additional rules of good mass e-mailing that marketers should all follow. Our inspiration for these rules comes from the Direct Marketing Association, where they have guidelines for responsible use of e-mail. We've also kept the legal restrictions in mind.

- ✔ **Send e-mails only to those people who ask for them.** Your bulk e-mails should go only to those people who have given you permission. The law (The Privacy and Electronic Communications Regulations 2003) now requires that no e-mails are sent without prior consent. What does that mean? It means that everyone you send an e-mail to should have 'opted in' to receive e-mails from you, and each time you contact them you must give them an option to reply and be taken off the list.

  If you have a 'prior relationship' with that contact (such as them being a previous customer or them requesting information from you) the rules are slightly softer. You can get these requests by creating a useful e-newsletter and advertising it on the Web as a free subscription. Those people who sign up really want it, and they're happy to see the next issue arrive.

✔ **Remove addresses from your list immediately when people ask for them to be removed.** Remember that refusing to allow people to opt out is illegal. Also, people have such widespread distrust of Web marketers that you may consider writing the person a brief, individual e-mail from you (identify yourself and your title for credibility), letting them know that you have eliminated them from the list and are sorry if you've inconvenienced them. You shouldn't say any more in the e-mail. Don't try to make a sale – you just irritate the person even more. You generally make a positive impression by being so responsive to the person's complaint, so don't be surprised if your special attention to their request leads them to initiate a sale later on.

✔ **If you insist on buying e-mail lists, test them before using them.** We're assuming that the list you buy in is legal (check first that the people on it have agreed to being contacted by third-party advertisers, like yourself). Then try sending a very simple, short, non-irritating message to people on the list, like an offer to send them a catalogue or free sample, and ask for a few pieces of qualifying information in return. See what happens. Cull all the many bounce-backs and irritated people from the list. Now your list is a bit better in quality than the raw list was. Save those replies in a separate list – they're significantly better and more qualified and deserve a more elaborate e-mail, mailing, or (if the numbers aren't too high) a personal contact.

✔ **Respect privacy.** People don't want to feel like someone's spying on them. Never send to a list if you'd be embarrassed to admit where you got the names. You can develop an e-mail list in plenty of legitimate ways (from customer data, from Web ads, from enquiries at trade shows, from return postcards included in mailings, and so on), so don't do anything that your neighbours would consider irritating or sleazy.

✔ **Send out your bulk e-mails just like you send an individual one.** Use a real, live, reply-able e-mail address. We hate it when we can't reply to an e-mail – it makes us angry! And – a good rule of marketing – try not to anger customers and prospects.

✔ **Make sure that the subject line isn't deceptive.** Good practice and good sense dictate that you make the subject line straightforward. In marketing, you want to get to know straight away if someone isn't a good prospect, instead of wasting your time or theirs when they have no interest in your offer.

✔ **Keep your e-mail address lists up to date.** When you get a *hard bounce-back* (notice that a message was undeliverable) from an address, remove it immediately and update your e-mail list for the next mailing.

A *soft bounce-back* is an undeliverable message resulting from some kind of temporary problem. Track it to see if the e-mail eventually goes through. If not, eliminate this address from your list, too.

People change their e-mail addresses and switch servers. You can have bounce-backs on your list who may still be good customers or prospects. At least once a year, check these inactive names and try to contact them by phone or mail to update their e-mail addresses. Some of these people are still interested and don't need to be cut from your list; they just need their e-mail addresses updated.

If you're e-mailing to an in-house list of people who have bought from you, gone to your seminar, or asked for information in the past, remind them of your relationship in the e-mail – they may have forgotten.

We hate *spam* – junk e-mails that clog up our mailboxes. In fact, we change our e-mail addresses whenever the spam begins to find us. We bet you feel the same way. So don't let your Web marketing make you part of this problem. Use good quality lists, be polite and respectful, and integrate e-mail into your broader Web strategy so that you don't have to rely too heavily on e-mail. Real people live at the end of those e-mail addresses. Treat them as such!

Spreading your message virally

There is one way to bypass the tight restrictions on sending out e-mail messages to people you don't know – and that's getting the people you do know to do it for you. *Viral marketing*, as it's known, doesn't require any great technical know how. All you need is such a good idea, or compelling offer, that your customers are going to spread the word without you even asking! Viral marketing quite simply means an idea or an ad that is so good it spreads from one person to many more – like a virus, but in a good way!

One of the most brilliant examples of viral marketing is Friends Reunited. The idea behind it is simple, and depends absolutely on viral marketing to work. If you don't know it already, Friends Reunited is a Web site that lists tens of thousands of schools, colleges, and universities around the UK. When you register on the site, you supply your personal details plus the schools you went to and, optionally, a few lines about what you are doing now. You can then see a list of all those schools and, crucially, the names and details of everyone who was at those schools with you and where they are now. Because the success of the experience depends on as many people as possible registering, news of the site spread like wildfire. At the height of its fame, Friends Reunited was getting over a million hits a day – solely through word of mouth and some free newspaper publicity.

Getting Mobile with Your Marketing

Seven out of ten people in the UK use a mobile phone and 75 per cent of them send and receive text messages. *Mobile marketing* is held up as being one of the most important methods of the future, while the possibilities for now aren't half bad either. We emphasise that things are changing in mobile marketing constantly, so the technologies of today will certainly have been superceded by tomorrow.

The most basic, and therefore most developed, method of mobile marketing is by Short Message Service, or SMS – which most people simply call texting. You can send a personal, targeted message by text in the same way as you would send an e-mail (and subject to the same laws on privacy; see 'Understanding e-mail etiquette" earlier in this section) – and you can reach your customers 24 hours a day.

Of course, you can also use a mobile phone as the launchpad for a whole host of marketing wonderment. MMS, EMS, WAP, GPRS, Bluetooth, 3G – the terminology is almost as impenetrable as the average marketer's ability to take advantage of it. These technologies will become commonplace, but for the time being, if you're interested in trying out mobile marketing you should stick to the tried and tested methods (or at least as tried and tested as a four-year-old method can be). The following list gives some pointers and ideas on how to use mobile marketing:

- ✔ **Keep it short and to the point.** An SMS message can only be 160 characters long – so your message has to be quick and clear. That's enough, however, to provide customers with a money-off message, for example.

- ✔ **Know who's using the mobile.** People of all ages use mobile phones, but texting is still most commonplace among the young, so use it for products or services that are going to appeal to that type of customer and communicate them in an appealing way.

- ✔ **Be prepared for a good response.** If you do plan to offer a mobile token or other giveaway, be aware that response rates can be as much as 15 per cent higher than direct marketing – and a large chunk of that response will be immediate.

- ✔ **Respect privacy at all times.** Mobile marketing is subject to the same laws as e-mail marketing, covered earlier in this section. You must have the permission of the person you are texting. Even though there are some loopholes where the technology is ahead of the rules and you can send location-based messages to non-customers, it's good sense to respect the principles of permission-based marketing.

- ✔ **Get help (you'll need it).** You can build your own database of mobile numbers and send messages directly to them, but this is time consuming and, for all but the smallest databases, uneconomical. Consider buying in a list of numbers from a company like 12Snap, and then get an SMS broadcast provider to send the messages for you. Like a mailing house or call centre, these companies can give you feedback on the campaign and manage the customer response.

Knowing How Much to Budget for the Web

If you're in a business-to-business marketing situation, we strongly urge you to put at least 10 per cent of your marketing budget into the Web, both for maintaining a strong Web site and for doing some Web advertising and search-engine placement purchases. If you add an e-newsletter, Web distribution of press releases, and occasional announcements to your e-mail list, you may need to make the percentage as high as 20 per cent.

The Internet Advertising Bureau is trying to secure 4 per cent market share for online advertising in the UK by 2007, which is nearly double its current level. As a result, the IAB recommends marketers spend 10–20 per cent of their total budget on online advertising. Our own recommendations are more modest because you must find the budget to allocate to the full range of e-marketing activities, and online advertising is just a part of that. Unless you're an online-only trader, the 10–20 per cent range for e-marketing will bring you the benefits of these new media without blowing the budget for traditional forms of promotion.

But you can find exceptions to every rule, and being the exception often gives you the most profitable and powerful strategy in marketing. If you find that your Web ads, search engine listings, or e-mails are pulling well for you and making a profit, try doubling your effort and spending on them for a month and see what happens. Still working well? Double again. You may find that the Web can do a lot more of your basic marketing work than you think. Many marketers hold Web spending down to a small minority of their budget for no good reason other than tradition and fear of all things new.

One Final – but Important! – Thought

The single most important point to remember about Web sites and e-marketing in general is that you must invest routinely so that you're always changing and improving your presence. Whether you're a do-it-yourself online marketer or are willing to hire a professional online agency, your e-marketing needs to be a living thing. Don't let parts of your site get old and stale. Don't continue to run a *banner ad* (an ad that appears on a major Web site or service) or bid on a *key term* (a word people use in searching for Web sites, which you can pay to have your message linked to) if you aren't getting results in clicks and sales. Do adapt and change every month. The Web is a dynamic marketing medium. Be dynamic!

Chapter 11

Direct Marketing and Telemarketing

· ·

· ·

Direct marketing is easy to do, but difficult to do well. You have to master direct marketing to the degree that you can beat the odds and obtain higher-than-average response rates. We share multiple ways to achieve this goal in this chapter as we help you review the varied problems and practices of direct marketing. This chapter focuses on conventional media – print ads, conventional mail (versus e-mail, which is covered in Chapter 10), and the telephone. Remember these media can be integrated with (or sometimes replaced with) Web-based marketing, which we discuss in Chapter 10.

Beating the Odds with Your Direct Marketing

Direct marketing, relationship marketing, one-to-one marketing: They're all the same thing at heart, so we don't care what term you use. To us, direct marketing occurs whenever you, the marketer, take it upon yourself to create and manage customer transactions through one or more media.

The odds of success in direct marketing aren't particularly good. The average direct appeal to consumers or businesses goes unanswered. Yet if you can up the response rate even a little bit over the average, you can make some serious money in direct marketing.

Practice makes perfect

Practice makes perfect in direct marketing if you make sure to keep records of what you do and track the responses. That way, you can tell when a change improves response rates. Even if you have little or no experience in direct marketing, have faith that a small initiative can generate enough information for you to get a grip on how to direct market better and on a larger scale. The best way to become good at direct marketing is to start doing it.

Ease into direct marketing with a modest campaign to minimise your risk, and start growing from there. This principle is true, whether you're big or small, a retailer or wholesaler, a for-profit or not-for-profit business. When Levi Strauss & Co. started a direct-marketing initiative, they started simply, by including a registration card with each pair of jeans they sold. Equipment marketers know this technique well, but no one in other markets has used it very much. As cards came back, Levi Strauss & Co. built up a database of customers that they could use in their direct marketing.

The importance of civility in direct marketing

Many marketers are rushing to direct marketing in the often-mistaken belief that they can handle their customers better than any intermediaries can. But if you aren't accustomed to dealing directly with customers, you're likely to mess up your attempt at direct marketing. The most common way to mess marketing up is to be too direct. If you're in your customers' faces, you're probably getting on their nerves, as well. Direct marketing should build a bridge between you and the customer. No matter what direct marketing you do, always keep it civil and polite, and you get much better results. Avoid impolite calls, errors on labels, and anything else that may offend the average person. Cull lists to eliminate duplications and errors. It costs just a bit more to do direct marketing well, but you get far better results.

You have to make a positive impression if you want to achieve high response rates. Here's the most important principle of direct marketing. Please repeat after me: It's better to contact a hundred people well than a thousand people poorly!

Developing benchmarks for your campaign

Because your goal is to stimulate consumers to respond to you, your direct marketing has a fairly difficult task to accomplish. You need to understand that most of the interactions between your ad and your prospects fail to stimulate the response you want. Failure is the most common outcome of direct marketing! So your real goal is to minimise failure. Look at the statistics if you don't believe me:

- ✔ A direct-mail letter, individually addressed, typically gets a response from 6.7 per cent of the names you mailed to. So you can expect, at most, 67 responses per thousand from an average letter.

- ✔ The average response from a direct-mail campaign to consumers (asopposed to a business-to-business campaign) is 7.1 per cent. For business campaigns you can expect a 6.2 per cent response rate.

- ✔ A door drop, where your message is delivered to home addresses but is not individually addressed, has an even lower hit rate – typically 5.0 per cent.

- ✔ Of all direct mail, 40 per cent goes into customers' bins unopened. Of the 60 per cent that does get opened, a further 20 per cent does not get read.

- ✔ A telemarketing call centre making *outbound* calls to a qualified list can typically achieve responses from up to 5 per cent of the households called for a consumer product, but can get as high as 10 per cent for some business-to-business sales efforts. However, telemarketing generates far more failures than successes, and its cost per thousand is often higher than direct mail because it is more labour intensive.

In short, direct marketing doesn't generate very high response rates, and you have to make realistic projections before deciding to embark on any activity. However, before you despair, know that good direct-marketing campaigns beat these odds and can be highly profitable – campaigns with over 50 per cent response rates aren't unknown. So don't be discouraged – just be dedicated to doing direct marketing better than average.

Boosting sales from your offers

Here are a few starting tips to help you get focused on the goal of generating high responses to your direct marketing:

✔ Send out a letter, special announcement, or brochure by first-class post once in a while to find out how well your customer list responds. The Royal Mail will return undeliverables if you use an advertiser mailing service such as *mailmedia*, so you can remove or update out-of-date addresses.

You should regularly update your mailing list. Not only will doing so keep your postage costs down, it is also the law since the introduction of the Data Protection Act (we write more on the law later in this chapter). The Royal Mail's Postcode Address File, or PAF, is the most accurate and up-to-date address database in the UK. You can license it direct or go through one of the many licensed resellers and *list brokers*.

✔ Run a very small display ad because they're the least expensive. Limit yourself to 15 words or less. Describe in a simple headline and one or two brief phrases what you have to sell and then ask people to contact you by post or phone for more information. (Include a simple black-and-white photo of the product to eliminate the need for wordy description.)

✔ Replace your existing advertising copy (your words) with *testimonials* (quotes praising your product or firm) from happy customers or with quotes from news coverage of your firm or product. These comments attract more buyers because they seem more believable than positive things you say about yourself.

✔ Give away a simple, useful, or fun gift in exchange for placing an order. People love to receive gifts!

✔ Swap customer lists with another business to boost your list size for free. Before you do this, make sure you're trading contact addresses for people who have given their consent to be contacted. We deal with the issue of data protection later in this chapter.

✔ Send a thank-you note or card to customers by mail or e-mail after they make a purchase. This polite gesture often wins a repurchase. This gesture also lets you test your contact information and gets the customer used to reading your messages so that they're more likely to pay attention to a sales-orientated message later on. In addition, it helps to reduce perceived risk and encourage word of mouth.

✔ Send out birthday or holiday greetings in the form of cards or gifts to your in-house list. If you consider them valuable customers, let them know it. You may be surprised how many contact you afterward to place a new order, even though your mailing to them was non-commercial. (Don't know their birthdays? Send cards on your company's birthday, instead.)

✔ Change the medium or form of your communication every now and then. If you always send out a sales letter, try a colour postcard or an e-mailed newsletter. Variations like this can increase customer interest, and you may also find that different customers respond best to different forms of communication.

✔ Use a photograph of a person's face, looking directly at the viewer with a friendly expression. The person should represent a user or an expert on the product, or relate to the product or offer in some other way. A face attracts attention and increases sales for most direct-response ads and direct-mail letters.

✔ Use a clear, appealing photo of the product. Showing what you have to sell attracts appropriate customers simply and effectively. And if some details don't show up in the photo, add close-up photos. Seeing is believing, and believing is a prerequisite for buying! Few businesses use largely visual direct-response ads, though we can't tell you why. Visual direct-response ads can outsell wordy ones by a wide margin.

✔ Try a radio advertisement asking people to call a freefone number or visit a Web site. Radio ads can be fun! And people really listen to them when they grab the listener's attention.

✔ Run your direct-response ad in Yellow Pages. Get a local number for each directory you list your ad in (you can have the calls forwarded to your central office; ask your local phone company for details).

And remember that behind every effective direct-marketing campaign stands a well-managed database of customer and prospect names. If you need some help with yours, see the sidebar, 'Using a database'.

Using a database

Almost all direct marketers use computerised databases. You should make the transition to this technology eventually if you don't already use it. But you don't absolutely need a computerised database unless you have thousands of names in your database, so if you're a small-time direct marketer who's allergic to computers, you can postpone the transition. In fact, a drawer of customer folders and box of index cards make up the simplest forms of databases, which can do just fine for many smaller businesses.

Your cheapest route to setting up a computerised system is to create one yourself using an everyday software package such as Microsoft Access. But if your business has a lot of contacts consider using one of the big-name, but still off-the-shelf, *Customer Relationship Management* (or CRM) systems designed for smaller businesses from Oracle, Navison, SAP, Peoplesoft, Microsoft, Onyx, Pivotal, and so on.

You could get a tailor-made system that works with your existing systems and even your Web site, but the cost and complexity of these make them unfeasible for all but the larger businesses. A final option is to use an *application service provider* (or ASP), which means they own the software but you buy the use of it for a fixed term. The advantages are that ASPs provide the expertise to build and maintain the database, and they can provide specialist services such as data mining (analysing patterns and grouping data within databases).

If you're designing or reviewing a database management system, make a list of the things you want the system to do. Write your list in non-technical terms. You don't care how the

(continued)

(continued)

system does its magic, just so long as it does it. For example, although different software packages and in-house systems use different techniques to keep track of past customer sales, you just want your system to be able to sort customers by frequency or recency of past sales or give you a sales history on specific customers. Some systems permit this sort of analysis; others may not – so make sure that the system fulfills that list of what you want it to do before you make a purchase.

The following are some of the most fundamental requirements of any marketing database:

✔ Report on and sort by recency of purchase

✔ Report on and sort by frequency of purchase

✔ Report on and sort by total value of past purchases in a selected period

✔ Support list management (merging and purging functions)

✔ Permit integration of new fields (including data from purchased lists or marketing research)

✔ Support name selection (through *segmentation*, which is dividing the list into similar subgroups; *profiling*, which is describing types of

customers based on their characteristics; and *modelling*, which is developing statistical models to predict or explain response rates)

✔ Make sorting, updating, and correcting easy

✔ Make tracking and analysing individual responses to specific communications easy, in order to test the effectiveness of a letter or script

✔ Allow operators at *call centres* (central collections of equipment and staff for handling incoming and/or outgoing calls more efficiently) to quickly pull up and add to profiles of all customers

The preceding list shows you that you may want to do a great many things with your database. So please seriously think about what you need from your database and give the software maker or distributor, or the consultant or in-house programmer you work with, a list of requirements.

As you list your requirements, however, don't get carried away creating a CRM system that holds more data than you could possibly ever use. A simple rule to remember is only collect what you can use, and use everything you collect. Everything else is just marketing money down the drain.

Designing Direct-Response Ads

Direct-response ads are ads that stimulate people to respond with an enquiry or purchase. You see direct-response ads most commonly in print media – magazines and newspapers – although they are a growing force in online advertising (there are more details in Chapter 13). You can also hear and see direct-response ads on radio and TV. As the response mechanism is just part of these broadcast ads, we deal with the area more fully in Chapter 12.

The people who respond to direct-response advertising have self-selected as customers or prospects. You need to do two things with these people:

✔ Try your best to close the sale by getting them to buy something.

✔ Find out as much as you can about them and put the information in your database for future direct marketing efforts.

Many businesses build a direct-marketing capacity through this very process. These businesses place ads in front of what they hope is an appropriate target market and wait to see who responds. Then these businesses attempt to build long-term direct-marketing relationships with those who respond (for example, by sending them brochures or direct-mail letters). Over time, these businesses add respondents to their direct-marketing databases, information about the respondents builds up, and many of those respondents become regular direct purchasers.

You can stimulate responses in ways other than direct-response advertising. We show you how to use direct mail and telemarketing in the same way in the sections 'Delivering Direct Mail' and 'Tuning in to Telemarketing' later in this chapter (and don't forget the Web's emerging capabilities in this area, too!). Both print and television advertising also have successful track records in this area – and radio may work, too, but you have to innovate to overcome the problem of people rarely writing down what they hear on the radio. You need to make the otherwise passive radio an action-orientated medium by making your call to action easy to remember. A memorable Web site address, such as `www.elephant.co.uk`, may do the trick.

A direct-response ad must do more than the typical image-building or brand-orientated ad. A direct-response ad has to create enough enthusiasm to get people to close the sale, on their own initiative, right now. How do you accomplish this goal? Make sure that your direct-response ad does the following:

- ✔ **Targets likely readers:** Your ad's readership dramatically affects your response rate. In fact, the same ad, placed in two different publications, can produce response rates at both ends of the range. So the better you define your target consumers, the easier it becomes to find publications relevant to those target consumers, and the better your ad performs.

    Highly selective publications work better for direct-response advertising. A special-interest magazine may deliver a readership far richer in targets than a general-interest magazine or newspaper. For instance, if you have a gardening product that you're trying to sell to women, select a publication read by them. *Good Housekeeping* reaches more than 400,000 women readers, or you could choose *BBC Gardeners' World*, which has a readership of more than 250,000, all of whom are gardeners and 60 per cent of whom are women.

- ✔ **Appeals to target readers:** A good story, a character target readers can identify with and want to be more like – these factors make up the timeless elements of true appeal.

- ✔ **Supports your main claim about the product fully:** Because the ad must not only initiate interest but also close the sale, it has to give sufficient evidence to overcome any reasonable objections on the reader's part. If you think the product's virtues are obvious, show those virtues in a close-up visual of the product. If the appeal isn't so obvious (as in the case of a service), then use testimonials, a compelling story, or statistics from objective product tests – in short, some form of evidence that is logically or emotionally convincing, or better still, both.

✔ **Speaks to readers in conversational, personal language:** Your ad must be natural and comfortable for readers. Don't get fancy! Write well, yes. Polish and condense, yes. Seek better, catchier, clearer expressions, yes. But don't be stiff or formal.

✔ **Makes responding easy:** If readers can make a purchase easily, ask them to do so. If the process is complicated or the product difficult to buy (because the product is technical, for example), then just ask people to contact you for more information and try to close the sale when they do so. Sometimes, you need an intermediate step. When in doubt, try two versions of your ad – one with an intermediate step and one that tries to make the sale on the spot. Then see which one produces the most sales, in the long run.

Delivering Direct Mail

Direct mail is the classic form of direct marketing – in fact, the whole field used to be called direct mail until the experts changed the term. *Direct mail* is the use of personalised sales letters, and it has a long tradition all its own. Direct mail is really no more nor less than a form of print advertising. So before you design, or hire someone to design, a direct-mail piece, please think about it in the context of being an ad (and see Chapters 7 and 10).

Actually, a direct-mail piece is not like a print ad – it's like two print ads:

✔ **The first ad is the one the target sees when the mail arrives.** An envelope, usually. And that ad has to accomplish a difficult action goal: To get the viewer to open the envelope rather than recycling it. Most direct mail ends up in the recycling pile without ever getting opened or read! Keep this fact in mind. Devote extra care to making your envelope

   • Stand out – it needs to be noticeable and different

   • Give readers a reason to open it (sell the benefits or engage their curiosity or, even better, promise a reward!)

Or send a colour brochure with a stunning front and back cover readers can't resist. Make sure the recipient can see the brochure's exterior by using a clear plastic wrap – don't hide it under a dull envelope.

✔ **The second ad goes to work only if the first succeeds.** The second ad is what's inside, and it needs to get the reader to respond with a purchase or enquiry. In that respect, this ad is much the same as any other direct-response ad. The same rules of persuasive communication apply – plus a few unique ones that we discuss in the following section.

Unlocking the secrets of great direct mail

A great many so-called formulas exist for successful direct-mail letters. None of them work. Instead, your letter must be creative copywriting and design at its best; don't make anything about your letter formulaic. Your direct-mail letter needs to use the secrets of direct-response advertising design (as described in the 'Designing Direct-Response Ads' section earlier in this chapter) and to employ the principles of creative marketing and good communications, which you can find in Chapters 5 and 7. However, certain strategies can help you employ these principles of good design in a direct-mail piece.

The most effective direct-mail letters generally include several elements, each with its own clear role:

- ✓ **Bait:** You should include some sort of bait that catches the reader's eye and attention, getting him or her to read the letter in the first place.

- ✓ **Argument:** You then need to provide a sound argument – logical, emotional, or both – as to why your great product can solve some specific problem for the reader. Marketers devote the bulk of many letters to making this case as persuasively as possible, and you should keep this sound practice in mind when drafting your direct-mail letter.

- ✓ **Call to action:** Finally, you should make an appeal to immediate action, some sort of hook that gets readers to call you, send for a sample, sign up for a contest, place an order – or whatever. As long as the readers act, you can consider the letter a success. So this hook is really the climax of the letter, and you need to design everything to ensure that this hook works.

These three essential elements can be described in various ways. One favourite of many copywriters is the star, chain, and hook approach. If you can't find and mark all three of these elements in your own letter, it isn't any good:

- ✓ **The star (aka, the bait):** A lively opening to your letter. It attracts attention and generates interest.

- ✓ **The chain (aka, the argument):** This part of the letter presents your argument – the benefits of the product and your claim about what it can do to make the reader's life better.

- ✓ **The hook (aka, the call to action):** This part ends your letter, and it asks the reader to do something immediately. If the letter doesn't make a purchase request, then it should offer an incentive for readers to send in their name or call for more information.

Do these principles apply to e-mail? Yes, but think screens, not pages, when writing the body copy of an e-mail sales letter. It takes as much effort (and involvement) to click on the next screen as it does to turn the page, yet a screen holds less than a page. So be more precise and less wordy, or your e-mail can't pull as well as the same letter in printed form.

These formulas refer specifically to the text of your letter itself. Remember to think hard about what else goes into your mailing, as well.

Enticing envelopes

The outside of the envelope needs to entice readers and get them to open the letter in the first place. Following are some techniques to make your envelope enticing enough to open:

- **The stealth approach envelope:** You disguise your letter so that it looks like a bill or personal correspondence – or just cannot be identified, at all. You're hoping the reader will open the envelope just to find out what's inside and like what they see enough to respond. You should use this approach cautiously, if at all; after all, it is a bit sneaky, and you don't want to annoy the recipient as it may ruin your chances forevermore!

- **The benefits approach envelope:** You include a headline, perhaps a little supporting copy, even some artwork, to let people know what the mailing is about and summarise why you think your offer is worthy of their attention. We like this approach best because it's honest and direct – and this is direct marketing, after all! Furthermore, this method ensures that those who do open the envelope have self-selected based on interest in your offer. But this technique only works if you have a clear benefit or point of difference to advertise on your envelope. If you can't say 'Open immediately for the lowest price on the XYZ product ranked highest by *Which*', then this method may not work.

- **The special offer envelope:** This envelope entices with your hook – never mind your offer. By letting consumers know that they can enter a competition to win a country cottage, or get free samples, or find valuable coupons enclosed, this envelope gives them a reason to read the letter inside. But the envelope itself doesn't try to sell the product – it leaves that to the carefully crafted letter inside.

- **The creative envelope:** If your mailing is unique enough, everyone wants to open it just to find out who you are and what you're up to. Consider an oversized package in an unexpected colour, an envelope with a funny cartoon or quote on the back, or a window teasing readers with a view of something interesting inside. You can make your envelope the most exciting thing in someone's letterbox by using any number of creative ideas. Yet this strategy is the least common, probably because creative envelopes cost more. But don't make false economies. If you spend 25 per cent more to double or triple the response rate, then you've saved your company a great deal of money on the mailing by spending more on the envelope!

Persuasive letters and reply forms

What else should go into your mailing? In general, a letter combined with a *circular* – a simple catalogue-style description of your product(s) – pulls more strongly than a letter alone. Circulars don't work for all products (don't bother for magazine subscriptions), but do work well for any product or service the consumer sees as expensive or complex. And make the circular more elaborate, involving, glossy, colourful, and large where involvement should be higher – big circulars for big-ticket items, little ones for simple items.

Also include reply forms. Allow readers to easily get in touch with you in multiple ways. Give readers some choices about what offers they want to respond to, if possible. Postage-free (or prepaid) reply forms generally ensure a higher response rate and thus justify their cost many times over. Don't skimp on the form because, after all, getting that response is the whole point of your mailing.

Getting your letter mailed

The first question to resolve is how to send the letter. Second class versus first class via Royal Mail? Should you use an overnight air service for an offer to business customers? Or maybe send the letter by e-mail or fax? In general, the postal service is still best. And, as direct mail is such a big revenue earner for Royal Mail, it has many different mailing systems and services for businesses of all sizes (such as mailmedia, where you can pay an upfront discounted price for outgoing mail and a certain level of postage-free response).

One little detail often puzzles first-time direct mailers – how to actually get your mailing printed, folded, stuffed, and mailed. If you don't know, you should probably hire someone who does. Your local telephone directory lists some companies that do this kind of work under 'mailing' or 'marketing' headings, and commercial printers often do this type of work, as well. Printers can often handle anything from a small envelope to a major full-colour catalogue. Talk to various printers to get an idea of the range of services and prices.

If you're planning small-scale mailings – say, less than 2,000 at a pop – then you may find doing the work in-house offers you a cheaper and quicker route. Many local businesses and not-for-profit organisations do small-scale mailings, and they'd be throwing away money by hiring printers. If you want to set up this in-house capability, talk to your local post office to find out how to handle metered or permit mail. And consider purchasing mailing equipment, such as the following (all these items can process standard-format mailings): Feeders, sealers, scales to weigh the mailings, and meters. Combine this equipment with your local photocopy shop's ability to produce, fold, and stuff a mailing, and you have an efficient small-scale direct-mail centre.

Purchasing mailing lists

When you don't have a database of your own, or you want to expand the one you do have quickly, you can use purchased lists to prospect for leads. Don't expect the purchased lists to work very well – response rates can be low, and you may get high returns or undeliverables. But that's okay because you're using these purchased lists just to build up your own higher-quality in-house list of purchasers. So, plan to send out relatively inexpensive mailings with easy-to-say-yes-to offers, and then focus on the replies. If you get any calls, faxes, or postcards from these purchased lists, qualify them as leads or customers, and move them to your own list.

We recommend buying one-time rights to mailing lists, with phone numbers (plus e-mail, if it's offered) to make replying to a response easier for you. One-time use means that you don't own the list, just rent it. But you do own the replies. As soon as someone contacts you from that mailing and you begin to interact with them and gather information about them, you can add that person to your own list.

You can buy lists from list owners (those who first developed the list and rent it out), list managers (who manage it on an owner's behalf), list compilers (whose business it is to create bespoke lists from a wide range of sources), or list brokers (who can point you in the direction of the right list for your purposes and advise you how best to use them). You can find hundreds of list brokers through the List Manager on the Direct Marketing Association (DMA) Web site, at www.dma.org.uk.

No matter how good your direct mail is, some people simply don't want to receive it. The Mailing Preference Service, or MPS, is a suppression file that exists for those people. There is no legal requirement for you to screen any of your mailings against the MPS (though there is for some other preference services, so we cover both in the 'Keeping it Legal (and Decent)' section later in this chapter) – but industry codes of practice say you should when renting third-party lists. Using the DMA List Manager will ensure you are getting lists that have regularly been checked against the MPS. Most importantly, you won't be aggrieving potential customers or wasting money. A preference service exists for phone, fax, and e-mail – so whichever direct channel you use, think about those people who don't want to hear from companies, full stop.

List suppliers usually have minimums. We recommend buying the minimum (it comes on sticky mailing labels or in a database, depending on what's easiest and cheapest for you to use in your business). Then test the list with a mailing and see what happens. If you get some good customers out of the list, go back and buy a larger number of names, excluding the ones you already used. Or if you're disappointed in the response, buy a different list next time. (And if your mailing is too expensive to test on the minimum – which is often 1,000 names – just mail to the first 250. That's enough names to find out how the list performs.)

You have so many lists to choose from that you can keep shopping until you find one that works for you. But remember the basic principle of list-buying: The best indicator of future purchase is past purchase.

So try to find lists of people who have purchased something similar to what you're selling, preferably through the mail, rather than people who fit your customer profile in other ways.

If you're new at the list-buying game, be prepared for some list sellers to refuse to send their names to you. These list sellers worry that they'll rent a one-time use of a list, but users won't honour this, so they sometimes want to work through a supplier they trust, like a graphic designer, ad agency, or printer in your area. You probably use the services of someone they do trust, so if you run into this problem, network around until you find someone the list-seller will send the lists to.

Establishing and Running a Call Centre

A *call centre* is the place where telephone calls from your customers are answered. A call centre can be a real, physical place – a big room full of phones staffed by your employees, or it can be a virtual place – a telephone number that rings to whatever subcontractor you're currently using to handle telemarketing for you. (A hidden advantage of keeping the call centre in-house is that managers can keep an eye on the accessibility issue and add more lines and staff quickly, if a problem arises.)

If you don't want to set up a call centre yourself, you can hire a consultant to design a call centre for you or simply use a service firm to perform the function for you. *Marketing* magazine publishes a league table every year of the top 50 telemarketing agencies. These agencies range in size from Vertex with a £320m turnover and 11,000 staff to Price Direct with a turnover of £500,000 and 50 staff. Many telemarketing agencies are members of the Call Centre Association, where you can access details through the Web site: www.cca.org.uk.

Every business is a call centre, but most don't realise it. If you have telephones and people calling in and out on them, you need to manage this point of customer contact very carefully. Small businesses may not operate on a big enough scale to hire or build a dedicated call centre, but they still must manage this function wisely if they want to win customers, rather than lose them, on the phone. So please, read and apply the principles of this section, no matter how large or small your business may be!

Being accessible to desirable customers when they want to call you

If you service businesses, then you can use business hours to answer business calls. If you service consumers, however, be prepared to take calls at odd hours. Some of the best customers for clothing catalogues do their shopping late at night – just before bed, for example.

And remember, being accessible means more than just having staff by the phones. You need to make sure that nobody gets a busy signal (your phone company will have a variety of services to help solve this problem – ask them for details). If you answer your phone faster than the competition does, you can gain some market share from them.

You need to measure and minimise customer waiting time. Don't leave people sitting on hold for more than what they perceive to be a moderate amount of time. Depending upon the nature of your product and customer, that time limit is probably less than two perceived minutes. A *perceived minute* is the time period a customer on hold thinks he or she has waited for a minute – and that time typically comes out to be more like 40 seconds when you measure it on the clock. You have to convert actual wait times to perceived wait times in order to appreciate the customer's perspective.

Capturing useful information about each call and caller

One of the most important functions for your call centre is to field enquiries or orders from new customers as they respond to your various direct-response advertisements – such as magazine ads, letters to purchased lists, and your Web site. This function is known as *inbound telemarketing* and these callers are hot leads. You don't want these customers' orders as much as you want their data. Don't let these customers escape from your call centre. Make sure that your operators ask every caller for his or her full name and address, how he or she heard of your company, and perhaps a few other qualifying questions, as well.

The best way to capture call-ins for your customer database is to have your operators online, so that they can enter the data directly into your database as they obtain it. At the very least, give your operators a printed information form they can fill in – or, if you're the one answering those customer calls, make yourself a form so you don't forget to capture useful information about the prospects, their needs, and how they found your number.

Recognising – and taking care of – repeat customers

It is generally accepted that it costs a lot more to acquire a new customer than it does to keep an existing one, and if you can find a way of identifying your most valuable customers (those that spend more with you over a long period of time) then you're on to a gold mine. We discuss this more in Chapter 4. So how do you know when the person calling you is a new customer or an old, valued one? In smaller organisations with a few regular customers it is just good business to know your best customers, what they regularly buy from you and what their business requirements are. The same is true for bigger businesses, but it's harder to keep track of all those different customers. We recommend you keep customer records, even if it's just a name, address and list of transactions held on a paper form. You can quickly identify who your loyal customers are and treat them accordingly – that's good business, and will win you even more repeat business. A better way is to keep records on a computer database, that you can call up instantly when a customer rings you. These databases can easily be transferred onto the computer systems of any call centre you may choose to hire.

Putting your operators online also solves the related problem of recognising repeat customers. Repeat customers' names pop up on-screen for the operator's reference. That way, the operators don't have to ask stupid questions, and they can surprise customers with their knowledge about past purchases or interactions with your company.

Gathering data on the effectiveness of direct-response ads and direct mail

We're often amazed by how little information marketers gather about the effectiveness of their own work. What you don't know does hurt you in marketing! You can easily find out which direct-response ads, call scripts, or mailings work the best. And by doing so, you make your direct-marketing campaigns more effective, over time. You only need to tell your operators to ask every caller where they heard about you (or ask repeat customers what prompted this latest call).

You can also use this more rigorous way to track the effectiveness of each marketing effort: Use a unique code number on each mailing to help trace each call or other customer response. You can broaden this technique to include all written promotions, if you want – even those on the Web. An identifying code links calls and sales to specific ads, allowing easy analysis of their effectiveness.

You can also use codes for each ad to support customised sales promotions. For example, one mailing may offer a special two-for-one price over a two-month period – with the code, your operator can quickly display the terms of this offer on screen. And because you have associated an offer with this code, you motivate the customer to give you this information.

Tuning in to Telemarketing

In the UK, a company with an 0800 freefone number will generate around three times as many calls as a business without one. With a free, or at least very cheap, phone number you are inviting customers to call you rather than giving them a reason not to. Telemarketing has gained a poor reputation in recent years, as many people think it just means unsolicited sales calls from companies they don't want to hear from. Those people don't think of the calls they make to companies as telemarketing, but it is. In fact, inbound telemarketing, as it is called, can be one of the most effective sales channels, as you're not wasting resources on people who don't want to do business with you and are simply making yourself available to those who do.

Inbound and outbound telemarketing

Inbound

Although telemarketing requires nothing but a telephone, combining it with free, or at least low-cost, inbound calling usually makes it most effective. You can offer free calling to your customers and prospects with all 0800 or 0808 numbers. You, the marketer, get to pick up the cost of the customer's telephone call so that you can remove a possible objection to calling. By using an 0800/0808 number, you can provide customers and prospects with a single, memorable and free (93 per cent of customers know about 0800 numbers) route to contact you. These numbers also mean you can direct all calls to a centralised call centre, which is why many marketers prefer *freefone* to other types of numbers.

There are other types of phone numbers you can use that keep down the cost of calling for customers, but allow you to route all calls through a single call centre. The following *freefone* or low-cost numbers are useful in *inbound telemarketing*, in which customers call you in response to direct-response advertising:

- ✔ **0800/0808:** Freefone is a zero-cost way to encourage customers to call. At its most basic, freefone can route all calls to a specific telephone line or can be linked to a call management monitoring programme to improve the way your business handles calls.

✔ **0845:** Lo-call allows customers to contact you from anywhere in the country, but they pay only the cost of the local call while you pick up the difference in price. The advantage is a single number for customers to remember and a single call-routing system for you.

✔ **0870:** NationalCall means customers pay a single national-rate call from anywhere in the country. While your customers pay a 'fair' price for the call, this type of number can actually be a revenue-earner. The advantage of a single, memorable number for your business still applies.

✔ **09xx:** ValueCall is a premium-rate phone number, charged at various rates to your customers, depending on the service being offered. While it is a single business number, customers associate 09xx numbers with higher-cost calls, so they are best used for competitions or advice lines.

Every direct-response ad should have a phone number as one of the contact options – with a trained telemarketing sales force or an eager entrepreneur at the other end. (We recommend posting a *freefone* number prominently on your Web site and printing it on packaging, brochures, business cards, and so on, in case someone prefers to talk rather than e-mail or mail you. Add a free fax number, if customers in your industry like to fax in orders, too.)

Everything you send out that could have your phone number and Web address on it should have it. It's amazing how often we find ourselves staring at a catalogue page, package, product, Web site, or memo trying to find a phone number that just isn't there. Then what? We may just call the competition instead. The solution? Audit and order!

1. First, *audit* your mailings and other customer communications to find those holes where you've accidentally left out contact information.

2. Next, *order* up some simple contact information stickers with your brand or business name, phone numbers, address(es), and Web site and e-mail information. Pop those stickers on folders, boxes, cards, products, scribbled notes, or anywhere else anyone may conceivably look when thinking of calling you with a question or order.

Outbound

The other form of telemarketing is *outbound telemarketing*, in which salespeople make calls to try to get prospects on the phone – and then pitch to them to try to make a sale; see Chapter 20 for how to design a good sales presentation. You can do a little bit of outbound telemarketing informally as part of a broader routine of contacting customers and following up on leads, or you may have a full-blown outbound telemarketing campaign set up in a call centre that you either run yourself or contract with (the bureaus are the same as for inbound telemarketing, covered earlier in this chapter).

One way or the other, though, every marketer makes some calls to customers and prospects and must be prepared for the reality that outbound telemarketing yields plenty of rejections. In fact, we don't generally recommend outbound telemarketing for *cold call* lists, or lists of strangers who have never done business with you before. You can buy such lists from *list brokers* easily, but expect lower response rates than from lists you build yourself.

You can improve the success rate of outbound telemarketing dramatically by developing a good list before you start calling. Preferably, this list is of people who have had some contact with you before (they've purchased, returned an enquiry card, tried a sample, or responded to a print ad or Web banner ad). With a good list, you can afford to put competent salespeople on the phones so that your company puts its best face forward. We don't know why most telemarketers haven't worked out that the first contact between their company and a prospective customer should not be in the hands of a temp worker who can't even pronounce the name of the product correctly. To avoid such problems, you need to develop lists and a calling style that give your callers at least a 15 per cent success rate – more than ten times the average for typical unfiltered consumer telemarketing operations.

Truth and decency in telemarketing

The pressure is on in telemarketing. Selling anything over the phone is much harder than it used to be. People (and businesses) are getting sick and tired of these sales calls and adding their names to *preference services* by the thousands. So marketers are experimenting with stealth techniques, and these techniques lead them into dangerous ethical and legal territory.

A formerly new distribution channel, the telephone, has matured. Many desirable consumers became jaded to direct mail, print ads, billboards, and radio and television ads decades ago. But the rise of telemarketing in the 1980s gave marketers something new and different to experiment with. Telemarketing was great fun – for a while. But now, most prospects have received hundreds, if not thousands, of telemarketing calls.

So today's telemarketers have only two choices: One, they can go on doing what they've always done, which can only lead to increasingly desperate and shady practices as their medium matures and their industry shakes out; or two, they can wake up and realise that it's a new dawn. Telemarketers need to find new strategies for their newly mature medium. Some of these strategies include

  ✔ **Use the phone to follow up on leads, not to find them.** Whenever possible, use your Web marketing activities (see Chapter 13), events (check out Chapter 16), and advertising (see 'Beating the Odds with Your Direct Marketing', earlier in this chapter, plus all of Part III in this book) to generate telephone or personal sales call leads. When you generate enquiries about your product or service, you have permission to call. The prospect takes your call gladly in 99 per cent of these cases, and you close a sale in many of them.

✔ **Don't overuse the phone.** Save calls for issues that really deserve personal contact from the prospect's perspective, and try to call people who actually know you or your firm or will welcome the call for some other good reason. If you have something truly important to talk about, then you don't need a misleading hook to keep people on the phone. Remember that every marketing campaign should use a balanced mix of media and methods. You can't do all jobs with one tool. And also remember that even where telephoning is appropriate, your customers and prospects don't want you to call constantly – give them a little breathing room.

✔ **Be respectful.** Remember that you're interrupting anyone you reach by phone.

✔ **Be human.** Some experts waste a lot of time debating whether outbound-calls should be scripted or not. As long as what your caller says sounds warm and natural, it doesn't matter whether it's written down or not. Get your callers to say 'you'll', not 'you will'. If the script is written in perfect English but still doesn't sound right, then throw the grammar book out of the window.

✔ **Compensate telemarketers for building relationships, not destroying them.** If telemarketers are paid only by the *kill* (commission on sales), then they can get frustrated and start berating and hanging up on your prospects and customers.

✔ **Guard existing customers from bad telemarketing.** Deceptive, high-pressure, or irritating phone sales tactics may produce a good-looking end-of-day sales report, but they are guaranteed to increase customer turnover. Why? These tactics bring in deal-prone customers, who can be taken away by the next telemarketer, and they irritate your loyal customers rather than reward them. At the very least, use two different strategies and scripts: One for existing customers and one for deal-prone prospects. At best, focus your telemarketing on building existing customer loyalty; for example, by really calling to see if you can improve the product or service quality.

✔ **Gain insight from other media.** Holding someone's attention long enough to deliver a marketing message is a major problem in every medium, not just telemarketing. And marketers have developed clever solutions in other media. Why not try some of them in telemarketing? You can write a script that includes entertainment – a very short story, a good joke, a warm and pleasant manner, or another engaging opener may build interest far better than a deceptive claim about the purpose of the call. Similarly, a sales promotion tie-in can hold attention. For example, your script can start with the offer of a contest or free sample giveaway and then go on to a pitch for the product. Get creative!

Keeping It Legal (And Decent)

In recent years there have been a host of new laws introduced to protect consumers and any data about them – and that affects a lot of what marketers do day to day. Whether you are storing or using customer data, mailing, e-mailing, or telephoning customers (new or old) – these laws make a difference to how you should be doing it. And it's not just the law you need to think about. There are industry codes of practice and preference services (which allow people to opt out of receiving a lot of communications) that you should abide by – you don't have to, by law, but we'll explain later why it makes good sense.

So what follows are the basics on new laws and codes that restrict what you can do when trying to contact your customers. We urge you not to treat these restrictions as the enemy – in many cases, making sure you're only using *clean* data and are not trying to contact consumers who don't want to hear from any businesses (not just yours) makes sense and will actually save you money in the long term.

Data Protection Act

So, do you process personal data? The answer to this simple question will determine whether the Data Protection Act (or DPA) affects what you do – and in most cases the answer is yes. Processing personal data covers almost any activity you can think of. A person's name and address stored in a marketing database is personal data, never mind consulting it, disclosing it, transferring it, or even deleting it. If you've got personal data it's safest to assume you're processing it, even if it doesn't feel like you are.

Before you can do anything with the data you hold, you need to formally notify the Information Commissioner's Office of who you are and what you're planning to do. This notification costs £35 per year. The Information Commissioner (www.informationcommissioner.gov.uk) is the office responsible for administering the DPA, and as well as registering there, you can find more detailed guidance on the Act.

The DPA is based on eight principles (actually they're enforceable, but it makes them sound nicer) of good information handling practice. They state that data must be:

- Fairly and lawfully processed
- Processed for limited purposes

✔ Adequate, relevant, and not excessive

✔ Accurate and up to date

✔ Not kept longer than necessary

✔ Processed in accordance with the individual's rights

✔ Secure

✔ Not transferred to countries without adequate protection for the individual

The good news is that while the DPA may look like a legal minefield you can, in fact, easily navigate it if you are only using the data for advertising and marketing purposes and if you have obtained the consent of the customers you plan to contact.

The 'fair and lawfully processed' principle in the DPA is the one that most relates to you and your direct marketing, as it's here where you must be able to prove 'prior informed consent' before contacting customers. 'Prior' means that you have obtained consent before you begin mailing or calling them, and 'informed' means you haven't buried the consent clause somewhere in the small print.

The Information Commissioner and the National Consumer Council have created an 'information padlock' symbol, shown in Figure 11-1, that companies are free to download and use wherever personal information is being collected to be processed, such as a coupon, application form, or to register on a Web site. Using this symbol will allow you to be open with customers and prospects, and show them you're taking your responsibilities seriously.

You should always try to be honest and upfront, not just legal. While it may pain you to allow your customers and prospects to easily opt out of further advertising from you, the fact that you have weeded out those customers from the ones that are happy to hear from you means your marketing campaigns will become much more efficient.

As long as you're clear in your communications, you can give customers the chance to *opt out* of, or *opt in* to your information – worded properly both count as informed consent. You have to give customers this choice every time you communicate with them. You will have seen tick boxes, of the opt in or opt out variety, on a lot of the mailings and e-mails you get from companies – and similar easily understood devices should be on all materials you send out to your customers (and if it's an e-mail, you must make sure the tick box actually works or you're in breach of the DPA).

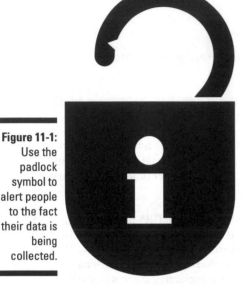

Figure 11-1:
Use the
padlock
symbol to
alert people
to the fact
their data is
being
collected.

While it's early days for the DPA, which passed into law in 2000, you can be sued if you're in breach of it. That means that you need to make sure you've got consent to contact your customers, but also that your suppliers have, too. If you're buying or renting a list, you should go through a reputable source such as the Direct Marketing Association (their site, at www.dma.org.uk, has a searchable List Manager of list suppliers), or make sure you have legal cover to indemnify you against bought-in data.

Preference services

You need to know about the existence of five preference services, which allow individuals (and in some cases companies) to register to opt out of receiving certain types of communication from you. (Don't take it personally; these people have chosen not to receive *any* marketing communications.) These services are the Mailing Preference Service (MPS), Baby MPS, Telephone Preference Service (TPS), Facsimile Preference Service (FPS), and Email Preference Service (EMPS).

You also need to know that not all preference services are created equal. There is no legal requirement for you to check your mailing lists for people that may be registered with MPS or Baby MPS (for bereaved parents to register not to receive baby-related mailings), but it pays not to contact people who don't want to hear from you, and most reputable list brokers and mailing houses will respect the MPS lists.

The other three preference services – TPS, FPS, and EMPS – fall under the Privacy and Electronic Communications (EC Directive) Regulations 2003, but, again, the same rules don't apply for each. Calling or faxing individuals or companies who have registered with TPS or FPS is prohibited by these regulations, so you need to check your database against both these registers. Check regularly, as a 'for the time being' clause means those who have registered can change their mind (to receive or not to receive) whenever they like. You are also responsible for making sure that any subcontractors using your lists to make calls are not phoning or faxing those names on the TPS or FPS registers.

We've written more about the Privacy and Electronic Communications Regulations in Chapter 13, but in terms of who you can and can't contact using e-mail, the Regulations introduce two new rules. The first rule is that you, as the sender of e-mail, must not conceal your identity and must provide a valid address for opt-out requests. The second rule is that you cannot send unsolicited e-mail marketing messages to individuals without their prior consent. This means that accordance with EMPS and this rule are slightly more relaxed if you have

- ✔ Obtained an e-mail address 'in the course of a sale or negotiations for a sale'

- ✔ Only sent promotional messages relating to 'similar products and services'

- ✔ Given the recipient the opportunity to opt out when the address was collected, and have given the opportunity to opt out with every subsequent message.

Consumer Protection Distance Selling Regulations

When you enter into an agreement with a consumer (not another business) to supply your product or service without having met face to face, you have entered into a distance contract. Contracts formed by mail order, digital television, over the phone, by fax, or on the Internet are all distance contracts and are subject to these Distance Selling Regulations (DSRs).

There are some sectors where DSRs do not apply, so if your business is in financial services, travel, or leisure (plane, train, concert, or sports event tickets or hotel accommodation) you can breathe easy. Otherwise, play it safe and assume that any direct business you do with customers is affected by DSRs and supply the following information – in writing or by e-mail – before a distance contract is formed:

- ✔ Your business name
- ✔ Your address – if you are seeking payment in advance

- ✔ A description of the goods or services you're offering

- ✔ The full price – including any taxes

- ✔ For how long the price or any special offers remain valid

- ✔ Details of any delivery costs

- ✔ Details of how payment can be made

- ✔ The arrangements for delivery or performance – when customers can expect delivery, for example

- ✔ Information about your customers' right to cancel

You will need to supply this information again, plus more detail on cancellation conditions, after-sales service, or guarantees, before the items are delivered or the services are completed. If you fail to do this step, your customer has longer to cancel – generally seven days from the time this *follow-up disclosure* is given. Persistent offenders of serious non-compliance with the DFRs could receive a court order to comply from the Office of Fair Trading (www.oft.gov.uk).

Chapter 12

Public Relations and Word of Mouth

. . . .

In This Chapter
▶ Generating positive publicity about products and organisations
▶ Writing an effective press release
▶ Harnessing the power of customer word of mouth

. . . .

*W*hen people bump into reminders of your company name, brand name, product, or service, they are more likely to buy. And if those exposures to your identity create a strongly positive impression, they can have a big impact on sales. So far, so simple.

But while advertising does work, most people who are affected by it don't like to admit to it. There are plenty of people who will deny ever having bought anything as a result of seeing an ad for it, but we'll bet you've never come across anyone who says the same about a magazine article, or who is so resistant to something a relative or friend recommends to them.

Independent endorsements for your product or service can be so much more powerful than 'pure' advertising, for the simple reason that consumers are more sceptical about a message that has been paid for and is self-serving.

In this chapter, we discuss the two key ways of gaining independent endorsement for your business: *Public relations* (when exposure to or mention of your company, service, or product becomes part of the news or an editorial feature) and *word of mouth* (what people say about you to others). Each endorsement can make a positive impression in a low-key, polite manner, and can do so (if managed well) for surprisingly low cost.

Public relations and word of mouth are both vastly underrated techniques for communicating with your customers. These endorsements are ignored or given only minor attention by marketers, but they belong in the front lines of your marketing plan because of their ease of use, simplicity, low cost, and potential.

Using Publicity to Your Advantage

Publicity is coverage of your product or business in the editorial portion of any news medium. Why would journalists cover a product as a story? Because the product is better or worse than expected. If, for example, *Which?* magazine runs an article praising your product as best in a category, that's publicity. Good publicity. If, in contrast, the evening television news programmes run a story saying that experts suspect your product caused numerous accidents, that's publicity, too. Bad publicity. Technical reviewer suggestion: But bad publicity can be turned to an organisations advantage – Johnson and Johnsons baby powder was found to contain traces of ground glass but they responded so promptly and responsibly that their image improved! Perrier on the other hand denied all suggestions that there were traces of benzene in their water and suffered the consequences.

In both cases, product quality is the key to the publicity. Keep this fact in mind.

When you use publicity, remember the all-important factor – the quality of your product development and production/delivery. You can gain positive publicity simply by designing and making a truly superior product. If you want to generate negative publicity, just make your product shoddy or do your service poorly. *Good publicity starts with a pursuit of quality in your own business!*

The following sections list ways that you can take advantage of good publicity (and, if the need arises, neutralise bad publicity) in your marketing materials.

Publicity and word together

The day before I started on this chapter I received an e-mail from a company called Rapha, which makes high-performance clothing for racing cyclists. Rapha was e-mailing all its past customers with the news that it had just won 'clothing brand of the year' in the `Roadcycling UK.com` Reader Awards. In other words, Rapha was letting its customers know that visitors to RoadcyclingUK voted its clothing line the best product of the year.

This is a perfect example of good publicity and word of mouth working in harmony. The company is passionate about making great products, and cyclists that use them tell other cyclists, who vote for Rapha as best brand. Rapha gets positive publicity, which attracts more customers and the cycle, if you'll excuse the pun, continues.

Tackling public relations

Public relations (PR) is the active pursuit of publicity for marketing purposes. You use PR to generate good publicity and try to minimise bad publicity. Generally, marketers have the responsibility of generating good publicity. If marketers create good stories and communicate them to the media effectively (see the following two sections), the media pick them up and turn them into news or entertainment content. Good publicity.

Although marketers or general managers wear the PR hat in smaller organisations, large companies generally have a PR person or department whose sole job is to manage its reputation – generating good publicity but also reacting promptly and effectively to publicity crises. Also, many businesses hire *PR consultancies*— agencies that can work for a number of clients, planning and delivering messages to the press or reacting to incoming enquiries.

If you need help writing a good press release and placing the story then it is worth enlisting this professional help – you may not get any coverage without it.

PR consultancies vary in size from international groups employing thousands to single owner-operator PR professionals. You can also find specialists, who have expertise in industry sectors such as IT or healthcare. There are around 3,000 PR consultancies operating in the UK, so you'll need help narrowing down your search. If you're serious about hiring one, the Public Relations Consultants Association offers a free online service called PReview (www. prca.org.uk), which matches your needs with the member consultancies that most closely match them.

Creating a good story

To a journalist, a *good story* is anything that has enough public interest to attract readers, viewers, or listeners and hold their attention. A good story for a journalist covering the plastics industry must hold the attention of people in that industry.

We're sorry to say that most of what you want to communicate to your market doesn't fall into the category of a good story. For that reason, you need to develop your story (by collecting the right facts and quotes and writing them down clearly and well) to a level that may qualify as good editorial content. And when you think of good editorial content, think like a journalist would.

Stories to avoid

Journalists and editors do *not* want stories about any of the following:

- Your new product or service and how it differs from competitors or your previous models (unless that's their coverage speciality)

- Why you or your company's senior executive think your products are really great

- Your version of an *old story* – one that they've covered in the same way before

- Anything that seems boring or self-serving to anyone who doesn't work for your firm

Yet reporters often get those kinds of stories because the people handling PR generally aren't skilled journalists (and aren't even trying to think like skilled journalists). You have to give the reporters what they want. Sniff out a story, put together sufficient information to back it up , and script a version of it that reporters in your target medium can realistically work with.

Finding the hook

The *hook* is what it sounds like: The compelling bit of information that snags your reader's interest and draws him or her to the story.

Here's a simple exercise to help you understand how hooks work. Scan today's newspaper (whichever one you like to read) and rank the top five stories based on your interest in them. Now analyse each one in turn to identify the one thing that made that story interesting enough to hold your attention. The *hooks,* the things that made each story interesting to you, differ. But every story has a hook, and all hooks have certain elements in common:

- Hooks often give you new information (information you didn't know or weren't sure of).

- Hooks make that new information relevant to your activities or interests.

- Hooks catch your attention, often by surprising you with something you hadn't expected.

- Hooks promise some benefit to you – although the benefit may be indirect – by helping you understand your world better, avoid something undesirable, or simply enjoy yourself as you read the paper.

Combining the hook with your marketing message

You need to design hooks to make your marketing message into stories that appeal to journalists. And your hooks need to be just like the ones that attracted your attention to those newspaper stories, with one exception: *You need to somehow tie them to your marketing information.* You have to make sure that at least a thin line exists connecting the hook to your brand identity, the news that you've just introduced a new product, or whatever else you want the public to know. That way, when journalists use your hook in their own work, they end up including some of your marketing information in their stories as an almost accidental side effect.

Journalists don't want to help you communicate with your target market – but they'll happily use any good stories that you're willing to write for them, and if your product gets mentioned or you get quoted as a result, they don't have a problem giving you the reference. So the secret, the key, the essence of good publicity? Develop stories with effective hooks and give those stories to overworked journalists with empty pages to fill.

Communicating your story to the media: Press releases

The most basic format for communicating a news story is the press release. The trouble is that journalists don't like press releases. I know this because I am one (a journalist, that is). As editor of *Marketing* magazine I get hundreds of press releases e-mailed and posted to me every day. Most of them are rubbish, which is exactly where they end up. At the head of every magazine, covering every imaginable professional or consumer interest there is the equivalent of me – a stressed-out editor with the next deadline looming. So you should look on your challenge as getting past me, or at least the equivalent of me.

When I say that journalists don't like press releases, what I mean is that we don't like admitting to being influenced by them – a bit like consumers with advertising, really. Now I'm not going to single-handedly attempt to hold back the tide of press releases, but I am going to give you some insider advice about how to get on the right side of journalists by giving them what they need and not troubling them with what they do not.

A list of dos

Here is a list of ways that you can get a positive response from the journalists you call.

✔ **Do offer exclusives.** The best way to make a journalist feel better about a press release is to offer the news as an *exclusive* (but remember, it still has to be a relevant story). An exclusive means that the journalist you are dealing with gets the story before it appears anywhere else, the story gets a more prominent position in the newspaper or magazine, and the journalist scores points with their editor. Everybody's happy.

You, or your PR consultancy, need to get close to the journalists that are most relevant to your business – this usually means calling them with the story first to discuss it, and then sending the press release when they've shown an interest. Most companies do it the other way round, or worse, simply blanket e-mail to every journalist on their database.

✔ **Do make it relevant and timely.** Target the right media and contacts. The food critic doesn't need a release about a new robotics manufacturing facility. And the business correspondent doesn't either, if the facility opened two months ago, because now it's old news.

You should have read the paper or magazine and be familiar with its content before making contact with its journalists.

✔ **Do build up a list of media contacts.** You need to create an accurate database of journalists, with all contact details so you can get in touch with them quickly. E-mailing your release can be sensible because journalists work on tight deadlines, so include fields for fax and e-mail numbers in your database. Think about developing a list identifying authors of stories you like that may be similar to stories related to your business. Now you have a smaller list that's a much tighter match with your content and target audience. You can get commercial lists and information on journalists from PR directories and list-sellers.

✔ **Do think creatively.** Journalists need stories; you need some positive PR – so think up a story idea that serves both needs. A common but effective PR tactic is to carry out a piece of consumer research that's relevant to your business and let a newspaper publish the results – for example, a list of people's favourite films ever, if you run a DVD rental company.

Include something helpful, such as tips, rules or principles, that the media can quote. (A chiropractor's practice may send out a release that includes five ways to have a healthier back. A management consultant may offer five tips for avoiding cash-flow crises. A home inspection firm may offer five tips to avoid costly surprises when buying a home.)

✔ **Do offer yourself as an expert commentator on industry-related matters, in case they need a quote for another article.** A journalist may just include one sentence from you, but if they mention your company name, you just got some good publicity. For example, an article on how to shop for a used car in the Sunday magazine of a newspaper may quote the owner of a large car dealership as saying, 'If you don't have an independent mechanic evaluate a used car before buying it, I guarantee you will be in for some unpleasant surprises.' The article may also mention that this dealership's repair department does free evaluations for car buyers. The combination of a quote and a bit of information about the free service is going to attract many new customers, some of whom will become steady users of the dealership's repair service, and some of whom will become buyers of new or used cars from the dealership.

✔ **Do keep it brief.** Journalists are quick on the uptake and work fast, so let them call or e-mail if they need more information.

✔ **Do post your press releases on your Web site.** Even if you have given your story as an 'exclusive', your press releases can do double duty on the Web, providing information for both curious journalists to follow up and potential consumers.

✔ **Do send releases to every local editor in your area, no matter how small their publication or station.** You can get local coverage more easily than regional or national coverage, and that local coverage can be surprisingly helpful.

And a few don'ts

These dos must be balanced by a few helpful don'ts that will help your information stand out from the junk that flies into every journalist's inbox:

✔ **Don't make a nuisance of yourself.** One of the worst pieces of advice that is seemingly given to every aspiring PR practitioner is to make a follow-up call. If your media contacts database is accurate, the journalist will have received your press release: If it's a good story they'll use it; if not they won't. There is nothing you can do to change your press release after the event, so make sure that what you send is as carefully crafted as it can be.

✔ **Don't ask for clippings.** Journalists don't want to send you clippings of the articles they write, so don't bother asking. Nor do they care to discuss with you why they didn't run a story, or why they cut off part of a quote when they did run a story. They're busy with the next story. Forget about it. You should focus on the next story, too.

✔ **Don't make any errors.** Typos throw the facts into question. And don't include any inaccurate facts. You want the journalist to have trust in the information you're providing. Prove that you're worthy of that trust.

✔ **Don't give incomplete contact information.** Be sure that you include up-to-date names, addresses, and phone numbers. Let the contacts know when they should be available and what they should say so that the journalist finds them helpful and co-operative.

✔ **Don't ignore the journalists' research needs.** The more support you give them, the easier they can cover your story. You should include high-quality photographs of the expert you quote in a mailed release (include the date, name of person, and information about the supplier of the photo on the back or the margin of the photo). Also consider offering plant tours, interview times, sample products, or whatever else may help journalists cover your story.

✔ **Don't forget that journalists work on a faster clock than you do.** When a journalist calls about your release, return the call (or make sure that somebody returns it) in minutes or hours, not days. If you handle media requests slowly, a journalist will just find another source or write another story by the time you've returned the call.

Considering video and electronic releases

You can get a story out to the media in ways other than press releases. You can generate a video release, with useful footage that a television producer may decide to run as part of a news story. You can also put a written press release on the PR Newswire or any other such service that distributes hard copy or electronic releases to its media clients – for a fee to the source of the release, of course. You can also pitch your stories to the Associated Press and other newswires (but we recommend hiring a major PR firm before trying to contact a newswire).

Being interviewed for TV and radio

So now you've got a hook or a reputation for expertise within your sector, the requests for interviews will come flooding in. Okay, it's not usually that simple, you need to be prepared for when a broadcast interview does come your way. There are a few people who are naturally confident and gifted when speaking publicly or on radio or TV – these people are not normal! You're going to feel nervous the first time you're in an unusual interview situation – that's only natural. You can prepare yourself by getting professional media training, where you will be put into mock interviews in front of real cameras and microphones and put through your paces by professional journalists. Or you could simply follow these basic (and much cheaper) tips:

✔ **Give no more than three key messages.** If you are tempted to blurt out everything you know about your subject, your main messages will get lost and people will remember nothing. Prepare in advance what you want to say and then say it.

✔ **Know your audience.** Find out as much as you can about the interview, the programme, and its audience. Is it live or pre-recorded? Light-hearted chat or serious comment? For business experts or housewives?

✔ **Be positive.** State your main messages in positive terms, and provide examples rather than go on the defensive. Whatever you do, don't say 'no comment' – the interviewer and audience will assume you've got something to hide. Watch how politicians manage this one when they're being interviewed. They repeat their key message and studiously ignore the question.

✔ **What not to wear.** Avoid patterns when on TV, as the cameras sometimes can't cope and viewers get a disturbing strobe effect. That means small checks and herringbone are out, but you should also avoid bold patterns as they will detract attention from what you are trying to say. Keep it simple and light – dark clothes can drain colour from your face.

✔ **Speak like a normal human being.** After all, normal people are watching or listening, so it pays to think about what they may or may not know about the subject and tailor your message to them. Imagine you're speaking to someone who is bright, but knows nothing about the topic. Don't patronise, but definitely don't overwhelm them with jargon and abbreviations.

Making the Most of Word of Mouth

Word of mouth (WOM) gives a consumer (or a marketer) the most credible source of information about products, aside from actual personal experience with those products. What consumers tell each other about your products has a huge impact on your efforts to recruit new customers. Word of mouth also has a secondary, but still significant, impact on your efforts to retain old customers.

If you survey customers to identify the source of positive attitudes toward new products, you generally find that answers like 'my friend told me about it' outnumber answers like 'I saw an ad' by ten to one. Word-of-mouth communications about your product don't actually outnumber advertising messages; but when customers talk, other customers listen.

How can you control what people say about your product? You can't very effectively encourage customers to say nice things about and prevent them from criticising your product – many marketers assume that no one can do it. But you can influence word of mouth, and you have to try. The most obvious way to influence word of mouth is to make your product special. A product that surprises people because of its unexpectedly good quality or service is special enough to talk about. A good product or a well-delivered service wins fans and turns your customers into your sales force. Other tactics for managing WOM about your business or product may not be so obvious. Fortunately, we discuss them in the following sections.

Do good deeds

If no aspect of your product itself is particularly wonderful or surprising, do some attention-grabbing activity and associate that with your product. Here are some strategies that have worked well in the past to generate positive publicity and word of mouth:

- ✔ Get involved with a charity or not-for-profit organisation that operates in your area (see Chapter 13).
- ✔ Stage a fun event for kids.
- ✔ Let your employees take short sabbaticals to volunteer in community services.

Get creative. You can think of something worthwhile, some way of helping improve your world that surprises people and makes them take notice of the good you're doing in the name of your product.

Spice up your sales promotions

A 20p-off coupon isn't worth talking about. But a competition in which the winners get to spend a day with the celebrity of their choice can get consumers excited – and can be cheaper, too. A premium like this generates positive PR and a lot of WOM. We cover this area more in the next chapter.

You can use special offers and competitions to get people to recommend a friend. BSkyB offered a special price for satellite TV installation if you did it with another household, and made this a feature of their TV advertising. The Web site Interactive Investor regularly runs competitions that require you to provide friends' e-mail addresses in order to enter. You're not going to do that unless you rate the product highly enough to pass on friends' details – so the competition just provides the motivation to do it. You see, you can influence word of mouth.

Identify and cultivate decision influencers

In many markets, some people's opinions matter a lot more than others. These people are *decision influencers,* and if you (hypothetically) trace back the flow of opinions in your industry, you may find that many of them originate with these people. In business-to-business marketing, the decision influencers are often obvious. A handful of prominent executives, a few editors working for trade magazines, and some of the staff at trade associations probably exert a strong influence over everybody else's opinions. You can find identifiable decision influencers in consumer markets, as well. In the market for football equipment, youth-team coaches, league managers, and the owners of independent sporting goods shops are important decision influencers.

To take advantage of decision influencers, develop a list of who falls into that category for your product or service and then make a plan for cultivating them. Match these people with appropriate managers or salespeople who can take them to events or out to lunch, just for fun. You just need to make sure that people associated with your business are in the personal networks of these decision influencers. Consider developing a series of giveaways and mailshots to send to these decision influencers. If we wanted to sell a football boot to youth players, we'd send free samples of a new cleat to youth coaches. When you know who's talking and who's listening, you can easily focus your efforts on influencing the talkers.

Seize control of the Internet

Okay, you can't actually take over the Internet, but you should be aware of what people are saying about your product or service on the Web. Weblogs, or blogs as they are commonly known, are one of the latest phenomena of the Internet age. What are blogs? The term *blogs* refers to personal Web publishing based on a topic or topics that attract a like-minded community of online participants. In other words, blogging is word of mouth on the Web. There are blogs dedicated to pretty much every subject you can imagine, from cars to politics to chocolate bars. You need to know this because there are two key ways you can use blogs to your advantage:

- **Get in on the discussion.** If there is a Web site dedicated to your market, then try to get your product mentioned or even establish a link between your site and the Weblog (blogs make extensive use of links to other sites). A recent survey among more than 600 blog publishers found that two-thirds would be happy to consider a direct public relations approach. The camera manufacturer Olympus uses blogs to market its new products, passing details to relevant blogs in order to generate interest among the camera-buying public ahead of the product being launched.

- **Create your own Weblog.** Blogs are cheap and easy to set up, which is why they are blossoming on the Web. You can download blog software for free from many sites such as `www.myblogsite.com`, and start publishing within the day. You can use this to promote your products and services and elicit feedback (bad as well as good) from potential customers. The computer games manufacturer Sports Interactive, which created the popular Championship Manager game, used this strategy to get feedback and make changes and additions before the game launched – publicity and customer research rolled into one.

Not all blogs or their users are business friendly, and you should remember this when making approaches or setting up you own blog. Blogs are run by enthusiasts and are usually independent of any corporate ties: That's the point, as well as the appeal of them. Many businesses have been hit by Web users criticising their products and services. That's the kind of word of mouth you don't want. Legally speaking, the Weblog publisher can be held responsible for libellous information but in reality there isn't much you can do about it – except improve your product!

Chapter 13

Face-to-Face Marketing

*I*n this chapter, we use the term *face-to-face marketing* to describe the way your business can have a personal impact on individuals and groups. Of course, you want that impact to lead to a sale, but the effect is not usually that immediate or direct, which is why there is an important distinction between face-to-face marketing and selling. When you set up a stand and display your wares at an exhibition, this is face-to-face marketing. Many potential buyers walk past that stand, and some will come in to examine and ask questions. That is a powerful opportunity to do good marketing. Face-to-face marketing has a personal, warm, human element to it that gives it special marketing leverage. We should say, however, that sometimes a special event may be a bit less personal than this – perhaps you sponsor a local football team, for example, in which case the individuals who play, and their families and fans, do certainly have a high level of involvement – but probably not with you or other representatives of your company. Still, that human contact and sense of bringing people together in some sort of community makes a sports team sponsorship especially effective, so I think it is fair to consider it a form of face-to-face marketing, too.

Face-to-face marketing serves many purposes, and it can take a number of forms. You can sponsor someone else's event or stage your own. You can buy exhibitor space in a trade show – a special kind of face-to-face marketing designed to put you in front of a lot of prospects in a hurry. And with the Web at your command, you can connect people with virtual face-to-face marketing that you don't need to spend a great deal of money on to integrate it into your marketing routine.

Whatever the exact nature of the face-to-face marketing, it gives you a temporary way to make a special connection with prospects and customers, putting you face to face with large numbers of customers or prospects. We recommend every marketer consider face-to-face marketing and every marketing plan have a section devoted to it. In this chapter, we show you how to bottle up the face-to-face marketing magic and put it to work in your marketing campaign.

Harnessing the Power of Face-to-Face Marketing

Face-to-face marketing has to have considerable drawing power. Think of it as theatre – a performance that entertains or stimulates people in a satisfying way (and sometimes includes people as participants, not just as an audience). At an exhibition or trade show, you may need to add interactive activities to your stand or invite a team of massage therapists to do their thing at specified hours to attract your target audience. In a store, appealing to your audience can mean bringing in an expert to give a weekend workshop. For a consulting firm, it may mean offering a special one-hour seminar led by your directors, accessible to all clients and prospects over the Web.

Face-to-face marketing is a great example of the real-world marketing principle that you should give away as much as you can. In the competition for consumers' attention, you often have to give them an interesting performance to win that attention. Here are more ideas for face-to-face marketing that you may want to promote:

- ✔ A client-appreciation event (what used to be called a party)

- ✔ A musical performance

- ✔ A weekend at a golf resort for your top customers, along with prizes for the winning golfers – and everyone else, too

- ✔ A fundraising dinner for an important charity

- ✔ A community event, like a fair or children's workshop

- ✔ An exhibit or hospitality suite at a major trade show for people in your industry

- ✔ A workshop in which you share your expertise or solve problems for participants

The possibilities are endless and varied. But they all attract people and hold their attention. And you need that attention to communicate and persuade as a marketer.

Planning it yourself or piggybacking

You have a great deal of choice – not only over the type of face-to-face opportunity you can participate in, but also over the level and nature of your participation. At the highest level of commitment, you can plan and manage your own events. Depending on the scale of the event, that process can be costly and difficult, but sometimes it's the best solution – especially if you want to have enough control to keep any other marketers from using the audience attention that the event generates. But you may also choose an event that others are organising and sign on as a sponsor. That's easier, and often cheaper, but may be less powerful in terms of marketing impact.

Automaker Volvo has a separate company, Volvo Event Management, which has been working to build excitement for several years in advance of the November 5, 2005, start date for a major event – the Volvo Ocean Race. Beginning in Spain, contestants from dozens of countries will sail around the world with close media coverage the entire way. It is to be the biggest event in sailing in the 2005–2006 season and a major source of media coverage for Volvo. But the coverage started years earlier with a major Web site tracking the progress of the sailing teams as they designed and built special boats for the race, and marketing of subscriptions for the Volvo Ocean Race Magazine. This example shows you event sponsorship on a large, exciting scale.

Then there's the Gill Abersoch Dinghy Week, organised by the South Caernarvonshire Yacht Club. It may not have the glamour of the Volvo Ocean Race but this regatta is one of the largest and most popular dinghy races in the UK – and that works just perfectly for the new title sponsor, Gill. The company makes specialist outdoor clothing for marine (and bicycle) enthusiasts, so this regatta is an ideal event for Gill to piggyback. The experts call this excellent *brand fit*, which simply means that Gill gets its name plastered all over an event where every single participant is a possible current or future customer. Gill is also leveraging that sponsorship by adding a prize draw for all regatta entrants to win a £3,200 sailing dinghy – quite a difference from the Volvo Ocean Race total prize fund of £35 million!

Business and industry opportunities

Turn first to your professional groups and industry trade associations for appropriate business-to-business marketing. These venues differ for each industry but have the benefit of collecting your prospective customers in one place in common. Attend conferences and trade shows if your budget is small and do plenty of informal networking. If you can afford to, also rent display space at trade shows, present at conferences, and sponsor industry events. The more visible you are at your own industry events, the more customer attention and credibility you can generate.

Trade shows are great because they draw people who are wearing their business hats, ready to make purchase decisions for their companies. You can also put on special events for your own customers or employees. (In fact, employee events often provide that extra motivating power that you need to get your people fully behind your marketing plan.)

Whatever the business-orientated opportunity, remember that you're still trying to attract and hold the attention of people, not businesses. You're interested in the people in any business who make the purchase decisions.

Getting stuffy and businesslike is very easy, but do people really want to sit through two days of lectures on the impact of new technologies in their industry? You're better off offering them optional, one-hour panel discussions on the topic, with a backbone of outdoor sports and recreation events or a visit to a nearby golf course.

Sponsoring a Special Event

Some people assume that special events are only useful in special circumstances, when you can justify a major effort and expense. Not so. Staging small-scale events or (as I discuss in this section) riding on the coattails of somebody else's event can work, too. (I also think of this as piggybacking on others' investments in events, a helpful term in visualising the benefits.)

Why create your own event when so many wonderful events already exist? Many companies that sponsor events as a way to expose their names to desirable audiences think that way, at least. But please make sure you get a clear, detailed agreement in writing about where, how, and how often the event identifies your brand name. That identification is the return on your sponsorship investment. Too often, sponsors end up complaining that they didn't get as much good exposure as they expected, so make sure you and the event directors understand the exposure level, up front.

You can find local organisations by following the events notices in local papers and on local radio stations. A number of Web-based companies now help you locate possible events to sponsor. For example, check out www.sportsmatch.co.uk or www.uksponsorship.com for hundreds of possibilities in everything from sports to the arts. You can find an exciting new event sponsorship out there that fits your budget and customers.

Finding cause-related events

You can attract a lot of positive attention from the media and the community by sponsoring a fundraising event for a charity. This event sponsorship is, for obvious reasons, called *cause-related event sponsorship.* You can generate extremely valuable goodwill by cause sponsorship – at least, if the cause and event are appropriate to your target market.

However, too much of this money is thrown away on events that appeal to somebody at the sponsoring company but don't appeal to its customers. Be careful to pick causes that appeal not only to you and your associates, but also to your target customers. Maybe your CEO really gets excited about raising money for Red Nose Day. But have you checked with your customers to see what charities they're excited about? The biggest and best known events aren't always the most effective for your business – try looking for something smaller and more local. Your customers may be more impressed if you raise a small amount for a local initiative than they are about a lot raised for a high-profile national or international charity.

Donations to controversial causes or to political campaigns are likely to offend people. Stay away from anything controversial. Causes having to do with health, children, preventing diseases and drug abuse, helping animals, and conserving the natural world generally pass the controversy test – unless the particular organisation takes an overly controversial approach.

If you don't have the marketing budget to sponsor a local charity, consider donating your time, instead. You can join the board of a charity and offer your energy and business savvy.

Be careful to examine the charity's books and tax-exempt status before sponsoring it or running an event to benefit it. Make sure it has full charitable status (you can check registered charities with the Charity Commission, at www.charitycommission.gov.uk) and that its audited financial statements show it has relatively low overhead and moderate-looking executive salaries. You don't want to support a charity that turns out to be poorly or dishonestly run. Some charities are more effective and well run than others and you never really know until you look. Their records and financials should be available for public inspection, so all you have to do is ask. If an organisation hesitates to share this information, don't get involved with it.

Running the numbers on an event

Be careful to pick a cause-related event or other event that reaches your target customers efficiently. Like any marketing communication, an event sponsorship needs to deliver reach at a reasonable cost. So ask yourself how many people will come to the event or hear of your sponsorship of it. Then ask yourself what percentage of this total is likely to be in your target market. That's your *reach.* Divide your cost by this figure, multiply it by 1,000, and you have the cost of your reach per thousand. You can compare this cost with cost figures for other kinds of reach, such as a direct mailing or a print or radio ad.

If you think the event sponsorship is more credible and convincing than an ad because of its affiliation with an appealing cause, you can adjust your cost figure to compensate. Doing so is called *weighting the exposure*. For example, say you decide one exposure to your company or brand through a cause sponsorship is twice as powerful as exposure to one of your ads. Then multiply the number of people the event reaches by 2 before calculating the cost. That way, you compare the cost of reaching 2,000 people through the sponsorship to the cost of reaching 1,000 people through advertising, which adjusts for the greater value you attach to the cause-related exposure.

In my experience, the right special event is often many times more effective than an advertisement. But the event has to be appropriate or it's worthless – so keep reading. And make sure you publicise the event well.

Evaluating the options for sponsorship

If you're considering event sponsorship, you're in good company. The total amount spent on sponsorship in the UK in 2004 was £861.5 million, according to the media agency Carat. Nearly half of that is spent on sponsorship of sports teams or sporting events (£411 million), while the next biggest chunk of investment (£165 million) was for arts events or tailor-made events for companies – such as Nike's Run London event. Sponsorship of TV and radio programmes and cinema accounted for over £220 million, and we cover this area of sponsorship in greater detail in Chapter 9.

If you take these numbers at face value, sporting events are the best place to spend your money, and the arts should get the smallest amount of your sponsorship money. That may be true – but I seriously doubt it. Why? Because these are just the totals, and what's right for your particular firm may be very different. If your product, service, or customer base is related to the arts, or if you happen to be particularly involved in the arts, you may want to ignore sports events and sponsor the arts exclusively. This is an example of letting your own particular interests and talents focus how you market.

To decide what is best for you, use the three-step selection process discussed in the three following sections.

By the way, as we go on to examine other forms of events, you find that the same three-step process is useful there, too. That's because you need to design all events through careful examination of your options, by running the numbers, and by screening for relevance.

Step 1: Explore the options

You can find sponsorship opportunities all over the place, so you owe it to yourself to take time to explore all the available options – and, as you would with any other aspect of your marketing, employ a little creativity. Web sites such as www.sportsmatch.co.uk can easily put you in touch with teams and events looking for business backing, or you could visit Business in the Community's site at www.bitc.org.uk for examples of what other companies are doing with charities in their local areas. Both these routes will give you ideas about what's available and achievable, but what about trying something new? Call organisations that seem like a good match with your product and customer to see if they put on appropriate events and would consider having them sponsored.

Step 2: Run the numbers

Carefully analyse the marketing impact of each candidate for sponsorship. Cut any from your list if their audiences aren't a good match with your target market. Cut any that may be controversial and likely to generate negative as well as positive attitudes. Cut any that do not seem to have strong positive images – no point sponsoring something unless your customers feel passionate about it! Now compare what's left by calculating your cost per thousand exposures for each one.

And don't be afraid to negotiate. If a sponsorship opportunity appeals to you but is priced too high, show them your comparative numbers and ask if they can cut you a deal!

This process may lead you away from the most popular types of sponsorship. A big, popular event (like a World Cup football match) certainly exposes you to a lot of people – millions, if it is televised. But how many are really in your target market? And what is the cost of reaching them this way? Big sports and entertainment events often charge a premium because of their popularity and size. But they aren't worth that premium if you can buy similar reach for less by sponsoring several smaller events.

Step 3: Screen for relevance

Relevance is how closely the event relates to your product and its usage by customers, and it is the most important, but least considered, factor. Let me give you an example to illustrate the importance of relevance.

Here is an example of a simple, highly relevant, very successful sponsorship – and with added humour! A few years ago the world football body FIFA lifted the sponsorship ban on referees, suddenly and unusually opening up a new sponsorship 'space' in a high-profile sport – but who would be first to take it? Step forward the optical retailer Specsavers, which has been sponsoring match officials in the Scottish Football League for the past few years. The relevance, and comedy factor, of having an optical retailer sponsoring football referees is obvious but inspired. Specsavers gained high-value media coverage (especially after offering free eye tests to referees after some controversial decisions) and sales went up significantly – and all because the company had the 'vision' to sign a highly relevant sponsorship deal.

Putting on a Public Event

Sometimes, you have no alternative but to stage the event yourself. None of the sponsorship options fit your requirements. Or you really need the exclusivity of your own event – a forum in which no competitors' messages can interfere with your own.

More and more companies are putting on their own events so they can tailor them to their own products and customers. In the UK the energy drink Red Bull runs a series of branded events, from the Flugtag, where amateur 'pilots' attempt to launch home-made flying machines (the drinks ads end with the line 'Red Bull gives you wings') to 'The Art of Can', a competition for customers to make sculptures out of the product's packaging.

Selling sponsorship rights

A good way to make your event pay for itself is to find other companies that want to help sponsor the event. Not your competitors, of course. Many companies often have an interest in the same event as you do, but for different reasons, and these firms make good co-sponsors. Basically, if the event is relevant, novel, and is likely to draw in their target audience, then you have a good pitch. Now you just need to go out and make sales calls on potential sponsors. Or consider hiring an event management firm that can sell sponsorships as well as help to organise and run events.

Getting help managing your event

Some people specialise in managing special events; they work on a consulting basis, from conception through completion, to make sure that everyone comes and everything goes just right. Many such specialists exist, from independent experts to major companies, like those listed in the following bullets. We recommend bringing in a specialist of some sort to help you design and manage any event that involves a lot of people, shows, speeches or activities, meals, conference and hotel room reservations, security, transportation, and all those sorts of details that you have to get right in order to avoid disaster.

You can find event management companies through the Association of Exhibition Organisers (AEO) at www.aeo.org.uk. The AEO has a listing of all suppliers to trade and consumer exhibitions through its sister associations the Association of Exhibition Contractors and the Association of Exhibition Venues.

Exhibiting at Trade Shows and Exhibitions

Do you need to exhibit at trade shows? If you're in a business-to-business selling situation, I assume that you do. Exhibiting is almost always necessary, even if you only do so to keep competitors from stealing your customers at the show! Business-to-business marketers in Europe devote a quarter of their marketing budgets, on average, to trade shows (these figures are from a study in the *Journal of Marketing*). Date?

Other sources suggest that trade shows generate 18 per cent of all sales leads, on average. As a way to control your own trade show spending, why not compare per cent of budget and per cent of leads, adjusting the per cent of budget figure until you find the spending level that yields the best return in leads? If you spend 20 per cent of your budget on trade shows, you want to try to beat the average and get more than 20 per cent of your leads from these shows. That means being a savvy event manager – selecting appropriate shows and staging excellent booths at them.

Some retail or consumer industries also have major shows. Boat manufacturers use boat shows as an important way to expose consumers to their products. County fairs attract exhibitors of arts and crafts, gourmet foods, and gardening supplies. Computer shows showcase new equipment. If your industry has a major show for the public, we highly recommend that you try to exhibit there. Send your in-house list of customers and friends an invitation, too – the more traffic you can get to your stand, the better. (In fact, you should plan to begin direct marketing to announce the event and give people incentives to come, starting at least two months before the show!)

Knowing what trade shows can accomplish for you

You can generate leads, find new customers, and maintain or improve your current customers' perceptions of you at trade shows. You can also use trade shows to introduce a new product or launch a new strategy. And they give you great opportunities to introduce back-office people (like the sales support staff or even the chairman!) to your customers face to face.

Use trade shows to network in your industry. You usually find the best manufacturers' representatives and salespeople by making connections at trade shows. And if you're secretly hoping to find a better employer, a little mingling may yield an offer at the next big trade show. Also, be sure to talk with a lot of attendees and non-competitive exhibitors in order to find out about the newest trends and what your competitors are doing in the market. The information a good networker gleans from a trade show is often worth more than the price of attendance. Never mind selling – get out there and chat.

In short, you should see trade shows as essential to your marketing campaign for many reasons. Even if you think you may lose money on the project, a trade show can be worthwhile in the long run. And a well-designed exhibit, well promoted in advance and staffed with people who are prepared to find leads and close sales, usually produces an almost immediate return on investment.

Building the foundations for a good stand

Marketers focus on the stand when they think about how to handle a trade show. But you should consider the stand just a part of your overall marketing strategy for the show. And you don't have a show strategy until you've written something intelligent down to answer each of these questions:

- ✔ How do we attract the right people to the show and to our stand?
- ✔ What do we want visitors to our stand to do at the show and in our stand?
- ✔ How can we communicate with and motivate visitors when they get to the stand?
- ✔ How can we figure out who visitors are and how to handle them in the stand?
- ✔ How can we capture information about them, their interests, and needs?
- ✔ How can we follow up to build or maintain our relationship with them?

The strategy has to start by attracting a lot of prospects and customers, and the easiest way to do so is to just go with the flow by picking a show that potential customers already plan to attend. Ask yourself what shows your customers are going to attend. For example, if you import gift items and your customers include the buyers from retail gift stores, then where do they go to make their purchases? Can you cover enough of the market by exhibiting at one of the Top Drawer shows or do you need to specialise, by going to The Baby Show, for example? You can ask the sponsoring organisations for data on who attended last year's show and who has registered for this year's show, using this information to help you decide. You need to see high numbers of your target customers. Otherwise, the show wastes your company's time and money.

You can also ask a sampling of customers for their opinions about your stand. You may want to use the simplest research method, which researchers call informal *qualitative interviews* – what real people refer to as conversations. Just talk to some customers, preferably at the show because their memory of your stand is still clear. See what they think. Or you can do some *intercept interviews* at the show. You conduct an *intercept interview* when you walk up to people as they pass by your stand and ask them if they will answer a few questions, such as "Do you like the such-and-such stand?" and "How exciting is this stand's design?"

Attractive company seeks compatible trade show for romantic weekend

How do you find out about possible trade shows? I thought you'd never ask! If you subscribe to trade magazines, the shows in your industry find you because the magazines sell their lists to the show sponsors. But don't go just by what gets sent to you because you may overlook something important. The Department of Trade and Industry backed organisation Trade Fairs & Exhibitions UK has a full free listing of shows coming up in the next two years, which you can search by category. You can find the site at www. exhibitions.co.uk. For international listings, try www.eventseye. com or www.exhibitions.com.

You do have another source, one that we find much more reliable than any other – your customers. The whole point of exhibiting at a trade show is to reach customers, so why don't you just ask them where you should exhibit? Call or drop by a selection of your best customers and ask them for advice on where and when to exhibit. They know what's hot right now and what's not.

Renting the perfect stand

You need to select a location and stand size. You want to aim for anywhere near a major entrance, the food stands, bathrooms, or any other place that concentrates people. Being on the end of an aisle can help you, too. And bigger is better – in general, you should get the biggest stand you can afford.

But even if you end up with a miniature booth in the middle of an aisle, don't despair. Many shoppers try to walk all the aisles of a show, and these locations can work, too, provided the show draws enough of the right kind of customers for you. In fact, smart buyers often look at the smallest, cheapest booths in the hope of discovering something hot and new from a struggling entrepreneurial supplier.

Setting up other kinds of displays

The firms that make trade show stands also can help with many other kinds of displays, such as lobby, conference room, and tabletop displays. These smaller-scale displays can be effective in the right spot and often cost you less than a trade show booth, so explore all the options before you decide what fits your marketing campaign and budget best.

Experts can help you design and build your stand or other display, manage the trade show activity, and handle the sales leads that result from it – consult business directories at a library or search the Internet for leads, starting with the members list at the Association of Exhibition Organisers (www.aeo.org.uk).

We recommend getting opinions and quotes from multiple vendors (and asking for credit references and the contact names of some recent clients) before choosing the right company for your job. We also recommend sharing your budget constraints upfront to find out if the company you're talking to is appropriate for you. Some can do very economical, small-scale projects with ease, and others are more orientated to large-scale corporate accounts.

Don't overlook the drawing power of simple things, like fresh flowers or food. A simple gesture like this can be remarkably effective at drawing traffic to your stand and putting visitors in a positive mood! Alternatively, try using comfort as your draw by setting up some comfortable sofas in the stand. People are on their feet for hours at these shows, so they appreciate a chance to rest – and of course, if someone sits there too long, you can launch into your hard sell and either win an order or politely drive them from the stand to open the seat to someone else. A massage chair or bottles of cold spring water can also draw weary visitors to your booth.

Doing Demonstrations

Seeing is believing. This old saying contains wisdom, and if you think a demonstration is applicable to your goods or services, you should definitely consider giving one. Demonstrations are often the most effective ways of introducing a new product, or even introducing an old product to new customers. This area of marketing falls under what the experts call *field marketing* or, even worse, *experiential marketing*. To you and me this means getting your product in front of the people that might buy it, and giving them a reason to do just that.

You can do a demonstration anywhere. Really. Even when you sponsor someone else's event, if you ask early on, they can often find a time and place for you to stage a demonstration. And when you control the event or a part of it, you have considerable freedom to design demonstrations. Let me show you some specifics.

In a retail store, mall, or other consumer-orientated location, a demonstration is often the most persuasive form of promotion. You can see run of the mill *sampling* take place at supermarkets nearly everyday – often a bored member of staff handing out bite-size pieces of cheese or a thimble full of wine from a temporary table. Give me a break. A proper retail demo should be:

- **Realistic!** Show the product in a natural use context – and that includes normal portions of foods. (*Natural use* means how the customer would normally use it. If you eat a food product for dinner, find a way to demonstrate it on a table with real place settings, for example.)

- **Wonderful!** The event should be worthy of attention, with real entertainment value that adds excitement to the product. Try a cooking demonstration with a lot of action, not just a one-bite taste. Or make the demonstration a taste test in which the product wins a contest and the tasters get the prizes. Imagine you're creating a skit for a television show – that's the sort of entertainment people pay attention to.

- **A marketing priority!** Here's your chance to sell your product directly to customers. Think of a political candidate going out to shake hands (notice the candidate always wears his or her best suit and biggest smile). Too often, companies put poorly qualified temps in charge of demos. Who do you really want out there selling your product – someone who makes the product look good or someone you wouldn't dare talk to if you sat next to him on the subway?

When you follow these three rules, you create great demos. But note that these demonstrations are more expensive than the lame ones we usually encounter. That's okay because they're more effective. Use them more sparingly, but put more into each one, and they can reward you with a surprisingly high level of customer enthusiasm.

Giving Gifts

Premium items, promotional items, incentives – however the industry refers to them, these are simply gifts you give to your customers, clients, prospects, or employees. Not bribes; gifts. We recommend that you send your regular customers some kind of premium they will appreciate at least once a year. Another approach is to distribute them in ways that spread the good word about your firm or product, making the premiums, and those who receive them, your ambassadors. A privately owned stationery and office supply store I know does this by offering free pens at its register. The pens are not fancy, but they work well and look nice, and they have the store's name, address, and phone number on them. Thousands of these pens are floating around homes and offices in their market area, helping to keep their store as visible as the new Ryman they must compete with.

Giving out a free pen at the register is as simple as putting a FREE PENS sign on a container, but when choosing a gift for your good customers, put more care into the selection and presentation of the premium to make sure it is appreciated. Think of gift giving as a form of theatre, as a special option among special events, and you can avoid the standard stupidities. You may even gain customer attention and goodwill.

A sister title to *Marketing*, which I edit, is called *Promotions & Incentives* and it does exactly what it says on the cover – identifying new promotional items and why and when they should be given. It's a bible if you can't think beyond pens (although it's got some good leads on those, too). Recent features on what's hot in branded promotional items identified:

- ✓ Solar Power rechargers for mobile phones or PDAs. £28.85 for 1,500, available from www.solio.com.

- ✓ Bath petals, confetti or mint bath leaves in branded packs. £4.40 per 45g tub (minimum 12); £1.25 per single sachet (minimum 24), from The Sourcing Team (www.sourcing.co.uk).

- ✓ Pocket or keyring roulette wheels. £6.50 each (pocket, minimum 500) or £3.95 each (keyring, minimum 500), from Silver Direct (www.silver-direct.co.uk)

- ✓ Pocket-sized WiFi reception finder. £14.50 each (minimum 50) from Insight Promotions (www.insight-promotions.com).

- ✓ The Computer Brushman branded keyboard cleaner, sits on top of your customer's computer monitor. 55p each (minimum 500) from Non-Stop Promotions (www.non-stoppromotions.co.uk)

Note that trade show stands usually give away some premium items, and you want to think about what you can give away if you exhibit at a convention or trade show. I recommend that you give a fun or interesting gift (a puzzle, joke book, or toy, for example) as a token of appreciation for filling in a registration form. You want to focus your marketing resources on finding and qualifying leads, so focus everything you do, from advance mailings and e-mailings to booth design and signs, on this goal. Giving everyone who wanders by your booth a gift is silly, and it requires such a large volume of gifts that you can't afford something nice. But there are exceptions to this rule. Free bottles of cold spring water or other draws can be offered to all as a way to attract people to your stand. Then add a more durable premium gift as a thank-you when you give out brochures and collect information from serious leads.

If you're selecting premium items for a trade show or other event to which people travel for long distances, stick with easy-to-carry items. Keep gifts small, durable, and suitable for airport security, and also make an effort to keep your marketing materials (brochures, for example) compact and durable enough that they won't be left in the hotel room or ruined in some-one's luggage.

As with all face-to-face marketing opportunities, you want to make a positive impact that customers remember down the road, so choose your gifts with this end in mind.

Part V
Connecting With Your Customers

"A great advertising gimmick, George, but who's going to see it up here on top of Everest?"

In this part . . .

*I*f you can design a great product, give it an appropriate brand name, package it well,, and then turn it over to a good salesperson, you may be able to dispense with everything else discussed in this book. The combination of an appealing product or brand, plus good sales and service, can make a business successful, all on its own. And so it seems fitting to devote an entire part to these topics.

We have an interesting story to illustrate this. A consultant was hired to consult to the chief executive of a speciality chemicals company. They wanted him to evaluate the overall business plan and suggest ways of making the business grow. After poking around the premises for a few hours and interviewing a bunch of the people, he discovered a startling thing: They apparently did no marketing at all. They had no marketing department, and the company had no brochures, no ads, no publicity, and no Web site. So, how had they gotten this far, and where in the world did their customers come from?

In this part, we explain the secrets of companies like this one. We show you how to maximize the impact of your product and its packaging, tell you how to price your products and services, keep you from underselling yourself by making common mistakes associated with distribution and pricing, and help you approach sales and service like an old pro.

Chapter 14

Branding, Managing, and Packaging a Product

. . . .

In This Chapter

▶ Designing and developing hot new products

▶ Fitting your products into product lines

▶ Finding the right name

▶ Creating strong identities under trademark law

▶ Packaging and labelling to boost sales

▶ Knowing when and how to improve or eliminate a product

. . . .

*T*he product is the heart and soul of any marketing plan. If the product is good – if the target customer is really pleased with it – then that marketing plan has a decent chance of success. But if the product is not good, or nothing special in the customer's eyes, then no marketing plan can make that product a winner in the long run – we call it the lipstick on the gorilla effect. Many people in the field of marketing, and in business in general, don't understand this point. These people underestimate their customers and overestimate the persuasive power of marketing. Something of real value has to be at the core of any marketing plan. The product needs to have some notable advantages from the consumer's perspective.

This chapter shows you how to develop winning products, how to manage them as part of a product line, and how to select your products' names to amplify their natural strengths and communicate those strengths to the target customer.

We use 'product' as an umbrella term that means a product, a service, or anything else your company wants to sell.

Finding Simple Ways to Leverage Your Product

One of the first and most important things you can do is take small steps to keep a product fresh and vital and to boost its visibility and appeal. Product management is a lot like gardening. You occasionally plant a whole new crop, and you tend the existing plants routinely, too.

Here's a list of simple and quick things you can do to build customer loyalty and grow sales by working on your product:

- ✔ **Update the appearance.** Many companies present good products to the world in poorly designed exteriors that don't dress those products for success. Look at the product itself (colours, attractiveness, and visibility of brand names). Apple's iPod isn't the most technically advanced MP3 player on the market, but it outsells all its competitors because it has a distinct and desirable design.

- ✔ **Update the packaging.** A consumer product that sits on a shelf waiting for someone to pick it up should be highly visible and appealing (remember, in-store buying decisions are made in seconds, or less). Can you add a brighter colour to the packaging to attract the eye? Can you mention key features on the outside? Or maybe you can add a clear window to show the actual product.

- ✔ **Make sure the product is attractive and easy to use.** Your product should also feel nice – smooth, polished, soft, or whatever texture is appropriate to the product's use. Even very minor changes in its look, feel, and function can improve customer satisfaction and product appeal.

- ✔ **Improve any printed materials that come with the product.** Can you improve their appearance? Dress them up? Make them clearer or more useful? Make sure they instill pride of ownership in the product.

- ✔ **Choose your product's best quality.** Coin a short phrase to communicate this best quality to the consumer and put that phrase on the product, its packaging, and its literature in prominent places. Have simple (but attractive) colour-printed stickers made up for this purpose – that's the quickest and cheapest way to add a marketing message.

- ✔ **Eliminate confusion about which product does what for whom.** Clarify the differences and uses of your products if you have more than one, by pricing and naming them distinctly (to make them obviously different). You'd be amazed how confusing most product lines look to the average buyer.

✔ **Make your logo beautiful.** Apple Computer switched from a somewhat dated-looking rainbow-coloured version of their distinctive apple-shaped logo to a beautiful, sophisticated version made of a clear plastic panel backlit with diffused white light. This logo sits on the top of all their newer laptops, giving those computers a more sophisticated appeal. Can you upgrade your image by improving the appearance of your logo on your products?

✔ **Pick up a related but non-competing product from another company and repackage and distribute it as part of your product line.** Adding another good product your customers like can increase the average purchase size significantly. And we recommend that you use distributor-style arrangements that eliminate the investment of product development, giving you a good way to expand your product line in a hurry, if you want to. Selling a new (or new to you) product to an existing customer is often easier than finding a new customer for an existing product.

We hope this list of simple ideas for action has your marketing blood circulating! You can do a lot with and for your products, even if you don't have the cash or time right now to develop and introduce an entirely new product.

You're only as good as your products, so try to update, upgrade, or perhaps even replace your current line of products. It's a long-term but vital activity that most marketing plans need to include, just as gardeners have to remember to plan the next planting along with their more routine weeding and watering duties.

Identifying When and How to Introduce a New Product

We wish we could say that you don't need to worry about new product development very often. But if your market is like most, innovations give you a major source of competitive advantage. A competitor's major new product introduction probably changes the face of your market – and upsets your sales projections and profit margins – at least once every few years. So you can't afford to ignore new product development. Ever. You should, therefore, introduce new products as often as you can afford to develop them.

One product strategy or multiple strategies?

One market or more? How you answer this question determines whether you need to have one product line and one strategy or multiple lines and strategies. Many businesses sell into multiple markets. PepsiCo sells into the beverage and snack markets. Car manufacturers sell to consumers and to fleet buyers. Small companies use this strategy, too: A local cleaning service may have both homeowners and businesses as customers, and the marketing (and specifically the product offering) needs to be different for each.

Coming up with the next great thing

Okay, you think you need a hot new product. But where do you get the idea? First, check out the basic creativity skills covered in Chapter 5. That chapter offers a host of brainstorming and idea-generating techniques that you can use. If you and your fellow marketers are stale, bring in salespeople from the field, production, repair, or service call centre. Try bringing in some customers for a brainstorming session. Your approach hardly matters, as long as it's new and different. New ideas come from new thought processes, which come from new approaches to thinking. Do something new to produce something new!

Also consider two cheap but valuable sources of new product ideas: Old ideas and other people's ideas. Oh, and don't forget to ask your customers for ideas (they're people, too!).

In with the old

Old ideas are any product concepts that you or another company have previously abandoned. These concepts may have been considered but rejected without being marketed, or they could even be old products that have fallen out of use but could be revived with a new twist. Because people have been struggling to develop new product concepts for decades in most markets, a great many abandoned ideas and old products are around. Often, companies fail even to keep good records, so you have to interview old-timers and poke through faded files or archived catalogues to discover those old ideas. But old ideas may be a treasure trove, because technological or marketing developments may have made the original objections less serious than when marketers originally scrapped the idea. Technical advances or changing customer taste may make yesterday's wild ideas practical today. Even if you can't use any of the old ideas you find, they may lead you to fresh ways of thinking about the problem – perhaps they suggest a customer need that you hadn't thought of before.

Also note that old products in one market may be new products in another. Old-fashioned hand-cranked cash registers sell well in some countries, even though they have been replaced by electronic cash registers in others. The use of electronic cash registers depends upon the nature of the local economy and the availability and reliability of local electrical service. You may be able to turn your dead products into winners in other countries, if you can partner with local distributors.

Stealing – er, borrowing – ideas

You can often pursue the second source, other people's ideas, through licences. A private inventor may have a great new product concept and a patent for it, but may lack the marketing muscle and capital to introduce the product. You can provide that missing muscle and pay the inventor 5 or 10 per cent of your net revenues as reward for their inspiration.

Many companies generate inventions that fall outside of their marketing focus. These companies are often willing to license to someone specialising in the target market.

Licensing is the official way to use other people's ideas; however, an unofficial way exists that's probably more common and certainly more important for most marketers. You simply steal ideas. Now, by steal, we don't mean to take anything that isn't yours. A *patent* protects a design, a *trademark* protects a name or logo, and a *copyright* protects writing, artwork, performances, and software. You must respect these legal rights that protect other people's expressions of their ideas. But it is not possible to legally protect underlying ideas in many countries where you're likely to do business.

If an idea makes it to your ears or eyes through a legitimate public channel of communication, then you can use it. (Just don't bug your competitor's headquarters, go through their rubbish bins, or get their engineers drunk – doing so may violate *trade secrecy laws* – ask your lawyer before planning any questionable research.)

Although a competitor may be upset to see you knocking off or improving upon its latest idea, nothing can stop you as long as your source was public (not secret) and you aren't violating a patent, trademark, or copyright. In most markets, competitors steal ideas as a matter of routine. And look at other industries for inspirations that you can apply in your industry. The good idea hunter has to be open-minded – you never know where you may find something worth stealing!

Note that you're less likely to violate these legal protections if you just take a public idea and develop it all on your own, but you may still want to have a lawyer (preferably one who specialises in intellectual property law) review what you've done before going public with it.

By the way, we call this activity 'stealing' in humour – it isn't really, if you do it legally. Some people call it *benchmarking*; some call it being inspired by others. Whatever you call this borrowing of ideas, try to be aware of new concepts and keep your product offerings up to date with them. For example, *Marketing* magazine comes up with new editorial concepts all the time. One of the most successful in recent years has been an annual ranking of the top 100 most influential people in the UK marketing industry. *Marketing* magazine staff didn't invent the idea of these lists, but they did effectively apply it to their business – and came up with the title 'Power 100'. Now there are 'Power 100' lists in many other titles – borrowing is a fact of life in business, so you may as well make it work for you.

Picking your customers' brains

A final source of new product ideas comes from your customers – although often they don't know it. Ask a customer to describe a brilliant new product you should provide for him or her, and you get a blank stare or worse. Yet frustrations with the existing products and all sorts of dissatisfactions, needs, and wants lurk in the back of every customer's mind. And you may be able to help them with these gripes.

How do you mine this treasure trove of needs, many of them latent or unrecognised? Collecting the customers' words helps you gain insight into how they think – so talk to them and take notes that use quotes or tape-record their comments. Get customers talking, and let them wander a bit, so that you have a chance to encounter the unexpected. Also watch customers as they buy and use your product. Observation may reveal wasted time and effort, inefficiencies, or other problems that the customer takes for granted – problems that the customer may happily say good-bye to if you point them out and remove them.

Using the significant difference strategy

New product development has a downside: Almost all new products fail. Every expert seems to have their own statistic about this, but the most common numbers that come up are that 8 out of 10 new product ideas fail and that half of line extensions fail. Before you give up and turn to another chapter, here's a different statistic to keep you reading: Industry-wide research shows that line extensions account for 62 per cent of total revenue but contribute just 39 per cent of profits, while 'real' innovation represents 38 per cent of revenue and 61 per cent of profits.

The odds aren't great but the potential rewards are. Make sure your new product beats the odds – that it proves much better than the typical new product. How?

Common sense and a large pile of research reports say that new products do better – make more money, for a longer amount of time – when customers see something strikingly new about them. Walk down the aisle of your supermarket and notice the number of packages proclaiming something new. Without the word splashed across them, you may never have been able to tell they were new. Same with services: We have the same trouble seeing what's really new in the financial services industry, for example. Take a look at the brochures and posters in your bank and see whether the 'new' services really seem more like repackaged old services with fancy new names and pricing.

To achieve real success, you have to introduce something that's not only new, but that looks new and different to the market. The product needs a radical distinction, a clear point of difference. Innovations that consumers recognise more quickly and easily provide the marketer with a greater return. Researchers who study new product success use the term *intensity* to describe this phenomenon – the more intense the difference between your new product and old products, the more likely the new product can succeed.

Branding and Naming Your Product

Once you have got your product, everything you do to it and everything the customer sees, counts as branding. What do you call your new product? Should you launch it under a brand identity your business already owns or give it a new one? Should you attempt to add value (and raise the price) by promoting a positive brand identity, or should you save your marketing budget and just get the product out to point of purchase? You have to make all these difficult decisions. Let us show you how to make them well.

Designing a product line

A *product line* is any logical grouping of products offered to customers. (Remember, products can be goods, services, ideas, or even people such as political candidates or stars.) You usually identify product lines by an umbrella brand name, with individual brand identities falling under that umbrella.

The Apple computer line includes many different products, called different things, from the iMac to the PowerBook to the Mac Mini, but they all bear the same brand logo (a trademarked asset of Apple Computer), and the company has made each product distinct enough that together they give the customer a wide range of choices. You can think of product lines like this one as families of products – and, like families, their relationship needs to be close and clear.

You have two key issues to consider when designing your product lines:

- ✔ **Depth.** How many alternatives should you give the customer within any single category? For example, should you make a single T-shirt design in a range of sizes? How about offering the design in a variety of colours? All these options increase depth because they give a customer more options. Depth gives you an advantage because it increases the likelihood of a good fit between an interested customer and your product. You don't want to miss a sale because somebody was too big to wear a size large.

  Increase depth when you're losing customers because you don't have a product for them. Increasing your depth of choice reduces the chance of disappointing a prospective customer.

- ✔ **Breadth.** This option allows you to generate new sales. For example, ifyou sell one popular T-shirt design, you can increase breadth by offering more T-shirt designs in your product line. When you add anything that the customer views as a separate choice, not a variant of the same choice, you're adding breadth to the product line. A broad line of T-shirts includes dozens of different designs. A broad and deep product line offers each of those designs in many sizes and on many different colours and forms of T-shirt.

  Increase breadth whenever you can think of a new product that seems to fit in the line. By *fit*, we mean that customers can see the new product's obvious relationship to the line. Don't mix unrelated products – that's not a product line, because it doesn't have a clear, logical identity to customers. But keep stretching a successful line as much as you can. Doing so makes sense for one simple reason: You sell new products to old customers. Of course, the line may also reach new customers, which is great. But you can sell to your old customers more easily (read that: more cheaply), so you definitely want to do more business with them in the future, and offering them products is a great way to do this.

Maintaining your product line: When to change

The secret to good product management is the motto, 'Don't leave well enough alone'. But if you keep growing your lines, you can obviously bump into some practical limits after a while. How do you know when the pendulum is going to swing the other way – when it's time to do some spring-cleaning?

You should decrease your depth or breadth (or both) if your distribution channels can't display the full product line to customers. Often, distribution becomes a bottleneck, imposing practical limits on how big a product line you can bring to the customer's attention.

The household and personal products giant Unilever has been cutting back its 1,600 brands to 400, but is focusing its main marketing efforts on around 40 *star brands*. This focus doesn't necessarily mean each line has fewer products within it; some, like Dove and Lynx, are expanding into different areas. But what Unilever is trying to do is concentrate its resources around fewer, well-thought-out product lines – making things easier for retailers and ultimately consumers, as a result. Too many choices frustrate customers and lead to confusion between products. Brand identities start to overlap, and you make customer decisions harder rather than easier.

Always calibrate your product line to your distribution channels and your customers. Don't overwhelm. Don't underwhelm. Keep talking to all your customers and watching how they behave with your product to see if you need to shrink or grow your product line.

Naming a product or product line

Naming a new product isn't simple, but you can use a number of effective methods. You can choose a word, or combination of words, that tells people about the exact character of your product – like Salty Dog crisps (see the nearby sidebar 'Potatoes with pedigree'). This approach is like giving a new puppy a name. You want to get a feel for its personality first and then give it a name that fits. A stand-offish poodle can be Fifi, but that name doesn't fit a playful mutt!

The Ford Mustang, an extremely successful brand name, used this strategy. Marketers presented the car as simply having the personality of the small, hardy horse of the American plains from which the car took its name. And those marketers hoped that the driver saw himself as a modern-day cowboy, akin to the real cowboys who broke and used the mustangs for their work. This strategy has a powerful effect because it uses existing terms whose meaning marketers apply to their product.

You can also name your product by making up a brand-new word that has no prior meaning. This approach gives you something you can more easily protect in a court of law, but it isn't necessarily effective at communicating the character of your product. You have to invest considerable time and money in creating a meaning for the new name in consumers' minds.

Potatoes with pedigree

You'd be forgiven for thinking that there's only so much you can do with the humble potato crisp. After all, how many ways are there to slice up and fry a potato (at least that Walkers hasn't already thought of)? Well, it's a good job everyone doesn't think like that – particularly the people at Chiltern Snacks, who created Salty Dog crisps. There's a lot of good marketing behind Salty Dog (although the owners would be first to admit they're no experts). The product's significant difference feeds into its name, which feeds into its packaging.

Every packet of Salty Dog carries the line 'The hand-cooked crisps that bite back', together with a cartoon of a dog on the distinctive silver-foil bags. The dog is based on the owner's real terrier puppy, and the 'bite back' phrase is based in truth as well. The company only uses the biggest and best potatoes, hand fries them in sunflower oil for extra crunch and gives them powerful natural flavours. So, you see, even for fairly ordinary product areas in markets that are oversupplied, you can succeed if you create something that is better and which tells its story in a powerful way.

Legally protecting your product's name and identity

You can gain legal protection by using, and getting legal recognition for, a unique identifier for your product, a line of products, or even for your entire company. This protection can apply to names, short verbal descriptions, and visual symbols. All these forms of identification are marks that can represent the identity of the thing you apply them to. A tangible product's name and/or visual symbol is a *trademark*. A business name is a *word mark* – again, with similar protection under the law.

You establish and protect your rights to exclusive use of any unique trademark by registering it and then by using it. There have been many improvements to UK and European trademark law in recent years. For starters, the definition of trademark has become very broad, giving companies better protection for all aspects of their brand than before. So trademarks can be words (including personal names), designs, letters, numerals, or the shape of goods or their packaging. This last point is particularly important to products that come in distinctive packaging (think of a classic contoured bottle of Coke, which is now a protected trademark).

What you should trademark

Consider registering as many different aspects of your product's identity as you think are important to its commercial success (you can even register colours and smells, though companies have had mixed success at this). Don't go overboard, though. You could register everything about your brand, if someone hasn't got there first – but don't register elements of your name or design that don't regularly feature. In trademark law, there's a simple rule of thumb to follow: Use it or lose it. For the law to apply, you have to register the trademark (and keep it registered, as registrations usually run out after ten years) and then you have to use it – regularly.

Registering trademarks in the UK and Europe

If you want to register a trademark of any kind in the UK, contact the UK Patent Office at www.patent.gov.uk or by calling their Enquiry Unit on 0845 9 500 505. There is a wealth of information on the Patent Office Web site, including information on copyright, designs, and patents. You can even use the site to help you in your name search, by typing in your desired product or company name and seeing whether it is already in use by a company in the same or similar line of business.

It is relatively easy these days to register your trademark for the main foreign territories. You can cover the whole of the European Community by applying for a community trademark (CTM). For information on how to do this, contact the Community Trade Mark Office at www.oami.eu.int. Or to cover an even wider international area, including the United States, you can have your trademark protected under the 'Madrid system'. Visit the Web site of the World Intellectual Property Organisation at www.wipo.int for a list of member countries – but the whole registering process can be done through the UK Patent Office. This eliminates the need for an expensive army of international lawyers (unless, of course, your application is challenged).

Packaging and Labelling: Dressing Products for Success

At some point in every marketing plan, the product has to take over and market itself. You reach that point when the customer and product meet and the customer makes a purchase decision – for or against your product. A customer enters a shop, glances over the shelves, pulls a package down, and carries it to the cashdesk. A customer opens a catalogue or brochure, flips through its pages, selects an item, and dials the freefone number. A customer goes online to purchase plane tickets and make a hotel reservation. At all these points of purchase, the marketer is out of the picture. The product must sell itself. But to do so, the product must be noticeable; it must be enticing; it must appear to be better than (and better value than) the competition.

To prepare your product for its solo role at this vital point-of-purchase stage, you need to give careful thought to how you display and present it. You can't play this all-important role for your product, but you can select the stage and design the set and costume. The *stage* is made up of the shop, catalogue, or other meeting place; the *set* includes the shelving, signs, display, or other point-of-purchase designs; the *costume* is the exterior package you give your product. Together, these elements make up what marketers refer to as the *packaging*.

Every product has a package! If you work in banking or real estate, sell windscreen gaskets to car manufacturers, or distribute your products by mail order rather than in a shop, you may be wondering if you can skip this chapter. But, sorry, you can't. Remember, the package is the product as the customer first sees it. And, therefore, marketers must give careful thought to package design, regardless of the product. Services, ideas, and even people (like musicians, job seekers, and political candidates) are included because they can all be products in the right context.

The importance of packaging

In spite of the vast sums of money and attention lavished elsewhere – on advertising, marketing research, and other activities – it all comes down to the package. Does the prospective customer see the package and choose it over others? Studies of the purchase process reveal that people rarely know just what they will buy before the *point of purchase* (POP) – the time and place at which they actually make their purchase. The majority of consumers are ready and willing for your product to sway them at point of purchase, as the findings in Table 14-1 (from a study by the Point-of-Purchase Advertising Institute) reveal.

Table 14-1	The Point-of-purchase Decision-making Process	
Nature of Consumer's Purchase Decision	*Percentage of Purchases, Supermarket*	*Percentage of Purchases, Mass Merchandise Shops*
Unplanned	60%	53%
Substitute	4%	3%
Generally planned	6%	18%
Total = Product selection made at point of purchase	70%	74%

As Table 14-1 shows, unplanned purchases make up the biggest category. Furthermore, specifically planned purchases (those purchases not included in the table) are less than a third of all purchases – all the rest can be influenced at least partially by the package and other point-of-purchase communications. (The study is for packaged goods in shops, but we find that service purchases can also be strongly influenced by the brochure, sales presentation, or Web site that packages the service.)

If more than half of final decisions about what to buy are made at point of purchase – where the customer is interacting with the product and its packaging – then the package may be more important than any other element of the marketing plan. Wow! In fact, you may want to stop and ask yourself whether you can dispense with all other forms of marketing communication, and invest only in packaging and point-of-purchase promotions and displays. If your target customer is open to a point-of-purchase decision, then this extreme is at least a possibility. And by focusing 90–100 per cent of your marketing attention on the point of purchase, you can handle the point of purchase better than less focused competitors. You may want to at least think about this option, if for no other reason than its radical nature means your competition probably won't think of it.

Can your packaging make the sale?

The packaging makes the sale in the majority of purchase decisions (along with any additional point-of-purchase influences to draw attention to the product – but you can look at those eye-catchers in Chapter 16). Here are some ways to make sure your packaging makes the sale (see Chapter 16 for more on point-of-purchase sales):

- ✔ **Bump up the visibility of the package.** Increasing the size of the brand name, the brightness or boldness of the colours and layout, or the size of the package itself helps make it more visible, as does arranging (or paying) to have shops display it more prominently. Look at the cover of this book for a good example. The *For Dummies* series is an amazing marketing success, partly because you can easily find the books in a bookshop due to their bold, clear cover designs.

- ✔ **Choose a colour that contrasts with competitors.** EasyJet's bright orange colour scheme stands out among the typically staid corporate liveries of the bigger airlines. Orange is a colour that shouts 'good value', a quality that has worked well for the Easy brand as it extended into hire cars, Internet cafes, and male toiletries. The colour only became a problem when Easy moved into the mobile phone market, where it is embroiled in a legal battle with network operator, Orange – all of which demonstrates how important colour can be to a business.

✔ **Improve the information on the package.** Less is more when it comes to clarity, so can you cut down on the number of words you use? Alternatively, ask yourself if the shopper may find any additional information useful when making a purchase decision.

✔ **Use the Web to package a product in information.** There are many products that are too technologically complicated to communicate any information of value on their actual packaging, so the Web sites for these businesses have become important 'packages' in their own right – think mobile phones and computers. You can use Web sites for more simple brands, too.

Innocent Drinks makes fruit smoothies and juices – hardly complex products that need further explanation, you'd think. But like their bottles, the Web site contains loads of useful and entertaining information about the recipes and ingredients used in their products.

✔ **Let the packaging sell the replacement, too.** Make some aspect of your packaging (if only a label on the bottom) be so permanent that it sends the user to your Web page or phone number for a reorder when the time comes.

✔ **Give your package or label emotional appeal.** Warm colours, a friendly message, a smiling person, and a photo of children playing are all ways to make the product feel good when someone looks at it. Purchases are about feelings, not just logic, so give your packaging a winning personality.

✔ **Add some excitement to the package.** You can learn a lot about what's hot in packaging with a simple trip to the local supermarket. Let us direct you down some of the aisles. Visit the bread section and look for Hovis (it's the loaf wrapped with a big picture of baked beans or tomatoes). Try stock cubes – see the Oxo display, with single, bold letters filling the side of the box? Products that stand out, sell well. Can you break away from category conventions with your product?

✔ **Increase the functionality or workability of the package.** Can you make your packaging protect the product better? Can you make it easier to open, useful for storage, or easier to recycle? Packages have functional roles, and improving functionality can help increase the product's appeal.

Use these ideas or your own to improve sales by upgrading your packaging. Whatever you do, do something. Packaging can be a significant cost in the manufacture of any product, so make sure it pays its own way by becoming a powerful marketing tool.

We can't do full justice to packaging in this book. That subject is big enough to justify its own book. But we can direct you to some of the leading resources out there for marketers looking to make their packaging work harder in the marketing mix:

- ✔ **Institute of Packaging** (www.pi2.org.uk). The main UK trade association for packaging professionals, it organises qualifications, conferences, and events, including the prestigious Starpack Awards.

- ✔ **Packaging News** (www.packagingnews.co.uk). The leading UK monthly magazine, with latest product news and case studies available through its Web site.

- ✔ **The Design Council** (www.designcouncil.org.uk). This Web site contains useful information and case studies on all aspects of packaging design.

- ✔ **Packaging Innovation Show** (www.packaginginnovationshow.com). This covers all areas of packaging and innovation relating to brand, retail, and consumer needs.

Modifying an Existing Product: When and How

Some products are so perfect that they fit naturally with their customers, and you should just leave them alone. For example . . . well, we can't actually think of an example at the moment. Our inability to name the perfect product tells you something important about product management: You'd better modify your products to improve performance, value, and quality with each new season and each new marketing plan.

You're competing on a changing playing field. Your competitors are trying hard to make their products better, and you have to do the same. Always seek insights into how to improve your product. Always look for early indicators of improvements your competitors plan to make and be prepared to go one step farther in your response. And always go to your marketing oracle – the customer – for insights into how you can improve your product.

The following two sections describe tests that a product must pass to remain viable. If it doesn't pass, you need to improve or alter your product somehow.

When it's no longer special

At the point of purchase – that place or time when customers make their actual purchase decisions – your product needs to have something special.

Your product has to reach out to at least a portion of the market; it needs to be better than its competition on certain criteria because of inherent design features; or it needs to be as good as the rest, but better value, which gives you a sustainable cost advantage. (Do you have such a cost advantage? Marketers generally underestimate the rarity of those cost advantages!) Or your product needs to be the best option by virtue of a lack of other options.

For example, if you sell sewing needles, your product may be about as good as most of the competition – but not noticeably better. But if you happen to be the company that a major retail chain uses to single-source needles for its small sewing section, then you have a distribution advantage at point of sale.

Don't assume your lack of special features means that your product isn't special. You can be special just by being there when customers need the product. You can justify keeping a product alive just by having a way of maintaining your distribution advantage. But a product at point of sale has to have at least something special about it if you expect it to generate a good return in the future – otherwise, it gets lost.

If your customers don't think your product is unique in any way, then you may need to kill that product. But don't set up the noose too quickly. First, see if you can work to differentiate your product in some important way.

When it lacks champions

Champions are those customers who really love your product, who insist on buying it over others, and who tell their friends or associates to do the same. But such loyal champions are rare. Does your product have champions?

The championship test is tougher than the differentiation test. Many products lack champions. But when a product does achieve this special status – when some customers anywhere in the distribution channel really love it – then that product is assured an unusually long and profitable life. Such high customer commitment should be your constant goal as you manage the life cycle of your product.

Products with champions get great word of mouth, and their sales and market shares grow because of that word of mouth. Even better, champions faithfully repurchase the products they rave about. And this repeat business provides your company with high-profit sales, compared with the higher costs associated with finding new customers. Check out the principles of good marketing in Chapter 1.

The hook? The repeat buyer must want to repeat the purchase. They need to be converts, true believers, advocates – whatever you call them, they're worth winning and worth keeping. Otherwise, you need to think of each sale as a new sale, and the sale costs you almost as much as selling to someone who's never used the product before.

How do you know if you have champions rather than regular, ordinary customers? Because when you ask them about the product, they sound excited and enthusiastic. 'I'd never drive anything but a Volvo. They're comfortable and safe, they don't break down, and they last longer than other cars.' Some customers say just that when asked about their Volvos, so Volvo has an excellent base of repeat buyers. The existence of customer champions gives Volvo the luxury of selling virtually the same car to people time after time, while competitors are madly retooling their factories every year or two.

Killing a Product

Unlike people and companies, products don't die on their own. Products never had a pulse anyway, and product bankruptcy just doesn't exist. Consequently, the marketer needs to have the good sense to know when an old product has no more life in it and to keep it going just wastes resources that ought to go to new products, instead.

Yet often you see weak products hanging around. Companies keep these products on the market despite gradually declining sales because everybody, from manufacturer to retailer, hates to face reality. Even worse, you sometimes see marketers investing treasured resources in trying to boost sales of declining brands through renewed advertising or sales promotions. If the product has one foot in the grave anyway, you should put those resources into introducing a radically improved version or a replacement product.

When to kill a product

You need to face facts: Many products would be better put out of their misery and replaced with something fresh and innovative. 'But,' you rightly object, 'how do I know when my particular product reaches that point of no return?'

In the following sections, we discuss the warning signs that you're due to replace a product.

The market is saturated and you have a weak/falling share

Saturation means that you and your competitors are selling replacement products. You don't have many new customers around to convert. Growth slows, limited by the replacement rate for the product, plus whatever basic growth occurs in the size of the target market.

Saturation alone is no reason to give up on a product – most markets are saturated. An obviously saturated market is that for the car. You find very few adults who don't already own a car if they have the means to buy one and the need for one. So manufacturers and dealerships fight for replacement sales and first-time sales to young drivers, which can still be profitable for some of the competitors – but usually not all of them. If you have a product that has a share of less than, say, 75 per cent of the leading product's market share, and if your share is falling relative to the leader, then you're on a long, slow, downward slide. (Market share means the percentage of all product sales in a defined market that one company captures for itself.)

Better to introduce a replacement and kill the old product than to wait it out. You have to replace the product eventually, and the sooner you do, the less your share and reputation suffer. Whatever else happens, you can't afford for customers to see you as a has-been in a saturated market!

We use the term *product* in the marketing sense, to include whatever you're offering, whether a good, service, idea, or person. Remember, too, that services, ideas, and even people sometimes need to be withdrawn from the market, just as goods do.

A series of improvements fails to create momentum

Often, companies try a series of 'new and improved' versions, new packages, fancy coupon schemes, contests, and point-of-purchase promotions to breathe life into products after they stop generating year-to-year sales growth. Sometimes these ploys work and help to renew growth; sometimes they don't.

Something is wrong with your product

All too often, marketers discover some flaw in a product, which threatens to hurt their company's reputation or puts its customers at risk. If your engineers think that the fuel tank in one of your vehicles can explode during accidents, should you pull the model immediately and introduce a safer version or keep selling it and put the technical report in your paper shredder? A major car manufacturer chose the second option. In the long run, the faulty fuel tank killed some of its customers, and the company had to stage an extremely unprofitable recall, along with a repair-the-damage publicity campaign, topped by several lawsuits.

Brand equity and profits take a licking whenever your customers do. But many marketers lack the stomach or the internal political clout to kill a bad product, even when the product may kill customers.

We don't know why some marketers keep making these mistakes, but we hope that you don't. Pull the product if you find out it may cause cancer, give people electrical shocks, choke a baby, or even just not work as well as you say it does. Pull the product immediately. Ask questions later. And write a press release announcing that you're acting on behalf of your customers, just in case the rumours are true. By taking this decisive step immediately, you let the market know that you have a great deal more integrity than most – and that can only make your brand equity stronger, not weaker. Trust us – pulling a product takes courage, but it's the best option, when the dust settles. And if you follow our advice and always invest creative energy and funds in your product development efforts – you should have something better to offer as a replacement.

How to kill or replace a product

Actually, getting rid of old products is the least of your troubles, because *liquidators* are happy to sell your inventory below cost to various vendors. Contact some of your distributors or your trade association for referrals.

But you may want to use a more elegant strategy – one that avoids the negativity of customers seeing your old products offered for a tenth of their normal price: Stage some kind of sales promotion to move the old inventory to customers through your normal distribution channels. We much prefer this option, especially if it also introduces consumers to the new product. But this method only works if you get started before the old product loses its appeal. So you have to aggressively replace your products. Don't wait for the market to kill your product; do the deed yourself. The following sections discuss more strategies that help you bow out gracefully.

The coat-tails strategy

The *coat-tails strategy* uses the old product to introduce the new. The variety of ways to put this strategy to use is limited only by your imagination. You can offer a free sample coupon for the new product to buyers of the old product. You can package the two products together in a special two-for-one promotion. You can do special mailings or make personal or telephone sales calls to old customers.

If the two products are reasonably similar from a functional perspective, you can call the new product by the old product's name and try to merge it into the old identity as if you wanted to introduce an upgrade rather than something brand new. In other words, you can dress the new product in the old product's coat instead of just attaching it to the coat-tails. You need to be able to defend this stealth strategy from a commonsense perspective, or your customers get angry. If you can make the argument that customers are getting a 'more and better' version of the same product, then the strategy should work.

The coat-tails strategy is a great promotional device for replacing an old product with a new one. Use it whenever you want to kill an old product in order to make room for a new one. *Room* can mean room in the customer's mind, room on the shop shelf, room in the distributor's catalogue, or room in your own product line. Products take up space, and physical or mental space can give you an important resource. But you do take a risk with this strategy – and it's a big one. When you make room for your new product, competing products can try to take that space, instead. Why? Any customers still faithful to the old product have to reconsider their purchase patterns, and they may choose a competitor over your new option. Similarly, retailers, distributors, or other channel members may give your space to another product. So you need to hold on to your space, even as you eliminate your product. Avoid any gaps in the availability of your products.

The product line placeholding strategy

You can use *product lines* to create clear product niches and hold them for replacement products. Keep pricing consistent with product positions in your product line, as well – a practice called *price lining*.

For example, a bank may offer a selection of different savings options to its retail customers – a mix of straight savings accounts, easy access accounts, fixed rate bonds, mini cash ISAs, and Child Trust Funds. If the bank organises these options into a coherent range of named products and lists them in a single brochure in order from lowest-risk/lowest-return to highest-risk/highest-return, then it creates a clear product line with well-defined places for these products. (The bank must be sure that each product sits in a unique place on that spectrum – no overlaps, please!)

Now, when the bank wants to introduce a new product, it can substitute the new one for an old one, and consumers accept that this new product fills the same spot in the product line. The bank can also extend the product line in either direction or fill gaps in it with new products. Whatever the bank does, the product line can act as a placeholder to ease the entry of new products. (See the 'Branding and Naming Your Product' section, earlier in this chapter, for more information on product lines.)

But we bet that your bank doesn't use this strategy – few do. As a result, you're always confused when you try to get your mind around your bank's offerings, and they therefore lose some business that they should have won. The fact is that, although product lines are a very important part of any marketing strategy, marketers often neglect them.

Make sure your offerings fall into a clear product line with an obvious logic to it and clear points of difference anyone can understand at a glance. What can you do, right now, to clarify the options you give your customers and make sure your branding and product offerings make good sense to everyone?

Chapter 15

Using Price and Promotions

S ome marketers believe that businesses fail most often for two simple reasons: Their prices are too high, or their prices are too low! Getting the price just right is the hardest task marketers face, but finding the right pricing approach makes success a lot easier to achieve.

The bottom line of all marketing activities is that the customer needs to pay – willingly and, you hope, rapidly – for your products or services. But how much will they pay? Should you drop your prices to grow your market? Or would raising the price and maximising profits be better? What about discounts and special promotional pricing? Getting the price part of your marketing plan right is hard . . . but the following pages help you through it.

Understanding the Facts of Pricing

Most companies fall prey to the myth that customers only choose a product based on its list price. As a result, they set their list prices lower than they need to. Or when companies need to boost sales, they do so by offering discounts or free units. If you insist on selling on the basis of price alone, your customers buy on the basis of price.

But alternatives always exist. To raise your price and still sell more, you can

✔ **Build brand equity:** Better-known brands command a premium price.

✔ **Increase quality:** People spread the word about a good product, and that can earn the product a 5 to 10 per cent higher price than the competition.

✔ **Use prestige pricing:** Giving your product a high-class image can boost your price by 20 to 100 per cent. See the 'Discounts and Other Special Offers' section later in this chapter for details on how prestige pricing works.

✔ **Create extra value through time and place advantages:** Customers consider the available product worth a lot more than one they can't get when they need it. (That's why a cup of coffee costs more at the airport – are you really going to leave the terminal, get in a taxi, and go somewhere else to save a pound?)

Price is important, but it doesn't have to be the only thing – unless the marketer doesn't understand this fact.

Avoiding underpricing

Lowering prices is always easier than raising prices. In general, you want to set price a bit high in relation to the competition and see what happens. If your product sells the way you want it to, great! If not, you can take back any price increase with a subsequent price cut. This strategy is wiser than setting the price low initially because you can take back price increases much more easily (if they don't work) than price decreases.

Customers may not be as price sensitive as you fear. They may tolerate an increase better than you think, and they may not respond to a decrease in price as enthusiastically as you need them to in order to make that decrease profitable. Customers may even assume that price correlates with quality – in which case, they don't buy your product unless the price is high enough. Instead of assuming that you need a price cut whenever you want to boost profits, start by experimenting with a price increase. Be a contrarian. They usually succeed!

Exploring the impact of pricing on customers' purchases

Price sensitivity is the degree to which purchases are affected by price level – in other words, how willing are customers to pay the price you're asking? You need to estimate how price sensitive your customers are in relation to your product or service.

How in the world can you estimate the price sensitivity of customers when you lack good data? The following checklist lists a series of *qualitative indicators* (clues we can guess from) of price sensitivity. You have to ask yourself a set of questions about your customer, product, and market, ticking the box next to each question that you answer with 'yes'. Then you add up the number of ticked boxes to see which way they lean. This study isn't scientific, but it's better than ignoring the problem altogether!

✓ **Does the customer view the price as reasonable?** If you're operating within an expected price range, customers aren't very price sensitive. Outside of the expected price range, they become more sensitive about price.

✓ **Is the product valuable at (almost) any price?** Some products are unique, and customers know that they can have a hard time finding a cheaper substitute. That fact lowers price sensitivity.

✓ **Is the product desperately needed?** I don't care how much fixing a burst pipe on a Sunday costs – at least, I don't care if my home is filling up with water! And I'm not too price sensitive about the cost of treatment by my dentist if my teeth are giving me pain. These products meet essential needs. But if your product is a *nonessential* (something that customers want but don't have to have right now), the customer is more price sensitive.

✓ **Are substitutes unavailable?** If the customer purchases in a context where substitute products aren't readily available, price sensitivity is lower. Shopping for price requires that substitutes at different prices be available. (For example, if you're the only company offering emergency plumbing repairs on weekends in your town, your customers will pay a high price for your services.)

✓ **Is the customer unaware of substitutes?** What the customer doesn't know costs her. And shopping is a complex, information-dependent behaviour. Customers can find the cheapest price available if they have the time and, these days, access to a computer and the Internet. But not everyone does. You don't have to charge the least if your customers are unable or unwilling to shop around for a lower price.

✓ **Does the customer find comparing options difficult?** Even where options exist, the consumer can have a lot of difficulty comparing products in some product categories. What makes one dentist better than another? I don't know – I have no idea which dentist is better able to treat me. The technical complexity of their work, plus the fact that you can't consume dental care until after you make the purchase decision, makes comparing options hard. And that difficulty makes dental care consumers less price sensitive – and dentists richer.

✔ **Does the product seem inexpensive to customers?** Customers don't worry too much about price when they feel like they're getting good value. However, if customers feel the pinch in their purses when they make the purchases, they pay close attention to prices. That's why you negotiate so hard when you buy a car or a house. Even products that cost far less can seem expensive if they're at the high end of a price range. For example, you're more price sensitive if you shop for a fancy, high-performance laptop computer than for a simple, basic desktop unit because the former probably costs 50 to 100 per cent more than the latter, making the laptop expensive by comparison.

The more boxes you ticked, the less price sensitive your customer is. If you ticked multiple boxes, you probably can raise your prices without hurting sales significantly. And that's great news!

You can supplement your estimate of price sensitivity (from the checklist) with actual tests. For example, if you think a 5 per cent increase in prices won't affect sales, try that increase in a test market or for a short period of time, holding the rest of your marketing constant. Were you right? If so, roll out the increase nationwide (or townwide, for you small-business people).

Finding profits without raising prices

When you think about profits, you may assume that your focus should be on the price. But many factors drive your company's cash flows and profits, not just the list price of your products. If your manager tells you to work out how to raise prices because profits are too low, don't assume that raising prices is the only or right solution. Here are some ways to boost profits *without* raising prices:

✔ Check to see how quickly you're making collections – are vendors paying within 65 days? If so, cutting that time by 25 days may make up the needed profits without any price increase.

✔ Look at the discounts and allowances your company offers. These can affect revenues and profits. Are customers taking advantage of quantity discounts to stock up inexpensively and then not buying between the discount periods? If so, you have a problem with your sales promotions, not your list prices.

✔ If you're in a service business that charges a base price, plus fees for special services and extras, look hard at the way in which you assess fees. Perhaps your company is failing to collect the appropriate fees, in some cases.

✔ Evaluate whether your fee structure is out of date and doesn't reflect your cost structure accurately. For example, an independent financial adviser who is making profits solely on commission from the products he sells may find profits stagnating if more and more of his time is spent offering complex investment advice. In such a case, the problem isn't with the commission percentage rate, which may be capped anyway. Switching to an annual retainer or charging for advice may even be more popular with higher value customers.

Five Easy Steps to Setting Prices

If you need to establish a price, you're stuck with one of the toughest things anybody does in business. Surveys of managers indicate they suffer from a high degree of price anxiety. So let's take you through the process logically, step by step. Price setting doesn't have to be a high-anxiety task if you do it right! Figure 15-1 illustrates the process that we describe in the following sections.

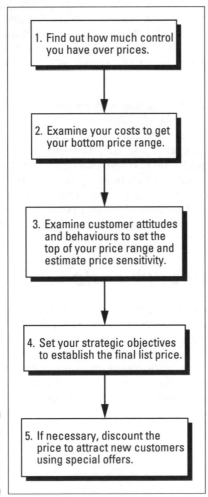

Figure 15-1: A helpful pricing process.

1. Find out how much control you have over prices.

2. Examine your costs to get your bottom price range.

3. Examine customer attitudes and behaviours to set the top of your price range and estimate price sensitivity.

4. Set your strategic objectives to establish the final list price.

5. If necessary, discount the price to attract new customers using special offers.

Step 1: Find out who really sets the price

The first step isn't obvious. You, as the marketer, can set a list price. But the consumer may not ultimately pay your price. You may encounter a distributor or wholesaler and a retailer, all of whom take their mark-ups. Furthermore, the manufacturer generally doesn't have the legal right to dictate the ultimate selling price. The retailer gets that job. So your list price is really just a suggestion, not an order. If the retailer doesn't like the suggested price, the product sells for another price.

So you need to start by determining who else may be setting prices along with you. Involve these parties in your decision-making by asking some of them what they think about pricing your product. They may tell you that you have constraints to consider. Know what those constraints are before you start.

For example, if you're setting the price for a new range of paints, you find that the big DIY chains expect a 40–50 per cent discount off the list price. Knowing that, you can set a high enough list price to give you some profit, even at a 50 per cent discount rate. But if you don't realise that these chains expect much higher discounts than smaller DIY shops, you may be blindsided by their requirement.

Marketers who operate in or through a *multilevel distribution channel* (meaning that they have distributors, wholesalers, retailers, agents, or other sorts of intermediaries) need to establish the *trade discount structure*. Trade discounts (also called *functional discounts*) are what you give these intermediaries. These discounts are a form of cost to the marketer, so make sure that you know the discount structure for your product before you move on. Usually, marketers state the discount structure as a series of numbers, representing what each of the intermediaries get as a discount. But you take each discount off the price left over from the discount before it, not off the list price.

Step 2: Examine all your costs

How do you know your costs? In theory, that's easy: Your company's excellent cost accounting system captures all your costs, and a man in a pinstripe suit with a calculator can simply give you the figure.

In practice, you may not have good, accurate information on the true costs of a specific product or service. Take some time to try to estimate what you're actually spending, and remember to include some value for expensive

Calculating discount structures

Confused? Let's show you how to calculate prices and discounts in a complex distribution channel. Say that you discover the typical discount structure in the market where you want to introduce your product is 30/10/5. What does that mean? If you start with a £100 list price, the retailer pays at a discount of 30 per cent off the list price (0.30 x £100 = £70). The retailer, who pays £70 for the product, marks it up to (approximately) £100 and makes about £30 in gross profit.

Now, the discount structure figures tell you that other intermediaries exist – one for each discount listed. The distributor, who sells the product to the retailer, has a discount of 10 per cent off the price that she charges the retailer (that's 0.10 x £70 = £7 of gross profit for the distributor).

And this distributor must have paid £70 (£7, or £63, for the product to another intermediary (probably a manufacturer's representative or wholesaler). The marketer sells to this intermediary. And the 30/10/5 formula shows that this intermediary receives a 5 per cent discount: 0.05 x £63 = £3.15 in profit for him.

Subtracting again, you can also determine that the marketer must sell the product to this first intermediary at £63 (£3.15, or £59.85. You, as the marketer, must give away more than 40 per cent of that £100 list price to intermediaries if you use this 30/10/5 discount structure. And so you have to calculate any profit you make from a £100 list price as costs subtracted from your net of £59.85. That's all you ever see of that £100!

inventories if they sit around for a month or more (assume you're paying interest on the money tied up in those products to account for the loss of capital wasting away in inventory).

After you examine your costs carefully, you should have a fairly accurate idea of the least amount you can charge. That charge is, at a bare minimum, your actual costs. (Okay, maybe sometimes you want to give away a product for less than cost in order to introduce people to it – what's known as a *loss leader*.) More often, you need a price that includes the cost plus a profit margin – say, 20 or 30 per cent. So that means you have to treat your cost as 70 or 80 per cent of the price, adding in that 20 or 30 per cent margin your company requires.

This cost-plus-profit figure is the bottom of your pricing range (see Figure 15-2). Now you need to see if customers permit you to charge this price – or perhaps even allow you to charge a higher price!

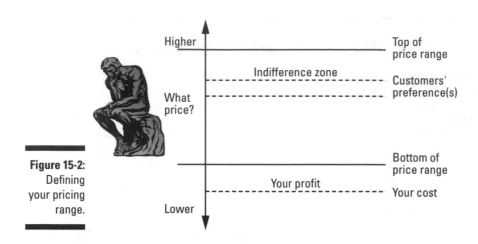

Figure 15-2:
Defining
your pricing
range.

Step 3: Evaluate customer perception of price

Your costs and profit requirements determine a lower limit on price. But your customers' perceptions determine an upper limit. You need to define both of these limits to know your possible price range. So you need to work out what price customers are willing to pay.

In Figure 15-2, I show the price that customers favour as *customers' prefer-ence*. Note that customer preference may not be the upper limit. If customers aren't too price sensitive, they may not notice or care if you set your price somewhat higher than their preferred price. (See the section 'Understanding how customers perceive and remember prices' later in this chapter.)

Pricing experts sometimes call the difference between the customer's desired price and a noticeably higher price the *indifference zone*. Within the indiffer-ence zone, customers are indifferent to both price increases and price decreases. However, the zone gets smaller (on a percentage basis) as the price of a product increases. How big or small is the zone of indifference in your product's case? Go back to the price sensitivity checklist. The zone is small if your customers are highly price sensitive, and large if they aren't that price sensitive. Just make some assumptions that seem reasonable for now. I know this process involves some guesswork, but still, breaking down the pricing decision into a series of smaller, educated guesses is better than plucking a number out of thin air! At worst, your errors on all those little guesses may be random, in which case they cancel each other out.

You can also get at customer preference by looking at the current pricing structure in your market. What are people paying for comparable products? Does a downward trend exist in the prices of comparable products? An upward trend? Or are they stable? Go shopping to get a grasp of the existing price structure; you'll get excellent clues as to how customers may react to different prices for your product.

Through these sorts of activities, you can at least get back-of-the-envelope figures for the customers' preferred price and an idea of how much higher you can price without drawing the wrong sort of attention. That means you have established the top of your price range.

The simplest approach to pricing is to set your price at the top of the range. As long as the price range is above the bottom limit (your preferred price plus the indifference zone is equal to or greater than your cost plus your required profit), you're okay.

But you can't always set your price at the top of the range. In the next step of the pricing process, we show you how to calculate what your final price should be.

Step 4: Examine secondary influences

You need to have your costs and the customers' upper limits as the two primary considerations. They set a price range. But you should consider many other factors, too. These factors may influence your decision by forcing you to price in the middle or bottom of the price range rather than at the top, for example.

Consider competitive issues. Do you need to gain market share from a close competitor? If so, either keep price at parity and do aggressive marketing, or adjust your price to be slightly (but noticeably) below the competitor's price. Also consider likely future price trends. Are prices falling in this market? Then you need to adjust your figures down a bit to stay in synch with your market. Similarly, currency fluctuations may affect your costs and, thus, your pricing options. If you're concerned that you may take a hit from the exchange rate, better to be safe and price at the high end of the range. Finally, product line management may dictate a slightly lower or higher price. For example, you may need to price a top-of-the-range product significantly higher than others in its line just to make it clear to the customer that this product is a step above standard alternatives.

Step 5: Set your strategic objectives

You may have objectives other than revenues and profit maximisation. Many marketers price near the bottom of their price range to increase their market share. (They price so low because a high market share later on will probably give them more profits – so it's an investment strategy. See Chapter 2 for details.)

This low-price strategy only makes sense if the customer is fairly price sensitive! If not, you're throwing away possible revenues without any real gain in market share. You should be pricing at the top of the range and using the extra revenues to invest in quality and brand-building marketing promotions in order to increase market share (see Chapter 2 for details on these and other strategy options).

In other cases, marketers have certain volume goals they need to reach – like when they need to run a factory near its capacity level. So they may price in the low end of the range in order to maximise unit sales, even if doing so doesn't maximise net profits per unit.

Sometimes, marketers even want to minimise unit volume – for example, when introducing a new product. They may not have the capacity to sell the product to a mass market and so decide to *skim the market* by selling the product at such a high price that only the very wealthy or least price-sensitive customers can buy it. Then they lower prices later on, when they have made maximum profits from the high-end customers and have added production capacity. Video games consoles, MP3 players, and 3G mobile phones are all examples of products that use the skimming strategy, entering the market at significantly higher prices than they settle down at later in the *product life cycle*.

Don't use a skimming strategy unless you're sure that you're safe from aggressive competition in the short term.

Understanding how customers perceive and remember prices

There is more to pricing than finding the highest price that most customers are willing to pay. You have to pick a pricing strategy that works for the context of your business and the market in which it operates. Do you need to beat your competitor on price? Do you have a vertical range of different quality products? The following list will give you an idea of how to pick a pricing strategy that works for you and your customers.

Whichever of the following strategies you use, remember: In pricing services, set a price that's consistent with your quality. Don't accidentally cheapen the perceived quality of your service by setting your price too low.

Odd–even pricing

In this strategy you use a price that ends with the number 9. Why? Because people perceive prices ending in 9 as cheaper – generally 3 to 6 per cent cheaper in their memories than the rounded-up price. You can take advantage of this perception about price. For example, if the top of your price range for a new child's toy is £10, you probably want to drop it down to £9.99 or £9.89 for the simple reason that this price seems much cheaper to most consumers. Assuming they're price sensitive at all, they buy considerably more of the lower-priced product, even though the price difference amounts to only pennies.

The only downside to using prices ending in 9 is that customers sometimes associate this pricing with cheap products that have worse quality. So don't use odd–even pricing when your customers are more quality sensitive than price sensitive. For example, odd–even pricing may cheapen the image of an original work of art for sale in an art gallery. But, in general, the strategy seems to work.

Price lining

You may also want to adjust your price to make it fit into your product line, or into the range of products sold by your retailers or distributors. The idea is to fit your product into a range of alternatives, giving the product a logical spot in customers' minds. Marketers know this common and generally effective strategy as *price lining*.

Competitive pricing

You may want to price relative to an important competitor or set of competitors. Marketers call this practice *competitive pricing*, for obvious reasons. If you're in a highly competitive market, you should exercise competitive pricing. Decide which competing products the customers may view as closest to yours and then make your price sufficiently higher or lower to differentiate your product.

How much difference is enough difference depends upon the size of the customers' indifference zone (see the section 'Step 3: Evaluate customer perception of price' earlier in this chapter to find out about the indifference zone).

Should you price above or below that tough competitor? That decision depends on whether you offer more or fewer benefits and higher or lower quality. If you offer your customer less or about the same, you need to make your price significantly lower so that your product looks like better value. If you offer greater benefits, you can make your price a little higher to signal this fact – but not too high because you want to be sure that your product seems like better value than the competition.

Sometimes you should just price exactly at the competitor's price. You may want to match prices if you plan to differentiate your product on the basis of some subtle difference. This way, customers focus their attention on the difference rather than on price.

In setting price it is important to try to anticipate the likely reaction to any price changes. A drop in price may be matched by the major player who may have deep enough pockets to match or better price reductions. Tesco dominates the UK food market with a 30 per cent share and at the time of writing is planning further price reductions. Asda, with the backing of Walmart, is spending even more on price reductions. The effect is being felt throughout the high street. In retail, discounting is the order of the day, so remember that pricing is affected by nationwide behaviours as much as by the outcome you would like to achieve.

Finally, some competitors try to convince customers that their product is better but costs less than the competitors' products. Nobody believes this claim – unless you present evidence. If you do, customers will love you – we all hope to get more for less, after all! For example, a personal computer with a new, faster chip may really be better but cost less. A new anti-wrinkle cream may work better but cost less if you've discovered a new formula. And a retailer may be able to sell the same brands for a cheaper price because it has larger stores that do more volume of business. As long as you have – and can communicate to the customer – a believable argument, you can undercut the competitor's price at the same time as claiming superior benefits. But make sure that you back up the claim, or the customer assumes that your lower price means the product is inferior.

Discounts and Other Special Offers

Special offers are temporary inducements to make customers buy on the basis of price or price-related factors. Special offers play with the price, giving consumers (or intermediaries) a way to get the product for less – at least while the offer lasts.

You may wonder, why play with the price? If you think the price should be lower, why not just cut the price permanently? The answer is because a price cut is easy to do, but hard to undo. A special offer, on the other hand, allows you to temporarily discount the price while still maintaining the list price at its old level. When the offer ends, the list price is the same – you haven't given anything away permanently. Here are some cases in which maintaining your list price and offering a discount is a good strategy:

✔ When your reason for wanting to cut the price is a short-term one, like wanting to counter a competitor's special offer or respond to a new product introduction.

✔ When you want to experiment with the price (to find out about customer price sensitivity) without committing to a permanent price cut until you see the data.

✔ When you want to stimulate consumers to try your product, and you believe that after they try it, they may like the product well enough to buy it again at full price.

✔ When your list price needs to stay high in order to signal quality *(prestige pricing)* or be consistent with other prices in your product line *(price lining strategy)*; see the earlier section 'Understanding how customers perceive and remember prices' for details on those pricing strategies.

✔ When your competitors are all offering special lower prices and you think you have no choice because consumers have come to expect special offers.

What happens when competitors get too focused on making and matching each other's special offers? They flood the customers with price-based promotions. Discounts and other freebies begin to outweigh brand-building marketing messages, focusing consumer attention on price over brand and benefit considerations. Special promotions can and do increase customer sensitivity to price. They attract *price switchers,* people who aren't loyal to any brand but just shop on the basis of price. And these promotions encourage people to become price switchers, thus reducing the size of the core customer base and increasing the number of fringe customers. So special offers have the potential to erode brand equity, reduce customer loyalty, and cut deeply into your profits. This slope is slippery, and you can easily lose your footing on it!

Despite these potential pitfalls, you still may have legitimate reasons to use special offers (see the preceding bulleted list). Or you may not have the power to change practices in your market and so have to go with the flow. If you have good reason to use discounts and deals, several options are available to you.

You can offer coupons, refunds, *premiums* (or gifts), extra products for free, free trial-sized samples, sweepstakes and other event-orientated premium plans, and any other special offer you can think up. If you're promoting to *the trade*, as marketers collectively term intermediaries like wholesalers and retailers, then you can also offer your intermediaries things like free-goods deals, buy-back allowances, display and advertising allowances, and help with their advertising costs (called *cooperative advertising*).

Because a large (and growing) majority of all special offers takes the form of *coupons*, we focus on them in explaining how to design special offers.

As you decide on a promotion strategy, be sure to check that the promotion is legal. Legal constraints do exist. You can't mislead consumers about what they get. And a sweepstake or contest has to be open to all, not tied to product purchase. The Institute of Sales Promotion (ISP) offers a legal checklist covering the basics of most types of promotional device. You can access it for free at www.isp.org.uk, but if you really want a guarantee that your promotion is legally watertight, you'll have to become a member to use the ISP's full legal advice service.

Designing coupons and figuring out how much to offer

Any certificate entitling the holder to a reduced price is a coupon, which gives a pretty broad definition – and that means you have a lot of room for creativity in this field. To get a good feel for the options and approaches to coupons, just collect a handful of recent coupons from your own and other industries.

How much of a deal should you offer customers in a coupon or other special offer? The answer depends on how much attention you want. Most offers fail to motivate the vast majority of customers, so keep in mind that the typical special offer in your industry probably isn't particularly effective. A good ad campaign probably reaches more customers.

But you can greatly increase the reach of your special offer simply by making the offer more generous (the higher the price sensitivity, the more notice you generate, of course). In consumer non-durables, whether toothpaste or tinned soup, research shows that you have to offer at least 50p off your list price to attract much attention. All but the most dedicated coupon clippers ignore the smaller offers. But when offers get over the 50p level, attractiveness grows rapidly – sometimes even reaching the 80per cent level! You can find within this larger percentage of interested consumers many brand-loyal, core customers – both yours and your competitors. And you should find these core customers far more attractive than the knee-jerk coupon clippers who flock to smaller offers.

So I think (and I disagree with many marketers on this point) that you do better to use fewer, bigger offers than to run endless pennies-off coupons. Too much noise exists already, so why add to the clutter of messages when you can focus your efforts into fewer, more effective coupons?

Forecasting redemption rates (good luck – you'll need it!)

Designing a coupon isn't the hard part – guessing the *redemption rate* (or percentage of people who use the coupon) is. And you raise the stakes when you use those big offers we advocate, which makes them riskier to forecast.

We can tell you that, on average, customers redeem a little over 3 per cent of coupons (and the average coupon offers 25p off list price). So you can use that as a good starting point for your estimate. But the range is wide – some offers are so appealing, and so easy to use, that customers redeem 50 per cent of those coupons. For others, the redemption rate can be close to zero. So how do you find out if your coupon will have a high or low redemption rate?

You can refine your redemption estimate by looking at your offer compared with others. Are you offering something more generous or easy to redeem than you have in the past? Than your competitors do? If so, you can expect significantly higher than average redemption rates – maybe twice as high or higher.

Also, look at your past data for excellent clues. If you have ever used coupons before, your company should have rich information about response rates. Just be sure that you examine past offers carefully to pick those that truly match the current offer before assuming the same response rate can be repeated.

Think about price sensitivity – again (refer to the earlier section 'Exploring the impact of pricing on customers' purchases'). A lower price isn't always better. Your offer really just shifts the price on a temporary basis – at some cost to the customer because of the trouble they need to go to in order to redeem the coupon. So the real new price is something less than the discount you offer on the coupon – adjust it a little to reflect how much the customer thinks it costs him to redeem the coupon. Now ask yourself if this real price is lower enough than the list price to alter demand. Does the price fall outside of most customers' indifference zones or not?

Many coupons do not shift the price very far beyond the indifference zone – that's why they generally attract those fringe customers who buy on price but don't attract the core customers of other brands. And that's why redemption rates are only a few per cent, on average. However, if your coupon does shift the price well beyond the indifference zone, you're likely to see a much higher redemption rate than usual – but erode your profit margin considerably. There is a happy medium, and your goal is to find out what level of discount is high enough to encourage trial of your brand without losing money.

Coupon deals gone wild is the most common reason for marketers to lose their jobs. So always check the offer against what you know of customer perception and price sensitivity to make sure that you aren't accidentally shifting the price so far that everyone and her brother want to redeem coupons.

Forecasting the cost of special offers

Okay, you've thought about the redemption rate: You believe, for example, that 4 per cent of customers will redeem a coupon offering a 10 per cent discount on your product. To estimate the cost of your coupon programme, you must first decide whether this 4 per cent of consumers accounts for just 4 per cent of your product's sales over the period in which the coupon applies. Probably not. Customers may stock up in order to take advantage of the special offer. And so you have to estimate how much more than usual consumers will buy.

If you think customers will buy twice as much as usual (that's a pretty high figure, but it makes for a simple illustration), just double the average purchase size. Four per cent of customers, buying twice what they usually do in a month (if that's the term of the offer), can produce how much in sales? Now, apply the discount rate to that sales figure to find out how much the special offer may cost you. Can you afford it? Is the promotion worth the money? That's for you to decide – and it's a judgement call; the numbers can't tell you.

Some marketers have their cake and eat it too when it comes to special offers. These marketers use what they call *self-liquidating premiums*, which don't cost them any money at all in the long run. A *premium* is any product that you give away to customers or sell at a discount as a reward for doing business with you (see Chapter 13 for ideas on how to use premiums). A self-liquidating premium is one that customers end up paying for – at least, they cover your costs on that product. Say you run a contest in which some of the customers who open your packaging are instant winners, able to send away for a special premium by enclosing their winning ticket plus £3.95. If your direct costs for the premium you send them are £3.95, you don't have to pay out of pocket for what the customer may see as a fun and valuable benefit.

Staying Out of Trouble with the Law

You don't have to be a legal whiz to know when pricing is illegal. Whenever a customer or competitor can make a good case for unfair or deceptive pricing, you're running the risk of legal action. However, just to keep legal eagles happy, I'm providing a short list of some of the more common and serious illegal pricing practices. (And, of course, because you want to run an ethical business.) Make sure that you read this correctly – these are things you should *not* do!

✔ **Price fixing:** Don't agree to (or even talk about) prices with other companies. The exception is a company you sell to, of course – but note that you cannot force them to resell your product at a specific price.

✔ **Price fixing in disguise:** Shady marketers have tried a lot of ideas. Those ideas don't work. If your competitors want you to require the same amount of down payment, start your negotiations from the same list prices as theirs, or use a standard contract for extending credit or form a joint venture to distribute all your products (at the same price) – realise that these friendly suggestions are all forms of price fixing. Just say no. And in the future, refuse even to take phone calls from marketers who offer you such deals.

✔ **Price fixing by purchasers:** Believe it or not, you shouldn't even treat marketers unfairly. If purchasers join together in order to dictate prices from their suppliers, this can very well be price fixing. Have a skilled lawyer review any such plans.

✔ **Exchanging price information:** You can't talk to your competitors about prices. Ever. Okay? If it ever comes to light that anyone in your company gives out information about pricing and receives some in return, you're in big trouble, even if you don't feel you acted on that information. Take this warning seriously. (By the way, *price signalling* – announcing a planned price increase – is sometimes seen as an unfair exchange of price information, because competitors may use such announcements to signal to others that everyone should make a price increase.)

✔ **Bid rigging:** If you're bidding for a contract, the preceding point applies. Don't share any information with anyone. Don't compare notes with another bidder. Don't agree to make an identical bid. Don't *split* by agreeing not to bid on one job if the competitor doesn't bid on another. Don't mess with the bidding process in any manner, or you're guilty of *bid rigging*.

✔ **Parallel pricing:** In some cases, it is possible that you could be charged with price fixing, even if you didn't talk to competitors – just because you have similar price structures. After all, the result may be the same – to boost prices unfairly. In other cases, the law considers similar prices as natural. Here's a rule that makes good sense: Don't mirror competitors' prices, unless everyone can see that you selected those prices on your own – especially if your price change involves a price increase.

Some people throw up their hands in despair because so many pricing techniques are illegal. Let me just add that trying to influence prices in certain ways is okay. You can offer volume discounts to encourage larger purchases.

And although you, as a marketer, can't force a retailer to charge a certain price for your product, you can encourage them to by advertising the suggested retail price and by listing it as such on your product.

Also, you can always offer an effective price cut to consumers through a consumer coupon or other special offer. Retailers usually agree to honour such offers. However, if you offer a discount to your retailers, you can't force them to pass that discount on to your customers. Retailers may just put the money in the bank and continue to charge customers full price.

Chapter 16

Distribution, Retail, and Point of Purchase

. . . .

In This Chapter

▶ Finding distributors and retailers

▶ Considering marketing channel design

▶ Maximising retail sales

▶ Thinking about point-of-purchase incentives and displays

. . . .

*T*he companies with a wide and efficient distribution are often the most successful, because that distribution system gives them access to so many potential customers.

Of course, reaching out into the world of your customers with your distribution does not guarantee success; it only makes success possible. The customers still have to know and like your product (which, we ought to remind you, can be a service as well as a tangible good). And customers have to view your product as affordable, too. So distribution is not the only important matter in marketing, but it is a big one.

In developing a marketing strategy (see Chapter 1), we encourage you to treat distribution as one of the key factors, or seven Ps, of marketing. For the purposes of fitting distribution into this list of marketing Ps, it is referred to as *place* along with *product, price, promotion, people, process* and *physical presence,* but the idea is the same. What you're doing in distribution is placing your offering when, where, and how prospective customers need and want it.

Distributing Advice

This book's distribution is a simple example of how powerful the right distribution channels can be. This book receives good placement on the shelves of bookshops, especially the increasingly important major chain stores like

Waterstone's, Barnes & Noble, and Borders, where it is placed in the marketing area of the business section, making it easy to find. *Marketing For Dummies* is also placed conveniently by topic, title, and author on searchable Internet bookshops like Amazon (`www.amazon.co.uk`). These two main distribution channels provide broad reach into the market of people who are looking for helpful advice and information about how to market their businesses and sell their products or services. Without this broad distribution, you may never have encountered this book, regardless of how well written, packaged, or priced it may be.

Keep these points in mind about maximising your distribution strategies:

- ✔ If you can add distributors or expand your distribution network, your product may become available to more people, and sales may rise as a result. (If not, consider the Web, direct-response marketing, and events as three alternatives, because they bypass distributors and reach out directly to customers. See Chapters 13, 14, and 16, respectively.)

- ✔ Boost sales by improving the visibility of your product within its current distribution channel, for example by making sure it is better displayed (if it's a product) or better communicated (if it's a service). Or perhaps you can find a way to shift your distribution slightly so as to give you access to more desirable or larger customers.

- ✔ Increasing the availability of products in your distribution channel can also help boost sales and profits. Can you find ways to get more inventory out there? Or can you speed the movement of products out to customers so that they feel that they can more easily find your product when they need it? These sorts of improvements can have a dramatic impact on sales by making finding what they want easier for more customers, when and where they want it.

- ✔ We urge you to make a list of every company that has a hand of any sort in making your sales and servicing your customers, and then to think about ways to strengthen your business relationship with them. Think about doing something simple, like sending them a gift at Christmas. Do something to invest in these relationships – they're very important to most businesses but too easily taken for granted.

- ✔ Using distributors is a low-cost way to keep expanding. Almost every business can sell through distributors if they're open minded and creative about cutting deals. If you already sell through distributors, you should find some more.

- ✔ Even if you have to give a distributor a deeper discount than you want in order to motivate them, you should consider doing it if you believe that your business hasn't achieved its potential until your products are readily available everywhere within your industry.

Getting Distributors on Your Side

Distributors want items that are easy to sell because customers want to buy them – it's that simple. So the first step in getting distributors on your side is making sure your product is appealing. A brilliant product and a clear way of presenting that product so its brilliance shines through is a great investment for growing any distribution system. You may still have to go out and tell distributors about it and work to support them, but if you start with a product whose unique qualities shine through, expanding your distribution will be a lot easier.

After you're confident that you have something worth selling, ask yourself which distributors may be successful at selling it. Who's willing and able to distribute for you? Are wholesalers or other intermediaries going to be helpful? If so, who are they and how many of them can you locate? Try these sources:

✔ **Local business telephone directories or an online equivalent such as Yell** (www.yell.co.uk). These directories often reference the category of intermediary you're looking for.

✔ **Trade associations and trade shows specialising in distributors in specific industries.** If you don't already know which trade associations serve your industry, you can search the Trade Association Forum at www.taforum.org.

✔ **google.co.uk (or any other search engine).** Go online and search for products like yours. Once you find them, work out who's selling them. Maybe they'd sell yours, too!

✔ **Major conventions in your industry.** These are the best places to find distributors. Take along product samples and literature, put on comfortable shoes, and walk around the convention hall until you find the right distributors.

✔ **Retail outlets.** The Yellow Pages phone directories can give you a listing of shops operating in your local area, grouped by the types of products they sell, or try www.yell.com to search further afield. These shops also have their own trade associations, such as the Association of Convenience Stores, at www.acs.org.uk. Consult any directory of associations for extensive listings (available in the reference sections of most libraries), or the Trade Association Forum at www.taforum.org.uk. Finally, consider wearing out a little shoe leather and tyre rubber to find out who the leading retailers are in any specific geographic market. Just visit high-traffic areas and see what shops are prominent and successful to identify the leading retailers in the area.

Understanding Marketing Channel Structure and Design

Efficiency is the driving principle behind *distribution channel* design. (*Channel* refers to the pathways you create to get your product out there and into customers' hands.) Traditionally, channels have evolved to minimise the number of transactions, because the fewer the transactions, the more efficient the channel.

As Figure 16-1 shows, a channel in which four producers and four customers do business directly has 16 (4 x 4) possible transactions. In reality, the numbers get much higher when you have markets with dozens or hundreds of producers and thousands or millions of customers.

You lower the number of transactions greatly when you introduce an intermediary, because now you only have to do simple addition rather than multiplication. In the example shown in Figure 16-1, you only need 8 (4 + 4) transactions to connect all four customers with all four producers through the intermediary. Each producer or customer has only to deal with the intermediary, who links him to all the producers or customers he may want to do business with.

Although intermediaries add their mark-up to the price, they often reduce overall costs of distribution because of their effect on the number of transactions. Adding a level of intermediaries to a channel reduces the total number of transactions that all producers and customers need to do business with each other.

This example is simplistic, but you can see how the logic applies to more complex and larger distribution channels. Introduce a lot of customers and producers, link them through multiple intermediaries (perhaps adding a second or third layer of intermediaries), and you have a classic indirect marketing channel. Odds are that you have some channels like this in your industry.

We have to warn you that we're suspicious of these traditional, multi-level channels. The longer and more complex they grow, the more types of intermediaries they have. The more times a product is handed from intermediary to intermediary, the less we like the channel. We prefer to see only one layer between you and your customers, if possible.

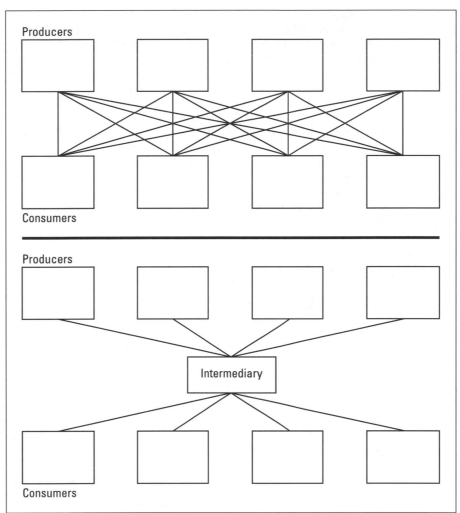

Producers

Consumers

Producers

Intermediary

Consumers

Figure 16-1:
Reducing
transactions
through
inter-
mediaries.

Why? We don't like traditional, many-layered channels because they separate you too much from the end consumer. We think that improved transportation; computerised links between channel members (through *electronic data interchange* or *EDI*); the creation of just-in-time inventory systems in which suppliers bring only what's needed, when it's needed; and the emergence of direct marketing technologies and practices all make running lean and mean channels much easier. Just as big companies are de-layering to become more efficient and get closer to their customers, the big distribution channels in many industries are trying to do the same thing.

The trend is toward simpler and more direct channels, and marketers need to be prepared to handle a large number of customer transactions on their own without as much help from intermediaries. Database management techniques alone do much to make this future possible.

So think hard about how to get closer to your customer. Can you reduce the layers in your channel or begin to develop direct channels (by mail, phone, or Internet) to supplement your traditional indirect channels? If so, balance the advantages of being close to the end customer with the benefits of broad reach from having many distributors. One way to do this is to add more distributors in the horizontal direction, where each new distributor buys directly from you, not through another distributor who then bundles their purchase with others and sends it on to you. Think broad distribution, not deep, if you want modern reach without traditional layers and all of the complexities and costs of those layers.

What do intermediaries do to earn their cut?

In deciding how to distribute your product, we recommend that you draw up a list of tasks you want distributors to do. For example, you may want distributors to find you more customers than you can find on your own. Finding customers is just one of the functions distributors may be able to perform. Decide what you'd like them to do, and then seek out distributors who say they want to do those things for you – that way, you'll be more likely to get a good match. Here's a starting list of functions you may want your intermediaries to perform. One or more of these functions may be important to you as you look for distributors:

- Finding more customers for your product than you can on your own
- Researching customer attitudes and desires
- Buying and selling
- Breaking down bulk shipments for resale
- Setting prices
- Managing point-of-purchase promotions
- Advertising at the local level (*pull advertising*, which is designed to bring people to a shop or other business)
- Transporting products
- Inventorying products
- Financing purchases

✔ Separating poor-quality leads from serious customers (marketers call this *qualifying sales leads*)

✔ Providing customer service and support

✔ Sharing the risks of doing business

✔ Combining your products with others to offer appropriate assortments

Channel design considerations

Yes, your intermediaries can do several useful things for you, as the preceding section indicates. You need to decide who can do which of these things. But, in addition to thinking about those various functions and who should perform them, you may want to consider the following strategic issues. How you set up and manage your distribution channel or channels affects each issue.

Market coverage

How well does your channel reach your target customers? If you go direct, doing everything yourself, you may be unable to cover the market as intensely as you want to. By adding even one layer of intermediaries, you suddenly have many more warm bodies or shopfronts out there. As you add more layers to the channel, the bottom of the channel grows ever larger, allowing you to achieve increasingly good market coverage.

In short, market coverage increases as you add layers and members to your distribution channel. As you increase market coverage, you increase your availability to customers, which in turn maximises your sales and market share. You can't fight that logic – so sometimes building a channel, rather than de-layering it, makes sense. Just make sure that you really do get better coverage and that the coverage translates into increased sales. Otherwise, those intermediaries aren't pulling their weight.

Level of intensity

Thinking about the issue of market coverage in terms of *intensity*, defined as the extent of your geographic coverage of the market, can help you work out how many and what types of distributors to use. Conventional wisdom says that three practical strategies exist:

✔ **Intensive distribution strategy.** This strategy attempts to put every customer within reach of your products by using as many intermediaries and layers as needed to create maximum coverage. You should use this strategy in mature markets where your competitors are trying to do the same thing, or in markets where the customer makes a convenience purchase – because intensive distribution makes your product convenient. Keep in mind that this strategy costs you a lot, and you may not need it in other circumstances.

✔ **Selective distribution strategy.** In this strategy you target the most desirable areas or members of your market. For example, the business-to-business marketer may decide to target a geographic region where many users of his technology are based. The consumer products marketer may decide to market to areas by postcode or counties where he finds heavy users of his product.

✔ **Exclusive distribution.** Here you cherry pick to find the best intermediaries and customers. This strategy is appropriate when you don't have any really serious competition and you have a speciality product that you want to keep providing at the same profitable level. This method doesn't grow your market or boost share significantly, but it does maximise profit margins, and that's not bad!

Exclusive distribution is also appropriate as you introduce an innovative new product, whether a good or service. You find a limited number of early adopters in any market, so a massive effort to mass-market a new innovative product usually fails. Start with exclusive distribution to those customers most interested in trying new ideas and then work up to selective distribution as competition builds and the product goes mainstream. Finally, push toward intensive distribution as the market matures and your emphasis shifts from finding first-time users to fighting over repeat business.

Speed to market

The longer the channel, the slower the product's trip from producer to customer. A relay team will seldom beat an individual runner in a sprint. If your customers need or want faster delivery and service, you have to prune the distribution channel until it's fast enough to satisfy the consumers. You may even need to replace physical distributors with a Web site where everything can be ordered immediately, for next-day delivery.

Think about the trend toward catalogue home-shopping in the clothing industry. Customers can obtain their choice of style and size from a large assortment and the company can deliver it within a few days. You may think that you can shop in a department store even more quickly because you can walk out with your purchase. But the busy consumer may not have time to visit a department store for days or weeks, whereas he can take care of a late-night call to Lands' End today. And you may need to visit several shops to find what you want, which eats up more days and more lunch hours. However, you can look through a stack of catalogues in a flash. Catalogue clothing sales are gaining over retail sales, in part because many consumers perceive catalogue shopping as the quicker and easier alternative.

Reviewing Retail Strategies and Tactics

If you decide to improve sales at a shop and you bring in a specialised retail consultant, you may soon be drawing *planograms* of your shelves (diagrams showing how to lay out and display a shop's merchandise) and counting *SKUs* (stock-keeping units – a unique inventory code for each item you stock). You may also examine the statistics on sales volume from end-of-aisle displays (higher sales) versus middle of the aisle (lower sales), and from eye-level displays (higher sales) versus bottom or top of the shelf (lower sales). Great. Go for it. However, we have to warn you that, although a technical approach has its place, you can't use this method to create a retail success story.

The real winners in retail are the result of creative thinking and good site selection – in that order. Those points are the two big-picture issues that determine whether your shop has low or high performance: A creative, appealing shop concept, in a spot that has the right sort of traffic, and a lot of it.

Traffic is a flow of target customers near enough to the shop for its external displays and local advertising to draw them in. You want a great deal of traffic, whether it's foot traffic on a pavement, car traffic on a road, or virtual traffic at a Web site. Retailers need to have people walking, driving, or surfing into their shops ('virtual' shops on Web sites need to have traffic in the form of lots of clicks and visitors; see Chapter 13). Customers don't come into a shop or onto a site in big numbers unless you have plenty of people to draw from, so you need to work out where high traffic is and find a way to get some of it into your shop.

An old joke about retailing goes like this: 'The retail business has three secrets of success – location, location, and location.' Not very funny, really, unless you've ever tried to market a shop in a poor location. And then you laugh pretty hard over the joke, but with a certain hysteria! Pick a location carefully, making sure that you have an excess of the right sort of traffic nearby. Think of designing a retail shop like digging a pond. You wouldn't dig a pond unless running water was nearby to fill it. Yet people dig their retail ponds in deserts or up steep hills, far from the nearest flow of traffic, all the time. You also wouldn't dig a huge reservoir beside a small stream. You must suit your shop to the amount and kind of traffic in its area, or move to find more appropriate traffic.

Developing merchandising strategies

Whether you retail services or goods, you need to think about your merchandising strategy. You do have one, whether you know it or not – and if you don't know it, then your strategy is based on conventions in your industry and needs a kick in the seat of the pants to make it more distinctive. *Merchandising strategy*, the selection and assortment of products offered, tends to be the most important source of competitive advantage or disadvantage for retailers.

What's your merchandising strategy? To answer this question, you need to recognise your own brilliance – what makes you especially notable – and make sure you translate that brilliance into visible, attractive aspects of both exterior and interior shop design.

We want to encourage a creative approach to merchandising. The majority of success stories in retailing come about because of innovations in merchandising. So you should be thinking of new merchandising options daily – and trying out the most promising ones as often as you can afford to. The following sections describe some existing strategies, which may give you ideas for your business. Perhaps no one has tried these strategies in your industry or region, or perhaps they suggest novel variations to you.

General merchandise retailing

This strategy works because it brings together a wide and deep assortment of products, thus allowing customers to easily find what they want – regardless of what the product may be. Department stores and general merchandisers (such as Woolworths) fall into this category, but so to do the large out-of-town supermarkets, which are expanding from groceries into non-food sales. In the UK, Tesco and Asda are leaders in this because they offer more variety (and often better prices) than nearby competitors. The warehouse store (such as CostCo and Matalan) gives you another example of general merchandise retailing. And as this varied list of examples suggests, you can implement this strategy in many ways.

Limited-line retailing

This strategy emphasises depth over variety. London's Planet Organic chain of grocery stores specialises in natural and organic food products; as a result, the chain can offer far greater choice in this specialised area than the average supermarket (and it picks locations where there is a high concentration of wealthy households). Similarly, a bakery can offer more and better varieties of baked goods because a bakery sells only those baked goods.

Mixing and matching

Can you think of the perfect new combination of shops? How about a gym and a launderette, so people can work out while washing their clothes? Or a connections shop that offers the combined services of a flower shop, jeweller's and gift shop, card and stationery shop, e-mail/Internet access service, gift-wrapping and shipping service, and a computerised dating/introduction service? With all these services under one roof, the shop can serve any and all needs having to do with making or maintaining personal relationships. See? Coming up with novel combinations isn't hard – give it a try!

Limited-line retailing is especially common in professional and personal services. Most accounting firms just do accounting. Most chiropractic offices just offer chiropractic services. Most law firms just practice law.

Perhaps you can combine several complementary services into a less limited line than your competitors. If you can expand your line without sacrificing quality or depth of offerings, you can give customers greater convenience – and that convenience should make you a winner.

After all, the limited-line strategy only makes sense to customers if they gain something in quality or selection in exchange for the lack of convenience. Regrettably, many limited-line retailers fail to make good on this implied promise – and they're easily run over when a business introduces a less-limited line nearby. What makes, say, the local chemist's or butcher's selection better than what a Boots or Tesco offers in a more convenient setting? If you're a small businessperson, make sure that you have plenty of good answers to that question! Know what makes your merchandise selection, concept, or location different and better than that of your monster competitors.

Scrambled merchandising

Consumers have preconceived notions about what product lines and categories belong together. Looking for fresh produce in a grocery shop makes sense these days because dry goods and fresh produce have been combined by so many retailers. But 50 years ago, the idea would seem radical because specialised limited-line retailers used to sell fresh produce. When grocery shops combined these two categories, they were using a *scrambled merchandising* strategy, in which the merchant uses unconventional combinations of product lines. Today, the meat department, bakery, deli section, seafood department, and many other sections combine naturally in a modern supermarket. And many supermarkets are adding other products and services, such as a coffee bar, bank, bookshop, dry cleaners, shoe repair, hair salon, photographer, flower shop, post office, and so on! In the same way, petrol stations combine with fast food restaurants and convenience stores to offer pit stops for both car and driver. These scrambled merchandising concepts are now widely accepted.

You can use scrambling as a great way to innovate. Scrambling gets at the essence of creativity because many people define creativity as the search for unexpected but pleasing combinations of things or ideas. We hope that you pursue this strategy.

We do want to warn you, however, never to employ the scrambling strategy just for your convenience as a marketer. Too often, retailers add a novel product line just because doing so is easy – they know someone in another industry who can handle the line for them, or they have a chance to buy a failed business for peanuts. Those reasons are the wrong sort to justify scrambling.

Scrambling only works if you approach it from the customer's point of view by seeking new combinations that may have special customer appeal. For example, several innovators around the world have stumbled independently upon the concept of combining a coffee shop and an Internet access service into one retail store. The result is a natural: A coffee shop where you can enjoy your espresso while cruising the Internet or flirting with another customer online. This new combination adds up to more than the sum of its parts, giving customers a pleasurable new retail experience.

Creating atmosphere

A shop's atmosphere, or *physical presence,* is the image that it projects based on how you decorate and design it. Atmosphere is an intangible – you can't easily measure or define it. But you can feel it. And when the atmosphere feels comforting, exciting, or enticing, this feeling draws people into the shop and enhances their shopping experience. So you need to pay close attention to atmosphere.

Sophisticated retailers hire specialist architects and interior designers to create the right atmosphere and then spend far too much on fancy lighting, new carpets, and racks to implement their plans. Sometimes this approach works, but sometimes it doesn't. And at any point in time, most of the professional designers agree about what shops should look and feel like. And that means your shop looks like everyone else's.

Instead, we think you should develop the concept for your shop yourself. If you think a virtual tropical forest gives the right atmosphere, then hire some crazy artists and designers to turn your shop into a tropical forest! Rainforest Cafe did so a few years ago, creating a fantasy environment they call 'a wild place to shop and eat'.

Maybe you really like old-fashioned steam engines. Great. Make trains the theme of your children's toy shop or men's clothing boutique. Run model train tracks around the shop, put up huge posters of oncoming steam engines, and incorporate the occasional train whistle into your background music. Some people will love it; others will think you're nuts. But nobody will ever forget your shop.

Atmospherics are important because consumers increasingly seek more from retail shopping than just finding specific products. In consumer societies, shopping is an important activity in its own right. Surveys suggest that less than a quarter of shoppers in shopping centres go there in search of a specific item. Consumers often use shopping to alleviate boredom and loneliness, avoid dealing with chores or problems in their lives, seek fulfilment of their fantasies, or simply to entertain themselves. If that's what motivates many shoppers, you need to take such motivations into consideration when you design your shop.

Perhaps you can honestly and simply provide some entertainment for your customers. Just as a humorous ad entertains people and, thereby, attracts their attention long enough to communicate a message, a shop can entertain for long enough to expose shoppers to its merchandise.

Examples of entertaining retail concepts include Niketown and the Apple store, two ways of combining a manufacturer's brand with an entertaining retail environment – resulting in a reason to linger and buy. Likewise, the mobile phone brands such as Orange and T-Mobile have outlets where you can recharge your phone and get training on how to make use of all of the functions of your phone – a form of entertainment. And some Barnes & Noble bookshops create comfortable, enclosed children's book sections with places to play and read or be read to, so that families with young children can stay and enjoy the experience.

Building price and quality strategies

Retail stores generally have a distinct place in the range of possible price and quality combinations. Some shops are obviously upscale boutiques, specialising in the finest merchandise – for the highest prices. Other shops are middle class in their positioning, and still others offer the worst junk from liquidators but sell it for so little that almost anybody can afford it. In this way, retailing still maintains the old distinctions of social class, even though the people who shop there may not.

As a retailer, this distinction means that customers get confused about who you are unless you let them know where you stand on the class scale. Does your shop have an upper-class pedigree, or is it upper-middle, middle, or lower-middle class?

 After you make a decision about how to place your shop, you're ready to decide what price strategy to pursue. Don't forget that building-in upmarket appeal can be an effective strategy for attracting the mass market – because you've built in desirability. In general, the higher class the shop's image, the higher the prices that the shop can charge. But the real secret to success is to price just a step below your image. That way, customers feel like they're buying first-class products for second-class prices – and that makes them very happy, indeed!

Pursuing retail sales

Many retailers take a passive approach. These retailers put the products on the shelves or display racks and wait for customers to pick them up and bring them to the counter. Other retailers are a bit more proactive: They have staff walking the aisles or floors, looking for customers who may need some help. But few retailers go all the way and actually put trained salespeople on the floor to work the customers.

We've heard that less than 20 per cent of retailers make active efforts to close a sale. The actual number is probably much lower. Even approaching customers to ask whether they need help is rare these days.

Sometimes that hands-off approach makes sense. But, in general, if people walk into a shop they're considering making a purchase, which makes them likely prospects. To us, that means that somebody should find out what their wants or needs are and try to meet them! The effort doesn't need to be pushy – in fact, the effort shouldn't be pushy or you reduce return visits – but you should make a friendly effort to be helpful. Find out what customers are looking for, offer them whatever you have that seems relevant, and ask them if they want to make a purchase. The last part, asking them for the purchase, is especially important. In selling, you call that question the *close,* and when you attempt to close sales, you usually up the sales rate. See Chapter 20 for more details.

If you want to get plugged into a wide variety of publications, conferences, and other events of interest to retailers, get in touch with the British Retail Consortium (BRC) at www.brc.org.uk. The BRC is the leading retail trade association in the UK, but you can also find specialist associations covering everything from bike shops to DIY centres. And if you need to find out more about shop planning or track down experienced shop planners, try the Shop & Display Equipment Association, at www.shopdisplay.org.uk. And don't overlook the useful book, *Retail Business Kit For Dummies*, by Rick Segal (Wiley), which goes into the topic in far more depth than we can here.

POP! Stimulating Sales at Point of Purchase

Point of purchase, or *POP*, is the place where customer meets product. It may be in the aisles of a shop, or even on a catalogue page or computer monitor, but wherever this encounter takes place, the principles of POP advertising apply. Table 16-1 gives you percentage figures relevant to retail design and point-of-purchase marketing, according to the Point of Purchase Advertising Institute (whose members are professionals working on POP displays and advertising, so the Institute does a fair amount of research on shopping patterns and how to affect those patterns at points of purchase).

Table 16-1	Nature of Consumer's Purchase Decision	
	Supermarkets' Percentage of Purchases	*Mass Merchandise Shops' Percentage of Purchases*
Unplanned	60	53
Substitute	4	3
Generally planned	6	18
Specifically planned	30	26

Customers plan some purchases outside of the shop – 30 per cent of supermarket purchases and 26 per cent of mass merchandise purchases fall into this category. In these cases, customers make a rational decision about what shops to go to in order to buy what they want. Because they have a clear idea of what they want to purchase, these customers' purchases aren't highly subject to marketing influence. Even so, the right merchandise selection, location, atmosphere, and price strategy can help get customers to choose your shop for their planned purchases rather than a competing shop. And the right shop layout and point-of-purchase displays help customers find what they want quickly and easily. So even with so-called specifically planned purchases, you do have an influence over what happens.

Furthermore (and this news is really good for marketers), you have a far greater influence over the majority of purchases than you probably realise. All the studies that we've seen, including the one from which we took those statistics in Table 16-1 (and also the oft-quoted statistic that 75 per cent of decisions are made at the point of purchase), all add up to the startling conclusion that . . .

> Shoppers are remarkably aimless and suggestible!

The fact that customers don't plan between a half and three-quarters of all retail purchases is really incredible. What happened to the venerable shopping list? How do consumers get their bank accounts to balance with all that impulse buying? And why do they wander aimlessly through shops, in the first place – don't they have jobs, families, or hobbies to keep them busy? Evidently not.

We don't pretend to understand our consumer society, we just write about it. Although we can't explain the fact that the modern retail shopper is in some sort of zombie-like state much of the time, we can tell you that this fact makes point-of-purchase marketing incredibly important to all marketers of consumer goods and services. Whether you're a retailer, wholesaler, or producer, you need to recognise that customers make an impulse decision – to buy your product or not to buy it – in the majority of cases. And that suggests you should do what you can to sway that decision your way at point of purchase. Another advantage is that not many companies seem to understand the power of point of purchase – we can't think of another reason why only 5 per cent of marketing budgets in the UK are spent on POP advertising. Can you?

For more information about POP, a directory of POP designers and manufacturers, or a calendar of trade shows and events for the industry, contact the Point of Purchase Advertising Institute UK & Ireland at www.popai.co.uk. You can come up with your own winning POP or retail concepts by perusing the latest winners of merchandising awards, such as the Instore Awards. Finally, don't overlook the interactions between package design and labelling and POP (see Chapter 17). Also check out Chapter 11 for details on how to design and use signs and banners.

Designing POP displays

You can boost sales by designing appealing displays from which consumers can pick your products. Free-standing floor displays have the biggest effect, but retailers don't often use them because they take up too much floor space. Rack, shelf, and counter-based signs and displays aren't quite as powerful, but shops use these kinds of displays more often. Customers are likely to notice any really exciting and unusual display, which means that display works very well because it has a general impact on shop traffic and sales, as well as boosting sales of the products it's designed to promote. Exciting displays add to the shop's atmosphere or entertainment value, and shop managers like that addition.

Because creativity is one of the keys to successful shop concepts, creativity also drives POP success. Let us show you what we mean through an example that worked well to boost retail sales and won design awards for its originality.

When Procter & Gamble introduced a new formulation of the Vicks 44 cough syrup, they created a point-of-purchase display (that shopowners could use as a free-standing display or as a wall rack) that featured a rotating frame in which two clear bottles were visible. Each bottle had some red syrup in it – one with Vicks 44, the other with a competing cough syrup. When customers rotated the frame to turn the bottles over, they could see that the Vicks 44 coated the inside of the bottle and the competition's syrup sloshed to the bottom. This interactive display was supposed to prove the unique selling proposition that Vicks 44 coats your throat better than the competition. We like this display because it's interactive – giving customers something interesting to do to build their involvement – and because it demonstrates the product's *USP* (its unique selling proposition – what makes it brilliantly different from all competitors). Like a good advertisement, this POP display attracts attention, builds involvement, and then communicates a single, powerful point about the product.

Too often, POP displays don't do everything the Vicks 44 display does. POP displays don't work well unless they

- ✓ **Attract attention.** Make them novel, entertaining, or puzzling to draw people to them.
- ✓ **Build involvement.** Give people something to think about or do in order to create their involvement in the display.
- ✓ **Sell the product.** Make sure that the display tells viewers what's so great about the product. The display must communicate the positioning and USP (make sure you have one!). Simply putting the product on display isn't enough. You have to sell the product, too, or the retailer doesn't see the point. Retailers can put products on display without marketers' help. Retailers want help in selling those products.

You may have noticed that we keep worrying about whether retailers like and use POPs. This concern is a major issue for marketers because between 50 and 60 per cent of marketers' POPs never reach the sales floor. If you're a product marketer who's trying to get a POP display into retail stores, you face an uphill battle. The stats say that your display or sign needs to be twice as good as average, or the retailer simply throws it away.

Answering questions about POP

The following sections give you some facts to help you develop and implement your own POP campaign.

Who should design and pay for POPs – marketers or retailers?

In some cases, marketers design POPs and offer them to retailers as part of their marketing campaigns. In other cases, retailers develop their own POPs. The Point of Purchase Advertising Institute (POPAI) reports that the industry is about equally divided. In other words, retailers directly purchase half of all POP displays, and marketers who offer their materials to retailers make up the other half. So the answer is a bit of both.

What kinds of POPs do marketers use?

The Point of Purchase Advertising Institute is a helpful source of data (www.popai.co.uk). POPAI surveys reveal that salespeople spend the most on POPs for permanent displays (generally, retailers make these purchases). Next in popularity (based on spending) are in-store media and sign options. And temporary displays come in third. Yet marketers generally think about temporary displays first when talking about POP. Maybe marketers need to rethink their approach and redesign their POP campaigns to emphasise permanent displays and signs first and temporary displays second.

How much can POP lift your sales?

Lift is the increase in sales of a product attributable to POP marketing. Researchers compare sales with and without POP to calculate lift (it's the difference between the two). You need to estimate lift in order to work out what return you can get for any particular investment in POP. First, we can tell you that, in general, accessories and routine repurchases have the highest lifts. Also, significantly, new products have high lifts if their POPs effectively educate consumers about their benefits. Table 16-2 shows you a range of lift statistics based on a detailed study of the question by POPAI.

Table 16-2	Lift Statistics
POP Displays/Signs For	*Typical Lift (%)*
Film/photo-finishing	48
Socks/underwear/tights	29
Dishwasher powder	22
Biscuits and crackers	18
DVDs	12
Butter/margarine	6
Pet supplies	6
Stationery	5
Salty snacks	4
Salad dressing	3

How much of your marketing budget should you allocate to POP?

We can't answer this question with any certainty because every campaign has to be shaped by its unique circumstances. But we can tell you that POP advertising accounts for only 5 per cent of UK advertising expenditure (and don't forget 75 per cent of buying decisions are made at point of purchase). Partly because retailers, distributors and wholesalers, and producers spread this spending out broadly between them, POP doesn't get the attention that other media do in most marketing plans. Big mistake. Try to identify who in your distribution channel is involved in POPs that affect your sales and work toward an integrated strategy and plan so that you can bring this hidden medium into the spotlight and make it work more effectively for your marketing campaign.

POP is just one example of what we consider to be proactive marketing. Getting a distributor to agree to sell your product, or writing a sale to a retailer are not enough. Now you have to get to work making sure that your product moves faster than others so that you win the enthusiastic reorders and loyalty that make for durable, profitable distribution channels. Channel management is an important part of most marketers' jobs and requires attention and a generous share of marketing imagination. One effective channel management strategy is to offer a varying selection of good point-of-purchase options to help your distributors succeed in selling your product.

Chapter 17

Sales and Service Essentials

*I*n marketing, the whole point is to make a sale. In fact, in business, the whole point is to make a sale. Nothing else can happen without that. But do you need to be doing personal sales and service, in which you interact with people directly as part of your marketing? The answer is always yes. Whether you have a formal sales role or not, selling should be a natural, everyday part of business life, and something you do whether you're interacting with clients, ringing sales at a checkout, meeting other professionals, or taking a phone call. So this chapter may be the most important one in the book.

Providing Strategic Leadership in Sales

The sales process is a journey for the buyer. Sometimes, she just takes a quick trip down the block, but she often has to make a difficult, even lengthy, journey – and then she needs the leadership of a good salesperson.

Some people think that the topic of leadership is not related to the topic of sales and marketing. Not at all! There are many similarities between great leadership and great salesmanship. As a salesperson (or an entrepreneur, consultant, or other professional who needs to wear a sales hat sometimes), you need to be prepared to help and guide your prospects toward purchase. You can't force your prospects to buy, but you can guide and facilitate their journey. To paraphrase the old saying, you can lead your customers to water, but you can't make them drink. You can't close their sales. Instead, your customers have to be prepared to close their sales with you, and that won't happen until they arrive at the end of their purchase journeys.

Every purchase of any consequence involves the whole human being – *including* her thoughts and feelings. You need to address the prospect's cognitive and rational thoughts, but you also need to address her irrational, emotional feelings. Think about buying a car, for example. You don't buy a car if you think it's ugly. The vehicle has to appeal aesthetically to you; that's the emotional side of the purchase journey. But even if the car looks good, you probably won't buy it if you think it's poorly designed or in poor repair and likely to break down – considerations that involve the rational side of the purchase journey.

Most people tend to focus on one or the other appeal when they sell – they orient their sales pitch more toward information and logical argument (that's the first dimension), or they focus it on relational and emotional elements in their approach (which is the second dimension). Advertising – and selling – needs to appeal to *both* the rational and the emotional dimensions of this journey, as we point out in Chapter 7. There is a third dimension to the sales process, which is after-sales support, and which will ease repeat sales. Doing this multidimensional appeal well, and at the appropriate times, can be hard without some special training and practice.

Sales strategies in a nutshell

Following are the four sales strategies and the three-dimensional sales process that you should use as the basic framework for all your sales challenges. Remember to ask yourself (or the prospect) what emotional (feelings) and informational (facts) barriers exist, and then choose a strategy to fit the strategic context. A great salesperson has (and uses) this core skill.

Appealing to your customers' feelings

The classic example of the feelings-orientated or intuitive approach is the super-friendly salesperson who knows people well, remembers their birthdays, entertains them, and brings them considerate gifts. This individual is a strong relationship builder and may do reasonably well in sales.

If you focus solely on building relationships you're, in essence, just a well-connected order taker. You run the risk of leaving the logical side of the purchase process to the prospect and not giving enough information and problem-solving support. This approach is best combined with an approach that addresses the cognitive side of selling, as explained in the next section.

Appealing to your customers' logical side

Some people naturally tend to emphasise the cognitive side of selling: They prepare by researching the prospect's needs, they present a lot of factual information, and they anticipate and refute objections. These people can be effective at selling, too. But sometimes their prospects balk – they refuse to complete the journey, even though it seems like all the evidence points that way.

Why do people sometimes fail to purchase when the purchase seems like a natural for them? Maybe the problems aren't rational or cognitive, but emotional. For example, you don't make a major purchase if you're feeling uncomfortable or uncertain – you postpone it or back out entirely. If you would describe yourself as a logical, fact-orientated salesperson, be sure to pair this strength with the characteristics of the intuitive approach to maximise your effectiveness.

Coaching your customer through the purchase

Perhaps you're one of the rare people who naturally combines both facts and feelings in their efforts to help a prospect move toward purchase. When the prospect has both factual and feelings-orientated issues or barriers, you need to use this strategy by encouraging the prospect to take small steps with plenty of support from you. For example, you may break the purchase decision down to make saying 'yes' to a small thing possible today. Positive results from a trial or test purchase or a small use of a service can reinforce both the factual and emotional dimensions of the prospect's journey, allowing her to reach the next level.

Think about selling like being a coach, patiently improving the performance of an athlete. What can you get the prospect to do today to increase her comfort and move her closer to a major commitment? Try to do something with the prospect each time you interact, even if you're only warming that person up to the big purchase. Salespeople have the most success using the coaching-orientated style, especially with complex purchases, so if you don't use this style already, make a point of using it in the future.

Delegating the sale to the prospect

Delegating means trusting the prospect to take the initiative and make the purchase. Delegators set up the opportunity for a purchase, and then step back and wait to see who buys. Many people overuse this delegate strategy and assume that, if the customer needs something, she asks for it. That strategy is not necessarily a good way to approach sales, because many prospects don't complete their purchase journeys without help.

Normally, you want to check on your prospects and assess their level of factual and feelings-based readiness for purchase – and then step in, using one of the three strategies listed in the previous sections. Otherwise, if you delegate and leave it up to the prospect, she may not make it to the end of her purchase journey. However, you can use the delegate sales strategy effectively when your prospect is really committed and ready on the emotional dimension, and also has all the information needed to decide what to do. In this situation, try a simple closing strategy, like asking if she wants to place an order or what kind of purchase she wants to make.

When the time is right, you need to trust your prospect to make a sound decision that's to her (and thus your) benefit. Try to close in several low-key ways until you secure the sale. Then make a flow of business occur easily by providing continuing access and service support.

Following up with customer support

Don't forget this all-important element of maintaining a flow of business through good customer support. If you ignore the customer after the order comes in, you'll probably lose her and have to start all over again with another customer – a much harder task than retaining a good customer would have been. Put all three of these dimensions together and you have an effective sales strategy, where you attend both to the facts and feelings of the sale and then support with ongoing service to retain the customer.

Knowing When to Emphasise Personal Selling

Sometimes you need *personal selling* – that is, selling face to face – as a part of the marketing process. In that case, you need to make sales the main focus of marketing plans and activities. Any advertising, direct mail, telemarketing, event sponsorships, public relations – or anything else you may think of – has to take a back seat to sales. To find out if your business should rely on sales, take the following quiz in Table 17-1.

Table 17-1		Are Personal Sales and Service the Key to Your Marketing Plan?
☐ yes	☐ no	Our typical customer makes many small purchases and/or at least a few very large ones in a year.
☐ yes	☐ no	Our typical customer usually needs help figuring out what to buy and/or how to use the product.
☐ yes	☐ no	Our typical customer's business is highly complex and imposes unique requirements on our products/services.
☐ yes	☐ no	Our products/services are an important part of the customer's overall business process.
☐ yes	☐ no	Our customer is accustomed to working with salespeople and expects personal attention and assistance.
☐ yes	☐ no	Our competitors make regular sales calls on our customers and/or prospects.
☐ yes	☐ no	We have to provide customised service to retain a customer.

If you gave multiple 'yes' answers to the questions in the previous table, then you can probably use personal sales (one-to-one with prospects) effectively, and you should make them an important part of your marketing plan and budget. You should focus your marketing plan on personal selling and good follow-up service. Although you certainly also want to employ many other marketing methods, be sure to think of the rest of your marketing activities as support for the personal sales process. That personal sales process is going to be the key to your success – or failure. And that means you need to give careful thought to how you hire, manage, organise, support, and motivate salespeople. Your salespeople's performance determines whether your marketing succeeds or fails.

Figuring Out Whether You Have What It Takes

Some people seem born to sell, and others are doomed to fail. But most of the population muddles along, struggling to improve their sales ability and wondering if they really have the right stuff. You can't categorise most people as either sales stars or no-hopers; they sit somewhere in the middle – capable of great performances but not so gifted that the performances come naturally. These potential salespeople can figure out how to do better, by practising the strategic approach that we outline with the three-dimensional sales process in the preceding section. You probably fall in this middle range and can increase your performance, too. We recommend that you check your sales talent in order to decide whether you should find someone else to do this challenging task for you, whether you're a natural sales star, or whether you're somewhere in-between and can easily improve with study and practice.

Table 17-2 gives you a simple version of a test of sales ability. Take five minutes to answer the questions and then another couple of minutes to score them. At the end, you have some useful feedback about your overall sales ability right now, plus an idea about the areas you need to focus on if you want to improve your overall score in the future.

Employers take note. Tests like this one don't guarantee someone's success – your management and the rest of your marketing plan affect an employee's performance as much as their sales ability does. Also, ability alone doesn't give you much without appropriate training and technique. But anyone who you think ranks low on this test probably shouldn't take over an important sales territory.

Table 17-2	Measure Your Sales Ability

Tick any statements that describe you well. If a statement doesn't fit you, leave it blank.

☐ 1. I feel good about myself much of the time.

☐ 2. I usually say the right thing at the right time.

☐ 3. People seek out my company.

☐ 4. I don't get discouraged, even if I fail repeatedly.

☐ 5. I'm an excellent listener.

☐ 6. I can read people's moods and body language with ease.

☐ 7. I project warmth and enthusiasm when I first meet people.

☐ 8. I'm good at sensing and bringing out the real reasons behind a negative answer.

☐ 9. I can see many ways to define a problem and understand its causes.

☐ 10. I'm skilled at drawing out other people's concerns and problems.

☐ 11. I know enough about business to help others solve their problems with ease.

☐ 12. I'm so trustworthy and helpful that I quickly convince people to work with me in true collaborations.

☐ 13. I manage my time so well that I'm able to get to everything that's important in a workday.

☐ 14. I focus on the big-picture goals that matter most to me and my company instead of always reacting to the latest crisis or chore.

☐ 15. I can balance the need for finding new customers with the demands of maintaining and strengthening all existing customer relationships.

☐ 16. I keep looking for and finding ways to be more effective and efficient.

☐ 17. I find that, for me, a sense of accomplishment is even more rewarding than money.

☐ 18. My internal standards and expectations are higher than any imposed on me by others.

☐ 19. I don't care how long it takes to succeed at a task – I know I can succeed, in the end.

☐ 20. I feel I deserve the respect and admiration of my customers and associates.

Scoring:

A. Positive Personality?

Total number of ticks on statements 1 to 4:

Less than three ticks means that you need improvement on personal attitude, emotional resiliency, and self-confidence.

B. Interpersonal Skills?

Total number of ticks on statements 5 to 8:

Less than three ticks means that you need improvement on communication and listening skills, including your ability to control your own non-verbal communications and read others' body language.

C. Solution-Finding Skills?

Total number of ticks on statements 9 to 12:

Less than three ticks means that you need improvement on problem-finding, creative problem-solving, and collaborative negotiating skills.

D. Self-Management Skills?

Total number of ticks on statements 13 to 16:

Less than three ticks means that you need improvement on organisation, strategy, and focus skills.

E. Self-Motivation?

Total number of ticks on statements 17 to 20:

Less than three ticks means that you need to build your personal motivation and figure out how to find rewards in the pleasures of doing a job well and accomplishing a goal.

F. Overall Level of Sales Ability?

Total number of ticks, all statements (1 to 20):

Total Number of Ticks	Score
0–5	Guaranteed to fail. Sorry, but you should let somebody else do the selling!
6–9	Low sales ability. Not likely to succeed.
10–12	Low sales ability, but with practice and study, may become moderately capable.
13–15	Moderate sales ability. Capable of good improvement.
16–18	High sales ability. Capable of rapid improvement.
19–20	Guaranteed to succeed. Superstar potential!

If you ticked a total of 13 or more, you have enough ability to be out there on the road making sales calls right now. However, this score doesn't mean that you're perfect. If you ticked fewer than 19 or 20 boxes, you should work on your weak areas – and when you do, your sales success rate should go up. (But be aware that rating yourself on such tests can be difficult and inaccurate. What do you think your customers would rate you on each item? Finding out may be useful!)

Technique can and often does trump natural ability. The salesperson who starts with high-quality prospects and then uses the right strategy at the right time with them, doesn't have as tough a sales task as the one who starts with less. You can close a sale far more easily when you start with good-quality leads and use the right strategy. These factors can make even someone with little natural talent perform like a star!

Making the Sale

The sales process can sometimes be painful. If you think of sales in this way, you can divide and conquer. You can divide sales into multiple steps and then focus on one step at a time as you prepare a sales plan or look for ways to improve your sales effectiveness. As with any complex process, a weak link always exists. When you look at the steps in your own sales process, try to find the one you perform most poorly right now. And focus on that one!

Figure 17-1 displays the sales and service process as a flow chart. Note that the chart doesn't flow automatically from beginning to end. You may be forced to cycle back to an earlier stage if things go wrong. But, ideally, you never lose a prospect or customer forever – they just recycle into sales leads, and you can mount a new effort to win them over. (By the way, the strategies we describe in the 'Providing Strategic Leadership in Sales' section earlier in this chapter can apply at multiple stages of this flow chart. The strategy gives you an overall approach and the steps give you a narrow tactical focus.)

This flow chart emphasises the need to integrate the sales and service processes. That's real-world selling. You can't stop when you close a sale and write the order. Your competitors certainly don't stop trying to win that client or account. So you need to think of a completed sale as the *beginning* of a relationship-building process. More sales calls, further presentations, and efforts to find new ways to serve the customer – you should focus on these points after you close a sale.

You also have to anticipate problems. You always do have a problem at some point – something goes wrong that upsets, disappoints, or even angers your customer. Trust me – problems happen, no matter how good your company is.

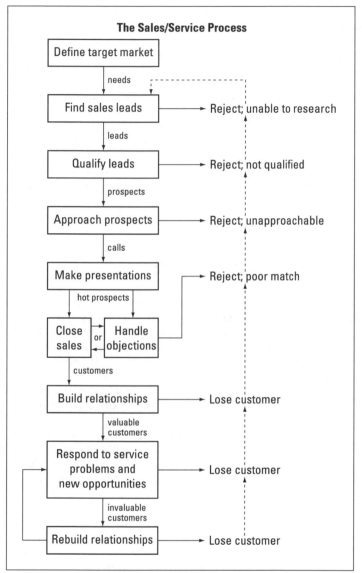

The Sales/Service Process

Define target market

needs

Find sales leads → Reject; unable to research

leads

Qualify leads → Reject; not qualified

prospects

Approach prospects → Reject; unapproachable

calls

Make presentations → Reject; poor match

hot prospects

Close sales — or — Handle objections

customers

Build relationships → Lose customer

valuable customers

Respond to service problems and new opportunities → Lose customer

invaluable customers

Rebuild relationships → Lose customer

Figure 17-1:
This flow chart shows you the process behind sales and service – try it!

Therefore, the sales process has to include a *service recovery* step. You have to figure out how to detect a service problem – how good is your communication with that customer? Make sure that the customer knows to call her salesperson when that problem occurs. If you think that you can use even more help in the customer service arena, start with the section 'Retaining Customers through Great Service' later in this chapter and then consider *Customer Service For Dummies* by Karen Leland and Keith Bailey (Wiley).

How well can the salesperson respond to a problem? If the salesperson finds herself overscheduled with sales calls, she can't take the time to solve problems. So budget, say, one in ten sales calls as *service recovery time* to prepare for this contingency. (Over time, you should be able to drive down the need for recoveries; perhaps you only need to budget 1 in 20 calls next year, if you make a point of trying to eliminate the most common root causes of these problems.) And keep in mind that the salesperson needs some resources, in addition to time, to solve customer problems and rebuild relationships. Give the salesperson some spending authority so that she can turn the customer's anger into satisfaction (or, if you're a small business, budget some funds for yourself to use on service recovery).

The most faithful customers are the ones who have had a big problem that you managed to solve in a fair and generous manner, so anything that you invest in service recovery is time and money well spent!

Generating sales leads

In many companies, the most important steps in the sales and service process are those steps in which you find and qualify sales leads because – as in any process – the *rubbish in, rubbish out* rule applies. *Qualifying* means gathering enough information about someone (or some business, if that's what you sell to) to make sure she is appropriate. By appropriate, we mean that the prospective customer fits a profile of a good customer. What is this profile? You need to decide, based on criteria like wealth, age, and interests (for a consumer sale), or size, industry, and location (for a business sale).

Don't throw low-quality leads into your sales and service process. Make sure that you feed your sales process with a constant flow of high-quality sales leads. Know what your customer profile is and seek out qualified prospects with questions or screening criteria that allow you to sift through and eliminate poor-quality prospects quickly.

Sales leads can come from any of the other marketing activities we describe in this book. In fact, we recommend that you try using as many alternatives as possible so that you can find out which works best for you. Your Web site may produce the best leads (see Chapter 10 for a discussion of Web site design). Or joining a professional group or association may help you network and meet potential clients. Perhaps a direct-mail campaign produces leads. And many marketers use direct-response advertising to find their sales leads. (Chapter 11 talks about both direct mail and direct-response ads.) Then you can consider telemarketing (Chapter 11), trade shows, event sponsorship (both discussed in Chapter 13), and so on.

You get the idea. You can use almost any kind of marketing to produce leads. You just have to find a good way to communicate with people who seem like good prospects for you and ask whether they're interested in your product or service. You also need to begin to ask for factual information: Who your prospects are, how to contact them, what they've bought or used in the past, and what their current needs are. Getting even a bit of information and an indication that someone is interested means that you have yourself a lead!

Here is a very simple way to generate leads:

1. **Select a magazine, newsletter, e-newsletter, or newspaper that the kind of people who should be interested in what you sell or do are likely to read.**

2. **Find the smallest, cheapest display ad in that publication and buy that ad space for the shortest possible time – one insertion, if you can.**

3. **Write a very simple, short description of what you do or sell, keeping it clear and factual.**

   Include a clear, simple photo, if you have a relevant one (you can show the product, if you're in a product business), or use your name and logo to illustrate the ad.

4. **End the ad with the following sentence: Please contact us to find out more about our offerings by calling 0800 xxx yyyy, or by using the enquiry form on our Web site at www.mywebsite.com.**

You run a no-nonsense direct-response ad if you use the preceding method. This ad is designed to generate some sales leads. This method may or may not work well – you always have to experiment to get your lead-producing formulas down – but it certainly gives you a good start. (If you already use some good lead-generation techniques, why not test something simple in a new medium? Everyone should be experimenting in marketing or they can't improve.)

Purchasing lists for lead generation

You can, of course, buy or rent names from list brokers. Mailing and call lists are widely available (you could start with the List Manager section on the Direct Marketing Association Web site at www.dma.org.uk). Don't make the mistake of thinking that these lists are leads in and of themselves. Nobody can sell you leads; you have to make them for yourself. Write a letter describing your offer and what you do and make sure your brilliance – what you're especially good at and want to be known for – is clearly and persuasively described in this letter. Send the letter out to a purchased list and ask recipients to contact you if they want more information.

To increase the response rate, try including a special short-term offer and a prepaid postcard or fax form for recipients' replies. Or try following up on the letter with a telephone call to the recipient. You may have to make two or more contacts to sort out the real leads from the rest of the list.

After you get some responses and capture their names and other information, you can call them leads. You own these leads and have the opportunity to follow up on them and see how many actually turn into customers. Good luck!

Remember, telemarketers are the first people from your company to talk with decision-makers at these prospects, so make sure that they're well spoken and polite. Better yet, have your salespeople select and train your telemarketers (or do it yourself, if you have a smaller business) so that you have plenty of control over that vital first impression.

Forgetting cold calling on households

The classic retail salesperson walks around a suburban housing estate, ringing doorbells to pitch brooms, encyclopaedias, or other household products.

Forget that approach. The method is still used, with some success, by gas and electricity suppliers and other utility providers who can make a case for cheaper household bills since their industries were deregulated. For most businesses, however, door-to-door selling isn't worth the effort that goes into it. Nobody's home at most houses in the daytime anymore, and the few people who do stay home are afraid to admit a stranger carrying a large suitcase – or should be. Some charities canvas door-to-door in the early evening with moderate success – if they pick areas where their name is well known and their cause popular. But this tactic doesn't work for most salespeople. Cold calling door-to-door is dead.

So how do you use personal selling to reach households? At *Encyclopaedia Britannica*, which eliminated its traditional sales force 20 years ago, they generate leads through advertising and referrals. They then follow up by telemarketing, or in person, if absolutely necessary. To eliminate cold calling, you need to get really good at generating sales leads – and to use many other marketing communications components for the purpose of getting leads.

You can also use a Web page or online newsletter to reach out for prospects and generate visits and enquiries that you can turn into leads. See Chapter 10 for more ideas on how to use the Web to supply your salespeople with better leads. Another idea is to ask your current customers to supply you with referrals and to thank them for this or even to reward them with gifts or discounts for it. Current customers often can find you good quality leads through their personal networks.

If you do consumer marketing, also consider following the lead of one of the most successful cosmetics companies. At Avon, they reach households by *networking*, using personal and professional contacts, in order to set up appointments – usually after working hours. This strategy gets through people's natural suspicions and busy schedules. In the UK, Avon has 160,000 salespeople and is looking to hire 20,000 more over the next five years – evidence that person-to-person selling isn't dead in the retail industry. You just have to do it differently, and with a bit more finesse, than in days of old.

Developing great sales presentations and consultations

At the sales presentation, the salesperson must convince the prospect to become a customer, which can be a challenge. Only the truly great sales presentation can persuade prospects to become customers with a high rate of success.

What makes a sales presentation great? Success. Any presentation that works, that gets customers to say 'yes' quickly and often, is an exceptional presentation. Be prepared to experiment and think creatively about this task. And make sure that you've designed the presentation to cover both basic fact needs and basic feelings needs. Your presentation needs to inform while also making the prospect comfortable (see the 'Providing Strategic Leadership in Sales' section earlier in this chapter for details). Sometimes, the right approach to sales presentations is to be consultative, meaning that you should first ask a lot of questions to work out what the customer needs, and then propose a somewhat customised solution, not just a generic purchase. This tactic is good in some cases – especially if you sell complex services. But consultative selling may not be right for your company. Maybe you can't see any obvious ways to sell customised services along with your product. You just want to deliver an excellent product and let the customer worry about what to do with it. If so, the last thing that you want your salespeople to do is to pretend that they're consultants.

Or – and this problem is increasingly common – perhaps you have the ability to solve customers' problems, but customers don't give you the time. Bringing a salesperson up to speed about a business so that she can solve the company's problems takes considerable time. In many markets, the buyers can't be bothered, in which case you can forget consultative selling. In that case, you need a good old-fashioned *canned approach* – that's when you write a detailed, specific, script that you (or your sales force if you have one) follow every time you give a sales presentation.

You can use a simple, canned approach as effectively as a sophisticated consultative approach, if the customer just wants an easy way to evaluate your offering. Be sure to tailor your sales style to accommodate your customers' needs, purchase preferences, and habits.

Organising Your Sales Force

If you have a large enough sales operation that you need to think about bigger-picture sales force management issues, look over this section.

Who does what, when, and where? Such organisational questions plague many sales or marketing managers, and those questions can make a big difference to sales force productivity. Should your salespeople work out of local, regional, or national offices? Should you base your salespeople in offices where staff provides daily support and their boss can supervise their activities closely? Or should you set salespeople free to operate on the road, maximising the number of calls they can make – and communicating with the company through high-tech laptop computers rather than through regional offices? Or – if you have a small business – should the owner do all the selling, or does bringing in a salesperson on commission make sense? We don't know. Honestly. These decisions depend on your situation. But we can help you decide by giving you an idea of the options available – several exist – and by sharing some of the conventional wisdom that helps you assess your particular situation.

Determining how many salespeople you need

If you have an existing sales force, you can examine the performance of each territory to decide whether more salespeople can help, or if perhaps you can do with less. Are some territories rich in prospects that salespeople just don't get to? Then consider splitting those territories. Also consider splitting territories, or adding a second person to create a sales team, if you're experiencing high customer turnover in a territory. Turnover probably indicates a lack of service and follow-up visits. Alternatively, if you see some territories that have little potential, you may be able to merge those territories with other territories. (Similarly, the small-business owner should consider adding commissioned salespeople if it isn't possible to cover all prospects adequately because of time or travel constraints.)

You can also use another, more systematic approach – which you really need when you have to design a sales force from scratch. Study your market to decide how many sales calls you want to make over a year-long period. The process isn't very complicated, and we explain it in detail in the sidebar 'How big a sales force do you need?'

How big a sales force do you need?

How do you determine the correct number of salespeople you need to sell your product or service? To find your personal answer to this burning question, follow these steps:

1. **Count how many potential customers you have in your entire market.**

2. **Decide what proportion or how many of those customers you want to call on.**

3. **Decide how many calls you want to make over the next year for each customer, on average (for example, 2 per month or 24 per year).**

4. **Multiply Step 2 by Step 3.**

   Doing so gives you the total sales calls you need for the entire year.

5. **Decide how many calls one person can reasonably make in a day.**

   The answer depends on the nature of the call and the travel time between customers.

6. **Multiply this daily figure (in Step 5) by the number of working days in your company's calendar.**

7. **Divide the total number of calls needed per year (from Step 4) by the number of calls one salesperson can make per year (from Step 6).**

   Doing so gives you the number of salespeople needed to make all those calls.

For example, 10,000 sales calls needed next year, divided by 1,000 calls per salesperson per year, means that you need a sales force of ten people to execute your plan. If you only have five on staff, you'd better hire five more or bring on some sales reps to help your staff – if you can't get authority for or raise funding for either plan, scale back your sales goals by half. You can never sell that light bulb to 10,000 customers with only five salespeople.

Hiring your own or using reps?

You have to make the most basic choice of whether to do it yourself or subcontract. Good sales companies exist in most industries that take on the job of hiring and managing salespeople for you. Called *sales representatives* (or reps), they usually work for a straight commission of between 10 and 20 per cent, depending on the industry and how much room you have in your pricing structure for their commission. Also, in areas where you need more work done – customer support through consultative selling and customised service – reps earn, and deserve, a higher commission.

If you have a small company or a short product line, we recommend using sales reps. Reps are the best option whenever you have *scale problems* that make justifying the cost of hiring your own dedicated salespeople somewhat difficult. Scale problems arise when you have a too-short product line, which means that salespeople don't have very much to sell to customers. Each sales call produces such small total orders that those sales don't cover the cost of the call. Reps usually handle many companies' product lines so that they have more products to show prospects when they call than your own independent salesperson would. Many product lines spread the cost of that sales call over more products, which may make the sales call more valuable for the buyer, as well. If you sell too few products, a busy buyer may not be willing to take the time to listen to your salesperson's presentation – so again, the rep has a scale advantage.

However, if you can possibly justify hiring and running your own dedicated salespeople, by all means do! You have much more control, better feedback from the market, and you find that a dedicated sales force generally outsells a sales rep by between two and ten times as much. Why? The dedicated salesperson is focused and dependent on your product. Often, the rep doesn't care what she sells, as long as the client buys something. And so reps tend to make the easy sales, which may not be yours!

Finding good sales reps

How do you find sales reps? The obvious doesn't work – you can't find them listed in any telephone directory. We don't know why, but rep firms prefer that you find them by networking. Doing so may avoid a lot of requests from companies that don't know the industry and don't have decent products. But if you want to find reps, you have to do it on the reps' terms, which means getting word-of-mouth referrals or meeting them at a trade show or industry conference. Or, even simpler, ask the buyers of products such as the one you sell for names of reps who currently call on them.

As far as word-of-mouth referrals go, we recommend asking the companies that reps sell to for their opinions about the best rep firms. After all, you need the reps to sell your product to these customers, so their opinions are the most important! You can also get referrals from other companies that sell (non-competing) products through the same kinds of reps.

We also highly recommend networking for reps at trade shows in your industry. Reps attend the trade shows, and many of them rent booths to represent their products. You can find reps just by wandering the exhibition hall, using your eyes and nose, and asking occasional questions.

Managing your reps – with an iron glove!

After you have reps lined up for each territory, your work has only just begun. You must, absolutely must, monitor your reps' sales efforts on a regular basis. Which rep firms sell the best (and worst)? Usually 10 or 15 per cent of the reps make almost all your sales. If you notice such a pattern developing, you can quickly put the others on notice. And if the other reps don't heat up in a hurry, you can replace them.

Renting a salesperson

Many businesses have made temps popular these days, so why not temporary salespeople? Temp agencies have been providing telemarketers on a temporary basis for years. Businesses often use those temporary telemarketers for a few weeks in conjunction with any special project that requires telephone prospecting or follow-up – such as generating leads for a new product or new territory.

Temp agencies can fill a short-term need for experienced telemarketers, salespeople, trade show staff, and other marketing people. Look in your local Yellow Pages telephone directory under *Employment Agencies*. One of the big, national temp agencies probably has an office nearby, as well, so you can also check your directory for Reed (`www.reed.co.uk`), Kelly Services (`www.kellyservices.co.uk`), or Manpower (`www.manpower.co.uk`).

Businesses don't use temporary salespeople that often, but we think they provide you with a great alternative because they allow you to put a lot of salespeople on the street quickly without making a long-term financial commitment. Use temps to help you open up a new territory, introduce a new product, or follow up on a backlog of sales leads from that big trade show you exhibited at last month. You probably want to hire these sorts of temps on a monthly basis to give them time to develop some continuity. And consider teaming temps with your full-time salespeople (if you have any) to ease the transition for new accounts when the temporary service period ends.

Compensating Your Sales Force

You face one of the toughest and most important management decisions in marketing when you have to figure out how to compensate salespeople. Compensation has a significant impact on the sales staff's motivation and performance, and (of course) salespeople's performance has a big effect on sales. The issue becomes difficult because compensation's effect on motivation isn't always obvious.

An important issue worth thinking about is how to make sure that you have relationship-orientated salespeople, not people who just go after the maximum number of transactions. Make sure that you aim your commissions and also your non-financial incentives (recognition, praise, and so on) at both finding and *keeping* good customers, not just writing the most new business.

If you want to recruit special salespeople, you may need to offer them a special compensation plan. Do something sufficiently different from the norm in your industry to make your job openings really stand out. For example, what if you want to make sure that your salespeople take a highly consultative, service-orientated approach, with long-term support and relationship building? You need people with patience and dedication, people who are looking for a stable situation and can build business over the long term. So try offering them less commission than they would earn elsewhere. Make your compensation salary based. If you give your salespeople sales incentives, consider bonuses linked to long-term customer retention or to building sales with existing customers. Your compensation plan stands out from your competitors and sends a clear signal about the kind of sales behaviour you expect. Similarly, if you want the hottest, most self-motivated salespeople, offer more commission than the competition.

Retaining Customers through Great Service

Sales and service go hand in hand. When your business relies on personal selling you can bet that you also need great customer service. Why? Although personal selling produces new customers, personal service keeps them. If you don't know how to keep new customers, you shouldn't waste your time seeking new customers. You will just lose them.

Measuring the quality of customer service

Do you know your *customer turnover rate* (the percentage of customers who leave each year)? If your turnover goes over 5 per cent in most industries, you need to build retention to lower that percentage. You probably have a customer service problem. If you don't already calculate *customer turnover (churn rate),* we tell you how in the following steps. Find out your customer turnover rate by comparing customer lists from two consecutive years – or asking your salespeople to gather the data if you can't do so easily from your central customer database or billing records.

Sometimes companies define a lost customer as one whose business has fallen by more than half, which gives you a more conservative measure than one based only on customers who have stopped ordering entirely.

To work out your churn rate or rate of customer turnover, follow these steps:

1. **Compare last year's and this year's customer lists to find out how many customers you lost during the year.**

   Ignore new customers for this calculation.

2. **Count the total number of customers on the first of the two lists, the list from the previous year.**

   That gives you your *base*, or where you started.

3. **Divide the number of lost customers (from Step 1) by the total number of customers (from Step 2) to get your turnover or churn rate.**

If you started the year with 1,500 customers and lost 250, your turnover rate is 250 ÷ 1,500, or nearly 17 per cent. If you find yourself in that situation, you fail our 5 per cent test and need to get to the bottom of your problem with customer service!

Delivering service recovery

Service recovery starts with recognising when service isn't going well. What makes your customer unhappy? Which customers are stressed or frustrated? Talking and thinking about these questions can lead to a list of the five top warning signs of an unhappy customer. We're not going to write your list for you because every company has a different one. Whatever your top warning signs, educate everyone to recognise them and to leap into action whenever they see one of them.

Service recovery needs empathy and polite sensitivity. Make the starting point just paying polite attention to someone. In fact, sometimes that action can be enough to turn the customer around.

You can practise service strategically, in the same way as sales (like we describe in the section 'Providing Strategic Leadership in Sales' earlier in this chapter), with the goal of winning back the customer by solving her problem or helping her feel better. Usually, you have to start with the feelings of the unhappy customer. Use your emotional intelligence to empathise with her. Let her vent or complain, and don't argue with her. The unhappy customer is always right.

After a customer has calmed down a bit and is ready to listen to you and look to you for help, you can ask factual questions and give information in return. But remember, every service recovery starts with working on the (hurt) feelings of the disgruntled customer, not on the facts. That important insight can save a lot of customer relationships and help you build a reputation as a great company to buy from.

Part VI
The Part of Tens

"In your marketing plan, you said you wouldn't spend unnecessarily. I thought that only applied to your business!"

In this part . . .

We could give you ten good reasons to read this part by why bother – it already contains more than 30.

In this part, we warn you how to avoid many of the common mistakes and causes of failures that have torpe- doed other marketers and their programs in the past. We suggest you re-read this section once a month, just to make sure that your marketing inoculations are up-to-date. It's easy to fall back into bad habits if you don't pay attention!

We bet you want to save as much money as you can on marketing. Believe me, almost every marketer shares this wish. But few accomplish it, at least without ruining next year's revenues and profits and sending customers away angry. So please consult this part of the book to find out how to save money by being an economical marketer. Given unlimited funds, any idiot can sell something, but doing it for less is a true art form.

Chapter 18

Ten Common Marketing Mistakes to Avoid

· ·

· ·

*Y*ou don't want to reinvent the wheel – especially if the wheel was square in the first place. Because you want your marketing to run smoothly, take a couple of minutes to find out about the all-too-common mistakes that so often derail sales and marketing efforts – and then avoid them!

Don't Sell to the Wrong People

We regularly get sent a catalogue from a company specialising in maternity clothes, and have done for several years. Clearly, we're not women and, as we've never ordered anything from them, you'd think they would give up sending out the expensive catalogues. At the very least, you'd hope someone at the company would realise that none of its customers can be pregnant all the time. At work we get sent all kinds of letters from office equipment suppliers and magazine publishers – none of which are relevant to our jobs. What a waste!

You can sort people by profession or gender pretty easily, thus eliminating the obvious mismatches. Face it, most people are the wrong people – meaning that they probably don't want to buy from you – and if you pull out the obvious mismatches, you can eliminate lost-cause prospects and not waste your money on them.

Don't Give Away Money

Many marketers devote half or more of their budgets to price-orientated promotions, and we can't tell you the number of times we've heard managers say things like, 'Sales seem to be off this month. Why don't we cut prices and see if that helps?' Discounts and price cuts have their role, certainly – but you should never use them unless you have clear evidence that the net result can be profitable. And it usually isn't, as we demonstrate in Chapter 15. Sometimes, customers are highly price sensitive, competitors undercut you, and you have no choice but to slash your prices, too. But, in general, you don't want to compete on price. You'll find making a profit (and staying in business) far easier when you compete on the elements that make you different and better.

Don't Forget to Edit Before You Print

If your letter, e-mail, Web page, print ad, sign, or poster has a spelling error in it, people will notice it and remember it. We often see signs outside businesses or on vehicles that have obvious typos, and a fair number of business cards have typos, too. Talk about making a bad first impression!

Don't Keep Repeating Yourself

If you send someone a mailing or e-mail once, they can chuck it or act on it quickly, no harm done either way. But what if they get the same communication two or three more times in rapid succession? Now they're going to respond in a third way – by getting irritated with you for bothering them.

Avoiding this error can be difficult. Check every list before you use it, looking for redundancies that may slip by and end up causing irritation at the other end. We don't need to get three copies of a sales letter addressed to us with three different misspellings of our names – but we often do (and you probably do, too).

Avoid the Wish-We-Could Trap

Every business has its core speciality and does best when it stays close to it. Sometimes you should expand into a new market area or try a new kind of product or service – but do this expansion with a careful, well-researched and funded strategic thrust (see Part I of this book). Otherwise, trying to play on someone else's patch is a big mistake. To fool around in an area that you aren't expert in just invites disaster. The grass may look greener on the other side of the fence, but someone put the fence there for a good reason. Make sure that you're prepared to fight with the dog that lives next door before you jump over that fence.

Watch Out for Impersonal Treatment

Every one of your customers is a person, and they like to be treated as such. Yet sometimes, businesses send out generic bills or mailings that have misspellings of customers' names. And perhaps the person who answers the phone doesn't know that the caller is an old customer. You can make these easy, casual mistakes often without even noticing that you make them. But put yourself in the customer's shoes and take a hard look at all your customer interactions. Are they as personal as they should be? If not, invest in better list-checking, a central list or software database of customers, training in how to pronounce customer names, and whatever else it takes to allow your business to treat good customers like important individuals.

Don't Blame the Customer

We recently received an overdue notice on an invoice from a cleaning and maintenance company that we'd used many months ago. Our bookkeeper was puzzled because she thought that she remembered paying the bill when it first came in. Reviewing her records, she called the company and gave them the cheque number, date, and amount of our payment and asked them to correct their records. This company met her polite efforts to correct this error with sullen irritation on the other end of the phone. A manager at the company told her off for 'sending a misleading cheque' and 'not making it completely clear which account it applied to' (even though she had returned their invoice with the cheque). In short, instead of apologising for the confusion, this contractor blamed us for the error. He may have felt better after letting off steam on the phone, but he just lost a customer forever. Don't make the same mistake with your customers, please!

Don't Avoid Upset Customers

You naturally want to avoid someone who's irritated with you – but don't. Customers can get unpleasant or abusive if they feel that they've been poorly treated – even if you don't think they really have been. Treat the unhappy customer as your top marketing priority. And don't stop working on him until he's happy again. If you win him back, he's especially loyal and brings you new business. If you let him walk away fuming, he becomes an anti-marketer, actively trying to drive others away from your business. The choice is yours.

Don't Forget to Change

You can easily fall into the trap of doing the same thing with your marketing communications every year – many companies do. If you are spending the same proportion of your budget on direct mail, telemarketing, and point-of-purchase materials every year, you've probably fallen into the trap of letting processes get in the way of effective change.

Don't throw out the marketing that does work, but at least find out which aspects work best, and adjust your spending accordingly. There are new communications ideas coming along all the time, too. You can't test out whether a Weblog or mobile marketing would work for you if all your budget is tied up in local press advertising.

Don't Stop Marketing

When things go well, you may be tempted to relax and let marketing costs slip down while you enjoy higher margin sales. If you have a loyal following and a recognised brand name, you can probably stop active marketing for a while without noticing any significant drop in sales. But whether you notice it straight away or not, this slip undermines sales and erodes your customer base. Keep up your marketing momentum at all times!

When things aren't going so well it's even more important to keep communicating with customers. Study after study shows that in an economic downturn, those companies that keep advertising through the hard times do much better than their competitors when business picks up.

Chapter 19

Ten (Or So) Ways to Save Money in Marketing

. . . .

In This Chapter

▶ Cutting costs and being creative

▶ Staying close to home

▶ Adding value to your product without adding cost

. . . .

*E*veryone wants to know how to do marketing on the cheap. In general, you can only find worthless advice on this topic out there. Yes, you can place photocopied fliers under people's windscreen wipers for.

However, you can find good ways to save money in marketing. Real next-to-nothing. But when you compare the impact of a cheap flier with a well-produced TV spot, you can easily justify the difference in price. In general, you get what you pay for in marketing. The cheapest consultants, designers, and researchers may be good professionals on their way up – but they usually aren't. And free exposures usually don't reach your target market or, if they do, don't make a favourable impression on that market. The real money-saving techniques aren't as obvious or easy as some people try to tell you, but these techniques can really work. In general, they involve doing real marketing, rather than substituting some cheap alternative. If you want an approach that really saves money, do the right things – better. This chapter gives you ideas for good ways to save money without reducing your effectiveness or embarrassing yourself.

Planning on Planning

We estimate that businesses don't plan half of their marketing expenses, meaning they spend the money without thinking about how it fits into the big picture of their marketing plan. Companies often reprint their four-colour brochures, renew their sales reps' contracts, buy expensive display ads in phone directories and trade magazines, inventory large quantities of poor-selling products, or spend money on fancy packaging without any idea of whether they're making good marketing investments. If you and your organisation make a commitment to spend nothing on marketing without knowing why – and considering alternatives – then you can avoid wasting money on marketing activities that don't have much impact on sales. The more time you spend on developing strategy and designing your plan, the more cost-effective and economical your marketing becomes.

Thinking Small in a Big Way

Grand gestures aren't necessary – there are lots of small tweakings you can make to your marketing budget. The following sections provide ideas to help you be more focused on your target market and thus save money.

- **Targeting your audience narrowly:** Most marketing campaigns waste much of their effort on people or organisations who can never become good customers because they aren't in the target market – or shouldn't be. Think about the waste involved in running an ad that thousands or millions view, when only a small fraction of that audience is your target. And think of the waste involved in direct marketing to a list that generates a 1 per cent response rate. Look for the narrowest, most specific, way to talk to your customers and prospects. If you switch from a list with 75 per cent wasted names to a list with only 25 per cent wasted names, you can have the same impact with a mailing that costs half as much but still reaches the same number of prospects!

- **Narrowing your territory:** You can also think small by focusing your resources on a smaller market area. In essence, you become a bigger fish in a smaller pond. Many entrepreneurs use this strategy successfully by marketing (at first) in a single metropolitan area. After they gain significant market share in a small area, these entrepreneurs can afford to roll out to other areas.

The trick to this strategy is understanding the effects of *scale* in your business. Most industries have a minimum profitable market size, and that size varies dramatically. So, do some quick calculations. Can a 10 per cent or 20 per cent share of the market in a single region, county, or city cover your fixed costs as well as variable costs and get you significantly above your break-even point? If your fixed costs aren't too high for that market, it can. Businesses with high fixed costs – a factory, for example – usually have to think bigger when choosing a market. Consultants can think very small because they have minimal overhead. Consultants can best boost consulting sales by focusing a local marketing effort on the members of just one chamber of commerce.

✔ **Concentrating your resources:** Don't spread yourself too thinly. Concentrate your salespeople, your shops, your direct marketing, or whatever you do in your plan into certain areas or periods of time so that you can cash in on economies of scale. *Economies of scale* means that your costs per ad or other marketing task go down as you do more of that task. Make sure that you do each marketing activity on a large enough scale to make it economical. Take advantage of discounts from printers, mailing list houses, and the media that sell ad time and space. If you print and mail 50,000 copies of your catalogue rather than 5,000 copies, your costs fall to less than half per copy. However, apply this advice only to aspects of your marketing that you know will work well enough to pay their own way, like mailing a catalogue that you have already tested and found to be profitable. Otherwise, be careful of over-committing.

You can concentrate your resources by rolling out sequentially. Even the biggest consumer marketers often use this strategy to concentrate their resources. Introduce your new product in one market at a time, and make a big impact in that market before going to the next one. This strategy works for more than just new product introductions. You can roll out an expensive advertising campaign in one or two markets and then wait for your returns from this investment before funding the campaign in additional markets. If you're patient, you can fund a much higher level of advertising and achieve far higher impact than you may think your annual budget permits.

✔ **Holding your target's attention:** Sometimes, you can make a big impact in marketing media by being smaller than anybody else. A little print ad sometimes out-pulls a big one – not on average, to be sure, but sometimes. And that means you should be able to develop a great small ad of your own if you work at it hard enough.

The same holds true in other media, especially media where they measure the size of an ad in time. Most radio spots run 30 seconds. And most of the time, radio ad writers struggle to hold the listener's attention for the full 30 seconds. Why not give up that battle and just make a ten-second radio ad?

Integrating Your Efforts

In the Japanese approach to total quality management, you sometimes hear the expression 'too many rabbits' to describe the situation in which a business has a lot of initiatives under way without sufficient co-ordination. Marketing plans usually have too many rabbits when they really want one big rabbit. To avoid the multiple rabbits scenario, you need to integrate all your marketing communications by doing the following:

1. **Identify all the channels of communication with your market.**

2. **Design an overall message strategy that says what your organisation should communicate through any and all channels and defines a general feel or style for all communications.**

You communicate far more effectively using integrated marketing communications, and you may find that you can cut back your budget and still get your point across. Have one (just one!) way to display your name and logo, plus one (just one!) key point you want to make to sell people on your benefits. Then be consistent in all your communications.

Spending Money Wisely and Cutting Judiciously

Well-designed marketing plans are an investment in future sales. You can most obviously save money on marketing by cutting the marketing budget, but across-the-board cuts rarely work. These cuts save money this year but hurt sales and profits disproportionately next year. If you don't reach out to customers, they don't reach out to you! So remember to view marketing as an investment in future revenues and profits.

✔ **Making smarter investments:** You can save money by making smarter investments, not by stopping the investments entirely. Take a look at your results from the past year (or month, or even week if you're looking at Web marketing, where you can get reports immediately) and figure out which investments are working the best. Then, simply cut low-return investments and shift the spending into the best-performing marketing activities. If you keep a vigilant eye on your activities, your returns keep growing from your marketing spending. Benefiting from experience in this way is surprisingly rare in marketing.

✔ **Cutting your fixed costs:** Consider cutting your *fixed costs* (those costs that you incur regularly, like rent, regardless of what you do or don't sell). Although this advice sounds more like accounting or operations management than marketing, you can use it as an incredibly powerful marketing strategy! Apply your marketing imagination to cost management and see if you can find a smaller-scale way to produce that product or perform that business process. If so, you can do small-scale and local marketing activities that your competitors can't profit from – but you can. If you're trying to work out how to introduce a new product on a shoestring budget, consider searching for a low-cost supplier who can make the product for you in small batches. Even if you end up with slightly higher total costs, you have much lower fixed costs because you don't have to order large quantities in advance or find storage for extra units. And so you can *bootstrap* (or grow on your own cash flow) by making and marketing a small batch in a small market and then reinvesting your profits into a slightly bigger second batch.

✔ **Cutting back where customers can't see:** To a customer, many of the line items in a company's budget seem unimportant. Yet nobody asks the customers what they think about the company's budget. Customers may tell you to cut back on many expenses that don't affect the product's quality or availability in ways that matter to them. From the customer's perspective, the landscaping outside the headquarters building doesn't matter (and many people inside that building feel the same way!). Most customers couldn't care less whether you print the department's letterhead in two colours or one, or whether salespeople drive new or used cars. Put money where customers will see it, not where they won't.

Focusing on Your Bottleneck

Many marketers spend their money on raising awareness of their brands when they don't actually have a problem in that area. If consumers already know about the brand, exposing them to it more often may not help sales – or, at least, not very much. Marketing more likely needs to work on the brand's image so that more of those people who do know about the brand decide that they *like* it.

Or you may have the problem that a lot of people try your brand, but too many of those people give up on the product without becoming regular users. Then the problem may lie in the product itself, and marketing money should go to an upgrade rather than to expensive sales or advertising. A weak distribution system poses another common problem that makes finding your product when a person wants it difficult. If you don't know where your bottleneck is, you aren't spending your money wisely. Make sure that you focus hard on the most important bottleneck. Spend your marketing money there, and you'll see the biggest return on your marketing investment, in the form of increasing sales and profits.

Giving Your Product or Service Away

You are in business to make money from sales, but sometimes making the sale involves giving would-be customers a taster of your product and service – for free. This idea works on at least a couple of levels. First, giving freebies encourages trial, which encourages purchase, which encourages repeat purchase. Second, this idea shows your prospective customers that you believe in your own product enough to let them have some of it now, and return for more later.

You can find ways to give away samples of your product or service no matter what business you are in. Consultants and professional advisers can provide basic documents and advice on their Web sites to pull customers in, food and drink manufacturers can give away samples in supermarket car parks, software and video games manufacturers can build in limited-time free usage. Let your product find you more customers. Give some of it away!

Rewarding Your Customers

Give your customers a treat as a reward for their business. Send them a bottle of wine, a cake, a bouquet of flowers, or some other treat you think they may like, along with a personal thank-you note. This tip is very simple, but it does a lot to let people know that you care about their business. This idea is worth its weight in gold because customers who feel you've treated them well always send new customers your way.

Using New Channels and Media

Whenever possible, find the up-and-coming thing and hop on for the ride. Or better still, create the new thing yourself. (Can you use an exciting new event with associated publicity instead of using advertising?) Your marketing money goes much farther when you do something novel for three reasons:

- ✔ New means unproven and advertisers are charged lower prices as a result.

- ✔ New means smaller, so you can be a big fish in a little pond. You have much higher visibility in a new medium than in an overcrowded mature medium. Advertise where no competitor advertisements distract the consumer from yours. That way, you get to be the star cheaply and easily.

- ✔ Your originality catches eyes and impresses customers. Be a market leader, not a follower!

Do direct marketing on the Internet instead of on the telephone – it's cheaper and more effective. Take advantage of that fact by shifting your marketing efforts to a new and better medium. Or be one of the first in your industry to switch from mailings to e-mail for new product announcements. Or be one of the first to experiment with direct marketing as a replacement for the traditional intermediaries in your industry. How about a radio ad, accompanied by a text message appearing on the digital control of the car radio? Not many marketers have used the emerging medium of digital radio yet.

Giving Solid Guarantees

If you really think that you have a good product or service, why not take the risk out of trying it? A money-back guarantee, without a lot of small print to qualify it, tends to get customer attention. And what's the cost? If you're right and they love it, the offer costs you nothing at all. If you're wrong occasionally, then you still have a pretty low cost and it isn't cash out of pocket. You can't lose on a guarantee unless you're selling a bad product – in which case, you need to upgrade it straight away because nothing is more expensive to market than a bad product!

Recognising Your Own Excellence

The one thing customers find most attractive about you is . . .?

If you don't know how to finish this sentence in your sleep, you need to invest in understanding, polishing, and communicating what it is your company excels at before doing any more marketing. You can't be all things to all people, and trying to be spreads your money and effort too thinly.

So, tell us, what *is* your most appealing quality? If you don't know the answer to this question, your marketing budget is poorly spent. Work out what your prime quality is, and then show and tell the story of what makes you special everywhere you do marketing.

Being Creative

All things being equal, the more you spend on marketing, the more you sell. Competitors with the largest marketing campaigns get more attention and sales so it's no wonder that winning the marketing war can get pretty expensive. However, one of the wonderful things about marketing is that you can escape this spending war – by being more creative than your competitors. A creative new product concept or package design, a clever approach to point-of-purchase advertising, a pop-up colour brochure with a musical chip – any such innovations can help you achieve big-money returns from small-time investments. You can get big results on a shoestring budget, but it's going to take some creativity!

Joining and Participating

We call this approach the *J and P strategy,* and many entrepreneurs say that it's the foundation of their success.

The average marketer goes home in the evening and watches two hours of television. Well, you're not average, and you can use those ten perfectly good hours each week (plus some weekend time) for more productive activities. Join community and professional groups, sponsor or coach youth sports teams, volunteer at a local community service agency, help raise funds for a local museum, or go to educational and cultural events (especially those events at which you can mingle with other professionals, like art gallery openings and ribbon-cutting ceremonies). Get out there and participate in these many fun and rewarding activities, and you find that your network grows quite naturally. Although your participation in such activities is its own best reward, you may also be pleasantly surprised at how often you bump into leads for your sales and marketing or discover that prospective customers have heard about your good works and call you up to introduce themselves.

Chapter 20

Ten (Or So) Ideas for Lower-Cost Advertising

In This Chapter

▶ Getting more advertising than you pay for

▶ Pulling in help from other sources

*T*hey say that 'you get what you pay for'. Well, they're missing the point. You want to get *more* than you pay for, and this book is all about how to achieve just that. In this section we give you 11 good ideas (for the price of 10!) on how to get free publicity, use your own 'media' space, and pay less for advertising than you have to.

Never pass up free advertising opportunities and always think about ways to create them. Handing out a business card and shaking someone's hand costs almost nothing – yet done in the right context, it can be the most effective marketing activity in the known universe.

Creating Billboards on Wheels

The vast majority of company-owned vehicles and vehicles of company employees don't have any signs on them, yet these same companies pay good money to buy expensive advertising space elsewhere. You can turn your vehicles into attention-grabbing business generators by being creative with them. Think vintage cars, full-livery paint jobs, giving each vehicle a separate name or identity (so kids can 'collect' them), or covering them in artificial grass. I can immediately think of a fast-growing company that has used each of these ideas, but I can't recall a single business that simply paints their phone number on the side of a white van. If you have to have the vehicles, you should make them earn their keep.

Using Free Placement for Your Name, Logo, and Tag Line

There is free advertising space all around you, but it's easy to mistake it for a wall, window, envelope, or e-mail. If your customers or potential customers see your building, or you are sending something to them, look on it as an advertising opportunity. Use buildings and windows for signs and posters, packaging and envelopes for stickers and stamps, and end each and every e-mail with a thought-provoking tag line (and your full contact details), such as 'Smart marketers read *Marketing For Dummies*'.

Getting Others to Advertise for You

Pass out window-sticker and bumper-sticker versions of your logo and company name (with Web address). Give out premium items (pens, mugs, caps, shirts, notepads, or whatever – but make sure that you've made them nice enough that people use them). This way, your customers and the people in their extended networks can all begin to promote your business for you.

Inviting a Customer to Lunch

You should have regular lunches with a customer. You can use this great way to stay in touch to keep your ears open for input and ideas. It also generates repeat or expanded business, in many cases.

If you don't know your customers or how to reach them because you distribute through intermediaries, take those intermediaries to lunch, instead. They're your immediate customers, and they deserve the same royal treatment that you want them to lavish on your end customers. Such attention will increase their level of motivation to promote and sell your products.

Taking Liberties with Launches

There are new magazines, papers, radio stations, Web sites – all kinds of media, in fact – launching all the time. And they need advertisers. The first few months of any media launch is a perfect time to strike a good deal for advertising space. If anything, they need you more than you need them: They're untested as a sales lead, they need to demonstrate they have the confidence of advertisers (like you), and they need some revenue. Keep an eye open for media launches targeting your customers or area – they can offer great value for money.

Ignoring the Ratecard

A ratecard is a card with some rates printed on it. An ad sales person uses the ratecard as a starting point, and so should you. If you like, a ratecard is a guide to how much of a rookie advertiser you are – and nothing makes an ad salesperson's day like someone who pays ratecard price. So, before you even think about buying media space anywhere you need to know what the ratecard is – and then negotiate down. Any media owner will happily send you their ratecard, so take the time to familiarise yourself with who charges what, and why. If you absolutely must have a certain ad slot, at a certain time then don't expect much leeway. If you express a nonchalant interest at possibly advertising sometime in the near future, they'll bend over backward. Pretend that you're haggling in an open air market. That shouldn't be too hard – you are.

Getting Publicity for Nothing

Magazines, newspapers, radio, and TV stations need editorial as much as they need advertising. It's easier to get your business on air or in print than you think. All you need is a good story, or even a strong opinion – there are professional letter writers who get their company names into BtoB magazines, like *Marketing*, more often than most. What has your company got that a local or specialist publication or TV channel might like to cover? Have you or one of your staff done something noteworthy? You can create 'good news' by doing some work in the local community, carrying out an original survey and publicising the results, or taking part in some sponsored event like a marathon. See Chapter 15 for more ideas for free publicity.

Standing Up and Saying Something

Most people hate public speaking, and consequently pass up the chance to get their business in front of a highly relevant and captive audience. Don't make the same mistake. Look out for opportunities to talk about your product or service. And if you're ever invited to speak on a conference platform, take it – there are few occasions where the audience is so self-selecting, and where you get to talk about your business and expertise without being interrupted. Talking about your product will also help give focus to your speech. It might not feel like advertising, but public speaking can be one of your most effective marketing activities – and it's free.

Running a Training Course

My local bonsai shop, Concrete Jungle, runs courses in bonsai cultivation, led by Japanese bonsai gurus. Brilliant. This brings out all the real enthusiasts, and hence highest-spending customers, and gathers us together in the shop, where we invariably end up buying new equipment every night the course is on. The idea works well for any kind of 'lifestyle' business, from wine-tasting to DIY. But with a little adaptation you can copy this idea and apply it to any product or service. A business-to-business company could offer specialist training courses to professionals who want to update their knowledge – you could even charge for it, but the real benefit is gaining loyal customers, and as we all know, those are the best kind.

Borrowing Good Ad Ideas

There is a breed of marketing agency that specialises in *ambient* or *non-traditional* media. Marketers in big, cash-rich companies pay them good money to come up with original (and often very cheap) ways of advertising. You can follow their lead and look for original ways of advertising and then do them yourself. Try hiring a pavement artist to draw your ad on a busy pedestrian pavement. It's legal (although some local authorities still don't approve of it) and you don't have to pay for the media space. Projecting your ad or logo onto a wall at night is a similar idea. Or how about getting some students who need the money to put a temporary tattoo of your logo on their foreheads? For more ideas on unusual and cheap places to put your ad, see Chapter 11.

Creating Your Own Network

Look out for marketers in complementary businesses that you can work with to a common aim – finding and retaining more customers. One of the easiest ways to do this is to put cards or flyers into retail outlets that serve your type of customers. Children's nurseries and babycare shops is one good example of a partnership where each can market the other's services easily and effectively, but if you think carefully, you will find complementary companies that you can team up with. If you have a shop consider using products from another shop as props for your window display. It will make your display more interesting and increase your exposure if the other shop does the same. In business to business, where the target market is relatively small and their time is precious, marketing a combined offer like this can benefit everyone involved – it's a wonder it isn't done more often.

Index

Notes

Notes

FOR DUMMIES®

Do Anything. Just Add Dummies

HOME

UK editions

0-7645-7027-7

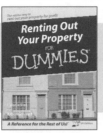
0-7645-7016-1

0-7645-7054-4

PERSONAL FINANCE

0-7645-7023-4

0-470-02860-2

0-7645-7039-0

BUSINESS

0-7645-7018-8

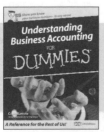
0-7645-7025-0

0-7645-7026-9

Other UK editions now available:

Answering Tough Interview Questions For Dummies
(0-470-01903-4)

Arthritis For Dummies
(0-470-02582-4)

Being The Best Man For Dummies
(0-470-02657-X)

British History For Dummies
(0-7645-7021-8)

Building Confidence For Dummies
(0-4700-1669-8)

Buying a Home On A Budget For Dummies
(0-7645-7035-8)

Cognitive Behavioural Therapy For Dummies
(0-470-01838-0)

Cleaning and Stain Removal For Dummies
(0-7645-7029-3)

CVs For Dummies
(0-7645-7017-X)

Detox For Dummies
(0-470-01908-5)

Diabetes For Dummies
(0-7645-7019-6)

Divorce For Dummies
(0-7645-7030-7)

eBay.co.uk For Dummies
(0-7645-7059-5)

European History For Dummies
(0-7645-7060-9)

Formula One Racing For Dummies
(0-7645-7015-3)

Gardening For Dummies
(0-470-01843-7)

Genealogy Online For Dummies
(0-7645-7061-7)

Golf For Dummies
(0-470-01811-9)

Irish History For Dummies
(0-7645-7040-4)

Kakuro For Dummies
(0-470-02822-X)

Neuro-Linguistic Programming For Dummies
(0-7645-7028-5)

Nutrition For Dummies
(0-7645-7058-7)

Pregnancy For Dummies
(0-7645-7042-0)

Retiring Wealthy For Dummies
(0-470-02632-4)

Rugby Union For Dummies
(0-7645-7020-X)

Small Business Employment Law For Dummies
(0-7645-7052-8)

Starting a Business on eBay.co.uk For Dummies
(0-470-02666-9)

Su Doku For Dummies
(0-4700-189-25)

Sudoku 2 For Dummies
(0-4700-2651-0)

Sudoku 3 For Dummies
(0-4700-2667-7)

The GL Diet For Dummies
(0-470-02753-3)

Wills, Probate and Inheritance Tax For Dummies
(0-7645-7055-2)

8232_p1